FILMMAKERS SERIES

edited by

ANTHONY SLIDE

52. *The Films of Michael Powell and the Archers*, by Scott Salwolke. 1997

53. *From Oz to E. T.: Wally Worsley's Half-Century in Hollywood—A Memoir in Collaboration with Sue Dwiggins Worsley*, edited by Charles Ziarko. 1997

54. *Thorold Dickinson and the British Cinema*, by Jeffrey Richards. 1997

55. *The Films of Oliver Stone*, edited by Don Kunz. 1997

56. *Before, In and After Hollywood: The Autobiography of Joseph E. Henabery*, edited by Anthony Slide. 1997

57. Ravished Armenia *and the Story of Aurora Mardiganian*, compiled by Anthony Slide. 1997

58. *Smile When the Raindrops Fall*, by Brian Anthony and Andy Edmonds. 1998

59. *Joseph H. Lewis: Overview, Interview, and Filmography*, by Francis M. Nevins. 1998

60. *September Song: An Intimate Biography of Walter Huston*, by John Weld. 1998

61. *Wife of the Life of the Party*, by Lita Grey Chaplin and Jeffrey Vance. 1998

62. *Down But Not Quite Out in Hollow-weird: A Documentary in Letters of Eric Knight*, by Geoff Gehman. 1998

63. *On Actors and Acting: Essays by Alexander Knox*, edited by Anthony Slide. 1998

64. *Back Lot: Growing Up with the Movies*, by Maurice Rapf. 1999

65. *Mr. Bernds Goes to Hollywood: My Early Life and Career in Sound Recording at Columbia with Frank Capra and Others*, by Edward Bernds. 1999

66. *Hugo Friedhofer: The Best Years of His Life: A Hollywood Master of Music for the Movies*, edited by Linda Danly. 1999

67. *Actors on Red Alert: Career Interviews with Five Actors and Actresses Affected by the Blacklist*, by Anthony Slide. 1999

68. *My Only Great Passion: The Life and Films of Carl Th. Dreyer*, by Jean and Dale Drum. 1999

69. *Ready When You Are, Mr. Coppola, Mr. Spielberg, Mr. Crowe*, by Jerry Ziesmer. 1999

70. *Order in the Universe: The Films of John Carpenter*, 2nd ed., by Robert C. Cumbow. 2000

71. *Making Music with Charlie Chaplin*, by Eric James. 2000

72. *An Open Window: The Cinema of Víctor Erice*, edited by Linda C. Ehrlich. 2000

73. *Satyajit Ray: In Search of the Modern*, by Suranjan Ganguly. 2000

74. *Voices from the Set: The* Film Heritage *Interviews*, edited by Tony Macklin and Nick Pici. 2000

STUART ERWIN

The Invisible Actor

JUDY CORNES

Filmmakers Series, No. 87

The Scarecrow Press, Inc.
Lanham, Maryland, and London
2001

SCARECROW PRESS, INC.

Published in the United States of America
by Scarecrow Press, Inc.
4720 Boston Way, Lanham, Maryland 20706
www.scarecrowpress.com

4 Pleydell Gardens, Folkestone
Kent CT20 2DN, England

British Library Cataloguing-in-Publication Information Available

Library of Congress Cataloging-in-Publication Data
Cornes, Judy, 1945–
    Stuart Erwin, the invisible actor / Judy Cornes.
        p. cm. — (Filmmakers series ; no. 87)
    Includes bibliographical references and index.
    ISBN 0-8108-4022-7 (alk. paper)
      1. Erwin, Stuart, 1903–1967. 2. Actors—United States—Biography. I. Title. II. Series.

PN2287.E787 C67 2001
791.43'028'092—dc21
[B]

                                    Library of Congress Control Number: 2001018880

♾️™ The paper used in this publication meets the minimum requirements of
American National Standard for Information Sciences—Permanence of Paper
for Printed Library Materials, ANSI/NISO Z39.48-1992.
Manufactured in the United States of America.

To

My father, for teaching me to love books;
My mother, for allowing me to be my own person;

and

My husband, for being so patient with me through the years.

1928

CONTENTS

PREFACE

"Walking down the street with sartorial sensations like Jimmie
Gleason and Pat O'Brien, I would be practically invisible."

—Stuart Erwin, *American Magazine* (1952)

STUART ERWIN, THE UNFAMILIAR

When I first told family and friends that I was writing a book about Stuart Erwin, I typically faced utter silence coupled with confusion, and not a hint of recognition with respect to my subject. Even among people in their seventies and eighties, there were likely to be inquiries about who this unknown actor was. "What was he in?" asked one acquaintance, a seventy-eight-year-old man. When I mentioned that Erwin had had one of his best roles as the newspaperman in *Viva Villa!*, a movie in which he appeared with Wallace Beery, my friend smiled and nodded, pleased that he had finally recognized the name. Then he assured me, "Oh, *yes*, I've heard of Wallace Beery." Among my colleagues in the teaching profession, only two or three had heard of him. "Maybe if I saw him in a movie, I'd recognize him," suggested one woman in her fifties, herself a fan of old movies. One colleague who *was* familiar with the name, a retired professor in his seventies, recalled that "he played in *Palooka*." But I was not surprised that this man had heard of Erwin; I was already aware that my fellow instructor knew a good deal about film history, including the names of the entire cast of *Rebel Without a Cause*.

On the other hand, my father, in his late seventies, thought that he remembered Erwin quite well as that man who usually played "silly parts" and died around 1942. My mother was not as certain about Erwin's identity as my father thought he was, so she asked some of her friends, all of whom are in their seventies and eighties. "None of them ever heard of him," she decisively informed me.

"I'll bet my great-aunt Ruby would have known who he was," I answered defensively. "She knew a lot about old movie stars; back in the early 1920s, when she was in college, she often went to the movies. She used to tell me about her favorite silent stars."

"That may be," my mother patiently responded, "but your Aunt Ruby is dead."

WHY STUART ERWIN?

Unlike some of those people of my parents' as well as of my own generation, I could recognize the name Stuart Erwin, even when I was a small child in the early 1950s. I loved the domestic comedies in those pioneer days of television, and I followed the fortunes and misfortunes of the characters on *I Love Lucy, The Adventures of Ozzie and Harriet, Father Knows Best, I Remember Mama, Our Miss Brooks*, and, a little later, *Leave It to Beaver*. But my favorite was *Trouble with Father* starring Stuart and June Erwin. Back then, I could not have explained why I liked the Erwin adventures the best, but in retrospect, I imagine the show's clever scripts and the genuine fondness displayed by the cast members for one another were the two features that appealed to me the most.

By the time I was a teenager in the late fifties and early sixties, I had transferred my loyalties from television comedies to classic movies, which proliferated on television during my adolescence and which were occasionally revived in theaters in my native Kansas City, Missouri. Even as an adolescent, I felt that I was living somewhere in the past. My heroes in those days were not such current teen favorites as Rock Hudson, Tab Hunter, Troy Donahue, Pat Boone, or Elvis Presley. Instead, I was in love with Ronald Colman, Paul Muni, William Powell, Mickey Rooney, Charles Chaplin, and his son Sydney, Lew Ayres, Cary Grant, and—my favorite—James Cagney. And Stuart Erwin? I knew the name, of course, but his movies were not among those often shown on television, so I rarely thought of him at all; I certainly did not include him among my heroes.

I was to get reacquainted with Erwin, however, a short time ago when I decided to buy on video some episodes of *Trouble with Father*. I was anxious to see if they were as funny as I remembered them. They were. But I was also struck by Erwin's performance as the caring but peculiar father. I knew that Stuart Erwin's reputation had been built around his longstanding screen persona as a boob who could not put on his shoes without a detailed instruction book. So I watched these shows for the first time in forty-five years, looking for that yokel who was supposed to be outsmarted by his wife and children. To my surprise, the bumbling fool was not there. What was there was a gentle, kind, loving man with a penchant for seeing the humor in everyday situations.

As I saw again those qualities that had evidently enchanted me as a child, I began to wonder about Erwin's place in movie history. I started searching through my collection of film books and found only brief references to his movies and equally brief biographical information. I examined indexes of film periodicals to see if career articles had been written about him, and I found nothing. Then I wondered if this critical neglect resulted from the fact that he had not been as truly effective in motion pictures as he had been on television. So I started collecting his movies to see for myself. And the more I watched and studied his work in motion pictures, the more convinced I became that he had always been a shrewd, skillful, versatile actor with both an intellectual and emotional appeal.

But perhaps I was suffering from spasms of nostalgia for the world that I associated with my childhood? So I decided to try an experiment with my students. I had been trying to explain to college freshmen in my introductory class in composition and rhetoric the finer points of developing an essay through specific representative examples. Exasperated with the traditional instructional materials I had been using, I had my students watch an episode of *Trouble with Father*. I then asked them to write their responses to the show and to give examples of what they saw in it that they felt revealed details of American life in the 1950s. Further, I asked them to contrast the family life of the television Erwins with family life as shown in television sitcoms today as well as with family life as it really exists in modern America.

The response I received from these students—many of whom were born in 1980 or 1981, thirty years after *Trouble with Father* premiered on television—was illuminating. Most of them really liked the show; one said that she thought it was better than either *Ozzie and Harriet* or *I Love Lucy* because the dialogue was sharper and funnier. Many expressed their delight in seeing a family whose members seemed genuinely fond of and comfortable with one another. In addition, and surprisingly, most said that they regretted the loss of a quality evident in the show: a quality embodying a world where family problems seemed to be less complicated, less serious than they are today. And they all enjoyed Stuart Erwin, whom none had ever heard of.

After reading their commentaries on a world that they knew only from history texts and from hearsay, I was more than ever convinced that Stuart Erwin needed a reevaluation—a serious study of his life and work. So here it is: a tribute to a man who, first, gave much pleasure to moviegoers of the 1930s and 1940s, and then to television viewers of the 1950s, and who returned via video to entertain their great-great-grandchildren in the first year of the next century. Because he needs to be more than a brief citation by film historians, because young people even today recognize his talent, especially his subtle sense of the absurd, and because he was an important part of my own childhood memories, I offer this recognition after so many years of neglect. I owe him that much.

PREFATORY NOTE ON MOTION PICTURE SOURCES

All of the quotations from Stuart Erwin's motion pictures are taken from dialogue from the actual movies themselves. Many of Erwin's films are still extant and available for viewing, either on video, on 16mm, or on television.

ACKNOWLEDGMENTS

Many people have helped me with this book. I am indebted to the staff at the Odessa College Learning Resources Center for ordering the material and providing the equipment for me to watch some of Stuart Erwin's movies. In addition, I appreciate the contributions of Sheila James Kuehl, William Schallert, and Toby Wing, all of whom graciously responded to my inquiries about their experiences in working with Stuart Erwin. I am especially grateful to the kindness and patience of Stuart Erwin Jr., who took the time to read my manuscript and who offered many valuable additions and corrections to my material concerning his father's life.

INTRODUCTION

"There he was, the man from an Iowa farm, the man from the Sioux Falls court-house, the man from Omaha, the man now fully ripe from Chicago. Here was no class, no race, nothing in order; a feature picked up here, another there, a third developed, a fourth dormant—the whole memorable but unforgivably ordinary."

—Robert Herrick, *The Web of Life* (1900)

"You're darn near perfect, you are."

—Joan Blondell to Stuart Erwin in *Make Me a Star* (1932)

A CASUALTY OF UNFORTUNATE CIRCUMSTANCES

They are stranded by an automobile breakdown in the desert somewhere in China—Stuart Erwin and Peggy Hopkins Joyce. Ms. Joyce is portraying herself, and she has just recently made Erwin the hapless victim of her determination to reach Wu Hu, China. When a washed-out bridge and subsequent train derailment force the Wu Hu-bound rail passengers to find other means of getting to their destination, Joyce latches onto Erwin and compromises his morals by persuading him to take her in his car on the twenty-four-hour trip from Shanghai to Wu Hu. And poor Erwin is already in trouble with his fiancée because he keeps catching childhood diseases and thus postponing their wedding. The movie is *International House* (1933), and the joke being played on Erwin's onscreen character would have been comprehensible to

1933 audiences but is quite remote today. The real-life Peggy Joyce, married six times, was an inconsequential actress but an elegant courtesan who played with wealthy men as though they were poker cards that might later be discarded for better ones. And Stuart Erwin, who was beginning to establish a movie persona as the unfortunate prey of vulgar opportunists, nevertheless lets Joyce know that, although they are isolated in the middle of no place, with Joyce pathetically trying to prepare breakfast, neither her aggressiveness nor her cooking skills impress him. When he examines the eggs she has just fried, which resemble cotton pieces that have been dipped in tar and left to congeal in the desert sun, he orders her to try again. The ensuing dialogue reveals their impatience with one another, but is also loaded with sexual tension:

JOYCE: You got a break. Miles away from everywhere. You spent half the night feeling around in the dark for nuts and bolts.

As Erwin tries to put her suitcase back into the car, it flies open, spilling her clothing on the ground. He starts to retrieve it:

JOYCE: Take your dirty hands off my lingerie. You start the engine and hurry.

ERWIN: What is your tearing hurry to get to Wu Hu?

JOYCE: Business. Dr. Wong's invention [television] is going to make millionaires. And I intend doing the same.

ERWIN (catching the sexual innuendo): You mean you're going to marry a millionaire?

JOYCE (speaking autobiographically): I never marry anything else.

ERWIN (growing increasingly agitated): Say, if my girl ever finds out I spent the night on the desert with a different girl. . . .

JOYCE: Oh, don't tell her. She might think you're having a good time.

ERWIN (disgusted, but still giving her a close look): *Good time*! Lady—I wouldn't enjoy a minute of this trip, even if you were Peggy Hopkins Joyce.

JOYCE (enjoying his discomfiture while triumphantly delivering the coup de grace): I *am* Peggy Hopkins Joyce.[1]

In *Going Hollywood* (1933), Stuart Erwin has to deal with another wily female. Here he is the producer of a motion picture: a recent college graduate who thinks that movies should be an "art" rather than a business, and who consequently appears out of place with the brainless denizens of the movie studio. He has developed a crush on would-be star Marion Davies, who in turn is clearly enamored of Bing Crosby. In one scene, director Raoul Walsh frames this triangle with Crosby on the left, Davies appropriately in the middle, and Erwin on the right. Erwin has had the good grace and judgment to give Davies the lead in his movie; Davies has just proved that he has not been mistaken in evaluating her talent, although Davies has precipitated Erwin's action by incapacitating Erwin's former leading lady Fifi D'Orsay, blackening her eye in a brawl.

Despite the high levels of testosterone just manifested by both of these ladies, Erwin still longs for Davies's affection, so he bravely invites her to a party. At first she agrees, knowing that Erwin is in a position to advance her career even more. But then, in steps Crosby, who has had an arrogant, cavalier attitude toward Davies up till this point, but who now senses an invasion of territory that he has not yet even staked out. Naturally, he invites her to the same party. Graciously conceding defeat, Erwin "remembers" a previous engagement for that evening and leaves Davies to the cunning of Crosby.

Meanwhile, Davies's friend Patsy Kelly has witnessed this exchange. As Davies and Crosby stroll happily off screen, she puts a thoughtful hand on Erwin's shoulder:

KELLY: Gee Mr. Baker, I'm awfully sorry you ain't taking her out instead of him.

ERWIN (outwardly calm but clenching his hand): Aw, that's all right.

KELLY: Oh no it ain't. If she had gone with you, it *would*'a been, 'cause you're harmless.

ERWIN (sarcastic but resigned to the unkind implication): Thanks.

KELLY: Oh, I mean—well—I can see that you're kinda stuck on Sylvia and—

ERWIN (defensive and hurt): Oh no, I'm not.

KELLY: Oh yes you are. Don't tell me. But *that* guy—tomorrow he'll be back with the French dame. I know men.[2]

Two years later, Erwin suffers a much more tragic defeat as he plays the doomed pilot in director Howard Hawks's *Ceiling Zero* (1935). As an airmail flyer, he philosophically accepts the dangers inherent in a job so dependent in those early piloting days on the uncertainties of weather conditions. Early in the movie, he returns from one of his runs, accompanied by his wife (Isabel Jewell), who always meets his plane and who is inexplicably but eternally suspicious of his activities when he is out of her sight. The brief screen presentation of the unfortunate Erwin/Jewell pairing is representative of Howard Hawks's dour view of marriage, a view that predominated in nearly all of Hawks's work. As Erwin enters the hangar, he asks his supervisor Pat O'Brien about Payson, a fellow flyer who has just bailed out and landed safely on the ground:

ERWIN: I heard Payson's jamboree over the radio. (Irrelevantly): Sure interfered with *Amos 'n' Andy*. What happened?

O'BRIEN: He got lost in the clouds and hit the silk. He's all right.

ERWIN: He ought to be tickled he's all in one piece.

JEWELL (facing Erwin and carefully looking him over while she suggestively fiddles with and pulls on his parachute straps): Hmph. I wish *you* were all in one piece.

O'BRIEN (looking irritated at her behavior): Hey! Do you always meet your husband when he lands?

JEWELL: Sure—and I sometimes wonder who meets him at the other end of the run.

ERWIN (placating her): Aw now, honey, all that I do when I get to Cleveland is call your mother.

JEWELL: You never call my mother.

ERWIN (wryly): You'd be surprised what I call her.[3]

Like the character that he plays in *Going Hollywood*, Erwin in *Ceiling Zero* is a decent guy, skilled at his craft, but painfully aware of life's precariousness and therefore fatalistically resigned to its uncertainties. In this philosophy, Erwin the actor appeared to agree with Hawks the director, whose movies usually reflected such fatalism. When ace pilot James Cagney wants to spend the day, and night, with his latest feminine conquest, he feigns heart trouble so that Erwin will go in his place on a mail run to Cleveland. The scene pits the scheming, frenzied melodramatics of Cagney against the concerned underplaying of Erwin. Supporting Cagney as he appears about to collapse, Erwin assures him that he can handle Cagney's run. When Cagney pretends to object, Erwin regretfully alludes to the night before, when too much drinking had gotten him in trouble with his wife: "I'm afraid to go home anyway." A few minutes later, after Cagney gleefully leaves, Erwin shrugs and muses offhandedly, "Guess I'll go to Cleveland."[4]

So Erwin surrenders once more to the reality of life's riskiness—except this time the risk is not worth taking. Returning from Cleveland, he confronts the horror of flying at 1,000 feet in a fog with his radio dead, while frantically, desperately—but vainly—trying to contact those on the ground to help guide him in for a safe landing. Unable to see the field, he stays with his aircraft all the way down, his plane exploding and burning as he crashes into the hangar. Erwin is never seen again onscreen in the movie, but we are told that he later dies in the hospital when his heart fails—an ironic touch that is not lost on the remorseful Dizzy Davis, the character played by Cagney, since the condition of Dizzy's heart has always been—and remains—just fine.

A TIME OF TRANSITION

To fully appreciate the personalities that Stuart Erwin created onscreen, it is important to understand the social background of the times in which Erwin shaped these characters. When he was born in 1903, Theodore Roosevelt was President, and according to Gail Bederman in *Manliness and Civilization*, Roosevelt considered himself a man's man, one who "grew up committed to Victorian codes of bourgeois manliness."[5] Further, as a child, Roosevelt "learned that male power was composed of equal parts kindhearted manly chivalry and aggressive masculine violence."[6] After the death of his first wife, Alice Lee, Roosevelt gave himself over more completely than ever to his cowboy-cum-aggressive hunter mentality. In *The Winning of the West*, his four-volume history of the eighteenth-century American frontier, Roosevelt applied the principles of Darwin to the Western experience and decided that the noble, manly American race had originated on the frontier. Likewise, it was this brave, violent, masculine race that had proved its worth through its ability to snuff out inferior races such as Indians and Black Americans.[7] Indeed, the brutal savagery of the white male paradoxically contributed to the advance of civilization because it enabled white American men to reclaim their continent and start building a better future.[8]

Stuart Erwin was born in Squaw Valley, California, an area that could be described at the turn of the last century as part of the western frontier. One of four children of a rancher, he came from the kind of primitive environment that so appealed to Roosevelt; in fact, he was often cast as a well meaning but unworldly country boy. But in many of his movies he also combined this paradoxical "kindhearted manly chivalry and aggressive masculine violence" that was found by Roosevelt to be so exemplary. Moreover, according to Bederman, this advocacy of the primal man goes back farther than Roosevelt, whose definition of true American masculinity might have been influenced by G. Stanley Hall. Hall was a prominent educator of the late nineteenth century and the founder and president of Clark University. Hall posited the pedagogical theory that little boys of the middle and upper classes should be encouraged to act like savages in order to counteract the feminizing influence of too much civilization. Hall cautioned that education

> was ... ruining schoolboys' health in civilized countries. American teachers were neglecting boys' bodies, allowing them "to atrophy, and chest, back, shoulders, hips, never to attain their fullest possible development." Hall warned that this "mutilation of civilized boys' bodies risked bringing a "sick and sterile epoch upon the world." If civilized American men lost their health and became neurasthenics, how could they lead the fight for further evolutionary advancement? Overcivilized effeminacy and racial decadence loomed.[9]

Hall's solution to this dilemma was a fuzzy resolution to this paradox. He explained that, if parents would raise their sons as primitives, these boys would somehow become tough but civilized men as adults. Hall believed that evolution would turn these violent young men into contemporary civilized (but by no means effeminate) men—his theory applying to men of the white race only, of course.[10] Hall showed his own indebtedness to Darwin through the implied reference to natural selection, especially in the mystical way in which Hall believed boys of the superior white race became productive men.

Much early twentieth-century literature reflects this prevailing belief with respect to American manhood. Willa Cather's short story "Paul's Case," written in 1905 when Stuart Erwin was still a toddler in rural California, traces the downfall of an adolescent who discovers that he cannot fit the mold of the virile male as extolled by President Roosevelt. In fact, Paul is depicted in much the same way as Hall had described the pathetic nature of boys' bodies due to the nineteenth-century trend toward the feminization of American education. He also appears to be afflicted by the traditional "woman's" disease of hysteria: "Paul was tall for his age and very thin, with high, cramped shoulders and a narrow chest. His eyes were remarkable for a certain hysterical brilliancy and he continually used them in a conscious, theatrical sort of way, peculiarly offensive in a boy."[11]

As portrayed by Willa Cather, Paul is a complete misfit, a boy who loves music, art, and theater. He hates the mundane, the colorless, the drab life of his native Pittsburgh; he craves bright lights, color, wealth. He does not want to marry, to reproduce himself like the boring, lifeless fathers that he sees sitting on the front stoops of Cordelia Street every Sunday, and to become a slave to the dull workplace. In short, Paul is passive, feminine, and artistic, but without even the aggressive energy required to learn how to draw, to write, or to play an instrument. Cather also strongly suggests that Paul is a homosexual, and that he has always been dimly aware that something that he fears within himself "was always there—behind him, or before, or on either side. There had always been the shadowed corner, the dark place into which he dared not look, but from which something seemed always to be watching him—and Paul had done things that were not pretty to watch, he knew."[12] Ultimately, Cather allows Paul only one option: suicide. Significantly, he cannot even bring himself to use the pistol that was his original choice of a way out. Perhaps because guns remind him of the masculine violence of Roosevelt's frontier, he chooses to jump beneath a train instead. He cannot live among the "savages" represented by his Calvinist father and by the dull, complacent men of Cordelia Street.

By the 1920s, Hollywood's presentation of masculine types echoed this depiction of Paul's confusion over his sexual identity; the way in which men were shown in movies of the late silent period was symptomatic of the changing nature of society's picture of the ideal, aggressive male. In the teens, the rugged western star William S. Hart, with a face that would have looked appropriate on a tin of chewing tobacco, had fit the Hall/Roosevelt turn-of-the-century model. Somewhat later, Douglas Fairbanks might have been the ideal "savage" as described by Hall and later by Roosevelt, but Fairbanks had a sense of humor and was having too much fun playing his athletic games. Elmo Lincoln, the first onscreen Tarzan, seemed a likely candidate for barbarity, but his hair was too long.

Then along came a group of handsome men who emerged in films of the 1920s and who were extremely popular with the ladies, including the flamboyant, effeminate, sexually ambiguous Rudolph Valentino and his Latin imitators such as Ramon Novarro, a publicity-shy homosexual off screen. Both of these actors represented the antithesis of the rugged man's man that Roosevelt had glorified. There were also two well-known Anglo "wise-crackers," William Haines and David Manners, who lacked the tough qualities so valued a generation earlier. Both were born in 1900—Haines in Virginia and Manners in Canada—both were extremely good looking and quite popular by 1930, both were homosexual, and both of them in their private lives entered into long-term relationships with their male companions. Haines was an "open" homosexual off screen, and the star of the ironically titled *A Man's Man* (1929). Manners gained popularity in horror films such as *Dracula* (1931) and *The Mummy* (1931), but he did some of his best work as the blind, gentle suitor of Barbara Stanwyck in *The Miracle Woman* (1931) and as the world-weary but passionate man in love with Loretta Young in

They Call It Sin (1931). Unlike Willa Cather's Paul, however, Haines, Manners, and Novarro were accepted by Hollywood in spite of their sexual preferences. Nonetheless, all kept their homosexuality relatively well hidden from the general public, especially during the thirties, when Hollywood became more conscious of its actors' morals than it had been during the flaming youth decade of the twenties. In addition, nonrugged actors with more traditional sexual orientation such as William Powell and Ronald Colman, both of whom first came to the public's attention in the 1920s, were nevertheless too debonair to accompany the likes of Roosevelt into the wilds of Africa for animal slaughter.

Although there was never anything at all sexually ambiguous about Stuart Erwin's characters, all of whom—even the wackiest, most offbeat comic ones—possessed a distinctly masculine orientation, the early decades of the century were ones which were constantly reexamining the role of the American male. And Erwin was to demonstrate from his very earliest pictures many sides to the men he portrayed.

Likewise, there were many parallels in American literature to society's changing definitions of manhood. For instance, by 1928, when Erwin made his first movie, two of the most popular authors in America exemplified this ambivalence about American men: Ernest Hemingway, already interpreting himself as a Theodore Roosevelt manqué, and F. Scott Fitzgerald, more at home with the cocktail glass than with the hunting rifle. Yet both novelists were puzzled by the riddle of sexual fulfillment. Hemingway partially solved this riddle by having his heroes and heroines enjoy their sexual encounters in odd and uncomfortable positions. Fitzgerald's characters remain so hysterically besotted that sex is either impossible or quite unnecessary to their happiness. Indeed, the two stars of the aforementioned *Ceiling Zero* would have been perfect choices to star in adaptations of Hemingway and Fitzgerald, respectively: Cagney is the ideal American version of Robert Wilson in "The Short Happy Life of Francis Macomber"—the opportunistic sexual predator with his double cot, always anticipating whatever "windfalls" might come his way. Stuart Erwin, on the other hand, is Fitzgerald's Jay Gatsby—idealistic, naïve, innocent, optimistic—as green as the green light at the end of Daisy's dock—forever seeking the woman as a vaguely Platonic concept, tragically unable to see the "foul dust [that] floated in the wake"[13] of his unattainable dreams. And, like Gatsby, Erwin was quite capable of depicting that paradoxical combination of fear combined with obliviousness to his own moral corruption, as he ably showed in 1934 in his portrayal of the newspaperman Johnny Sykes in *Viva Villa!*

In addition, as the dialogue from these three 1930s Erwin movies suggests, beneath the intelligence, beneath the sly humor and occasional amoral cynicism, beneath the kindness and decency and concern for others' happiness, there was also an undercurrent of longing for the elusive accolade, for that unattainable joy which was often just out of his reach. Yet, by the same token and somewhat ironically, Stuart Erwin was never confused about who he was. Comfortable with himself and certain of his own identity, his portrayals, no matter how strange or bizarre the character, always depicted the American male with no trace of confusion.

BEYOND THE NORM

This book, then, is an appreciation of the life and career of Stuart Erwin, a popular, dependable actor for over forty years, but largely neglected or treated only superficially by critics, possibly because he blended into the background so often that his performances were ignored. In fact, however, Erwin was a versatile actor who worked in virtually all of the most popular genres, and who was capable of playing serious roles as well as comedy. Moreover, he worked in many capacities; in addition to his movie work, he was at various times a stage manager, a stage actor, and a radio and television performer. He even starred in a 1947 industrial movie called *Doctor Jim*.

A physically attractive man with a certain diffident vulnerability about him, he lacked the polish of Ronald Colman, the curt cynicism of Bogart and Gable, the stalwart ruggedness of Gary Cooper and Victor Mature, the rough-edged, frantic violence of Cagney. Unlike Cagney, Erwin would never have splattered a grapefruit into a woman's face nor pulled her garters nor yanked her across the floor by her hair. But despite the differences with these popular leading men of the thirties and forties, he also demonstrated at various times the gentle manners of Colman, the world-weary attitude of Bogart and Gable, the sexual hunger and physical aggression of Cagney—even the tart-tongued humor of W. C. Fields. Further, like leading men such as Cagney, Bogart, and Victor Mature, and like the best of the heroic western stars, Stuart Erwin showed that, when called upon, he could die with style, as he demonstrates in *Ceiling Zero* (1935) and *When the Daltons Rode* (1940).

Although Erwin has usually been classified as a character actor—one who provided capable support for the dozens of leading men and women that he worked with—he often received top billing, playing many starring roles in films. Moreover, he was an astute, clever performer, combining the best parts of the Hemingway hero's bravado—what Hemingway called "grace under pressure"—and the Fitzgerald hero's wide-eyed openness and naiveté. But while Erwin's better-known contemporaries were always larger-than-life on the screen, Erwin never pretended to be more than an ordinary guy, sometimes so ordinary that he was nearly invisible. When he died shortly before Christmas in 1967, obituaries touted his reputation as the amiable "Mr. Average."

Except that Stuart Erwin was neither ordinary nor average. Not really. He was neither Sinclair Lewis's Babbitt nor W. H. Auden's Unknown Citizen. In fact, the appeal of his performances rests in his extraordinary qualities, on his versatility. Furthermore, Stuart Erwin was too guileless and straightforward to be average. One has only to read the literary critic Yvor Winters to understand that Erwin was an actor firmly established in the classical tradition. Writing in *The Sewanee Review* in 1948 about Robert Frost as a nonclassical poet who tended toward romantic sentimentality, Winters is rather critical of Frost, for Winters defines great artists as ones who have repudiated the normal or average:

> Classical literature is said to judge human experience with respect to the norm; but it does so with respect to the norm of what humanity ought to be, not with respect to the norm of what it happens to be in a particular place and time. The human average has never been admirable, and in certain cultures it has departed very far from the admirable; that is why in the great classical periods of literature we are likely to observe great works in tragedy and satire, the works of a Racine and a Molière, of a Shakespeare and a Jonson, works which deal in their respective ways with sharp deviations from the ideal norm; and that is why literature which glorifies the average is sentimental rather than classical.[14]

Indeed, Stuart Erwin consistently refused to glorify the average man. Furthermore, he eschewed the sentimental or maudlin; he distrusted the dishonest and phony. And if he can be said to have had a métier that he was most comfortable with, it was undoubtedly satire. He delighted in playing characters "with sharp deviations from the ideal norm." While Stuart Erwin the man was not one to promote himself as larger-than-life, Stuart Erwin the actor was many different characters, none of whom were ever average.

To illustrate, he was a radio operator on a submarine trapped beneath the China Sea, and he was a cameraman working in silent movies. He was a movie producer, and he was a rich Texan who bought a radio station, and he was an executive of an electric power company, fluent in a Chinese dialect. He was a pioneer airmail pilot, and he was a newspaperman who rode with Pancho Villa. He was a police reporter who solved a murder, and he was a lunatic who escaped from an asylum. He was a convict who helped a fellow inmate escape, and he was a western hero who accidentally killed a man threatening his territory. He was a prizefighter, and he was a football hero. He was an adventurer in the Congo who did not hesitate to work as an assistant to a female physician. He was a sailor who was sent to prison for mutiny. He was a persistent suitor offering unconditional love and marriage to a woman who he knew was pregnant with another man's child. He was a man with no fixed address; he lived everywhere and nowhere, yet he was always at home in the worlds he created, even as he was constantly shifting his identity.

In sum, what Stuart Erwin did achieve involved his traveling far beyond the boundaries that ordinarily surround Mr. Average Complacent American and finally coming to rest on television in the role of a loving but eccentric father. For Stuart Erwin, like Jay Gatsby, had his roots in slippery times, his young adulthood coinciding with the shifting moral standards of the Lost Generation in the 1920s. Unlike the fictional Gatsby, however, Erwin survived, ultimately to settle by the 1950s and 1960s into the relative stability of a satisfied, seasoned middle age. So too, unlike many other actors of his generation (Cary Grant, for instance), he was, from the start of his career, not only a man at peace with himself and unself-conscious (perhaps this is why he so easily and frequently changed shape), but also one who was modest to the point of self-effacement. As an example, throughout his long career, he never seemed to care where he was billed in the cast. Occasionally, he received top billing, but often he appeared third, fourth, fifth—or even further down in the credits. He was certainly not a man who demanded that his name be above the title. Possibly because he was so sure of who he was, he never felt compelled to engage in self-promotion.

In fact, through the years, Erwin gave interviews that suggested his innate modesty, notably when he referred to himself as just "a mere comedian." Perhaps this humble self-estimation contributed in part to his reputation with those film critics and historians who did not take him seriously enough to really study his work.

His overwhelming unpretentiousness, then, most likely kept him from getting the credit he deserved as an extraordinary comic actor, a regrettable oversight because he could handle quite expertly the incongruities of comic narrative. He was a master of both the verbal and physical non sequitur as he gave credence to the incoherent, usually with a perfectly solemn expression and absolutely effective timing.

Yet for all that, he was still capable of playing serious scenes and of exemplifying those "civilized" qualities promoted by G. Stanley Hall in his nineteenth-century description of the ideal man, the boy who has grown up from savagery to genteel manliness. And when he did turn serious, Erwin could make us hurt for him, while at the same time invariably refusing to hurt for himself. Furthermore, all of these traits were tempered by a sense of irony that was both cosmic and comic, wry and rueful. Erwin's characters often seemed to understand that our hold on the world is tenuous and that we have to keep our expectations realistic so as not to be disappointed.

In short, Stuart Erwin was a skillful, intelligent actor with a bittersweet emotional resilience and resonance that remain with the viewer long after specific details of the individual movies themselves have been forgotten. Thus, his appeal was both cerebral and visceral, for he was capable of evoking laughter while simultaneously slipping into his audience's emotional center and holding tightly enough to induce sadness. For too many years, he has been both overlooked and taken for granted. This book evaluates his vast body of film work, for he deserves much more recognition than he has ever received.

One of Stuart Erwin's early films, the tragically haunting *Make Me a Star* (1932), contains a memorable, crucial line. Erwin plays movie hopeful Merton Gill, who has just auditioned for a part in a film to be directed by a character called Jeff Baird (Sam Hardy). As Erwin is about to leave Baird's office, he shakes the director's hand, thanking him for his attention. Then he adds, "If you decide you want me, well, all I can say is I'll give you the best that's in me."[15]

And so he did. Again and again and again.

NOTES

1. *International House*. Dir. Edward Sutherland. Paramount, 1933.
2. *Going Hollywood*. Dir. Raoul Walsh. M-G-M, 1933.
3. *Ceiling Zero*. Dir. Howard Hawks. Warner Bros., 1935.
4. *Ceiling Zero*, 1935.
5. Gail Bederman, *Manliness and Civilization* (Chicago: University of Chicago Press, 1995), 172.
6. Bederman, *Manliness*, 172.
7. Bederman, *Manliness*, 178.
8. Bederman, *Manliness*, 182.
9. Bederman, *Manliness*, 90.
10. Bederman, *Manliness*, 91.
11. Willa Cather, "Paul's Case," in *Literature: An Introduction to Fiction, Poetry, and Drama*, ed. X. J. Kennedy and Dana Gioa (New York: Longman, 1991), 407.
12. Cather, "Paul's Case," 416.

13. F. Scott Fitzgerald, *The Great Gatsby*, with foreword and study guide (New York: Charles Scribner's Sons, 1961), 5.

14. Yvor Winters, "Robert Frost: or, the Spiritual Drifter as Poet," *Sewanee Review* 56 (1948): 565.

15. *Make Me a Star.* Dir. William Beaudine. Paramount, 1932.

1

LIFE AS AN ENTERTAINER

"From Mark Twain and Theodore Roosevelt to Steven Spielberg and Bill Clinton the evidence is overwhelming: the adult American male's dream of paradise is eternal boyhood."

—Russell Baker, in his review of *The Chief: The Life of William Randolph Hearst, New York Review of Books,* August 10, 2000

THE RANCHER'S SON

In 1922, the University of California at Berkeley was not the large, sprawling institution that it is today. But to young Stuart Erwin, recent high school graduate from Porterville, California, the campus was intimidating, formidable in size even then. Porterville is a small town close to the Nevada border, just west of Death Valley National Park, half way between Fresno, approximately fifty miles to the north, and Bakersfield, about forty miles to the south. It must have seemed particularly remote to young Erwin, for rural America in the early twentieth century was quite isolated, especially in those days before radio and good, paved roads. Especially awe-inspiring to Erwin when he arrived at the Berkeley campus were the slick, polished, sophisticated young men and women, among whom he felt awkward and self-conscious. "I was scared to death," he later admitted to an interviewer.

Even as a high school student in Porterville, Erwin had not been overbearing or intrusive; he had neither tried to be someone he was not nor aspired to be the most popular man on campus. One commentator, writing about Erwin in 1939, observed, "He never asks for more than his share of

1

anything in life."[1] So it was with the young Stuart Erwin, who was naturally reticent around others, but willing to observe them, to listen, and to learn. After he became a successful actor, he discussed with an interviewer the subject of *conversation*, and gave some advice pertaining to the best way to get along with others. It appears to have been advice that he himself had scrupulously followed from his high school days. "Don't use the word 'I' to excess," he cautioned. "Don't pretend you have read some book, seen some play or heard some music you haven't. Admit frankly you haven't, but are interested in what others have to say of them."[2]

Although young Erwin was basically shy, hesitating to throw himself into social situations, he did make an effort in high school to participate in extracurricular activities. He tried football; he played tennis and basketball. But he quit the football squad, and, by his own admission, preferred to play doubles in tennis. He found that in a singles game there was too much responsibility put on the individual player. He also played standing guard in basketball, but in those days, as Erwin later confessed, he rarely "crossed the center line"[3]; thus, he contributed a few points to each game, though not many. To the teenage Erwin, however, what was more important than athletics was the fact that his high school offered some opportunities to participate in student dramatics.

Bashful and timid, Stuart Erwin was not naturally fond of the idea of performing in front of others. But he had a way with words, a talent for expressing himself, so he forced himself to take part in his high school's drama activities. He felt that if he could manage to get up on a stage and play a role in front of a live audience, he could gain some self-confidence, be less self-conscious. And he soon discovered that he was happy on stage; in fact, the shy adolescent was sometimes happier on stage than off.

By the time he entered the University of California, he had decided to major in English and journalism. And, as he had done in high school, he concentrated on being less reclusive, on trying to overcome his natural reserve. In this endeavor he succeeded quite well; while he was at Berkeley, for instance, he was invited to join a fraternity. His best friend at this time and his fraternity brother was another young man with creative aspirations: Hamilton Luske, who was to become head of the animation department at Disney.

However, from the start of his college career, Erwin was always painfully aware of the probability of complications over which he had no control: complications that he had both anticipated and dreaded. These involved economic difficulties which were so severe that they eventually forced him to give up the idea of earning a degree. During his high school years, Erwin's parents had struggled financially; things had not gone well for them. Both wanted their son to go to the University of California, to get a first-rate education and to graduate. But they also reminded him that the costs involved would be very hard on them, that he might be forced to drop out at any time and go to work. And indeed, this is what happened, as Erwin had to leave college in his sophomore year.

According to Stuart Jr., his father rarely talked about the financial strain that attending college put on his parents. In fact, Erwin would later claim in interviews that he had left college because he had had a great deal of trouble getting the courses he wanted and that, as a result, he used the money earmarked for college to enroll in Egan's Drama School in Los Angeles. But, as Stuart Jr. pointed out, the "truth was he had no trouble getting his courses. However, there was no money earmarked for college. He was able to afford Egan's Drama School only after spending the summer crating cantaloupes near the California-Mexico border. He often did double shifts. The heat was oppressive, the work very physically demanding, but the pay was very good."[4] Confronted with abandoning his dream of a college degree, Erwin nonetheless desperately hoped that he could instead have a career on the stage. Moreover, once he had made his decision and earned the money to go to drama school, he always found ways to serve in some capacity in the entertainment business. Nor did he ever really leave his hard-working, rural background behind. Like Fitzgerald's idealistic Jay Gatsby, Stuart Erwin "believed in the green light, the orgiastic future that year by year recedes before us. It eluded us then, but that's no matter—tomorrow we will run faster, stretch out our arms farther. . . . And one fine morning—"[5]

Erwin was always one of those boats described by Fitzgerald at the end of *The Great Gatsby*: the one against the current, the one "borne back ceaselessly into the past."[6] As a consequence, there was always lurking somewhere in nearly every role that he played a boyish, childlike enthusiasm, an optimism that could rarely be stifled, even though the society surrounding him might fail to understand his oddly likable qualities.

Stuart Erwin was born on Valentine's Day in 1903 in Squaw Valley, California, fifty miles southeast of Fresno. On his mother's side, he was a third generation Californian. And, throughout his life, he continued to maintain ties to his native state, always preferring California to the East Coast. Yet he was not one to boast of his geographical origins. Once, when he was being interviewed about his estimation of women, he referred to his birthplace by adopting a mischievous pose and kidding the interviewer: "I was born in Squaw Valley, here in California. . . *Squaw* Valley, how do you like that?"[7]

His father was a rancher; both parents, according to Erwin's later account of them, were Victorian in attitude, very conservative, and apt to view their four children—Erwin, his two brothers, and one sister—as wild, uncontrolled members of the Lost Generation. Erwin claimed that both parents insisted that the children mind their parents, do their chores, and in general, do as they were told.[8] His father seems to have been the head of the household, moving them from the Squaw Valley ranch to a forty-acre peach orchard when Erwin was still a youngster. Later, when he was in his thirties, Erwin related the story by adopting a folksy, somewhat male chauvinist approach toward the young people hired to harvest the peaches. It was a humorous approach, one that belied the hard times faced by his parents in the teens and twenties: "Then we went to live on a *peach* orchard . . . and when the peaches were ripe for picking a bunch of girls and fellows used to hire out to us and pick 'em and, doggone, if the peaches that did the picking weren't more ructions and trouble than the peaches that were being picked. They were always having 'heart' troubles or something and the folks had to take more pains seeing that they didn't get bruised one way or another than they took with the fruit itself. . . . And still and all, they picked faster than the boys did. Even up a tree they had the fellows licked."[9]

ON STAGE

Such a bucolic setting as Erwin paints here is one that most audiences came to associate with the Stuart Erwin onscreen persona. But before he ever appeared on film, he first had a rather lengthy stage apprenticeship in front of him—one that would last from 1924 till 1928. His first break came in 1925, four months after he had been at Egan's Drama School. Erwin later recalled that he was given a chance to substitute in a play called *White Collars*, but without pay, not exactly the most promising of beginnings for the hopeful young actor. But it was a play that was known to New York theatergoers, for it had opened on Broadway in 1925 with Clark Silvernail and Cornelia Otis Skinner in the leads. What's more, Erwin's performance in *White Collars* was noteworthy enough that he eventually toured for forty-eight weeks in the play.

Erwin was fortunate enough to begin his career in the theater at a time when there was definitely promise in the air. The twenties was a fertile decade for American playwrights. Some of the best work ever produced on the American stage came out of the twenties. It was a decade of experimentation and innovation. The year 1923 was one in which Elmer Rice's expressionistic play *The Adding Machine* premiered in New York. Another expressionistic play that, like *The Adding Machine*, satirized the conformity of American life was the George S. Kaufman–Marc Connelly work *Beggar on Horseback*, which premiered in 1924. Likewise trenchant in its satiric commentary was George Kelly's 1924 play *The Show-Off*. The following year, George Kelly won the Pulitzer Prize for *Craig's Wife*. And *What Price Glory?*, the serious treatment of modern war by Maxwell Anderson and Laurence Stallings, opened in 1924. In 1926, Mae West's *Sex!!* caused such an uproar among the censors that, in 1927, Ms. West, charged with obscenity, served a short jail sentence in the Welfare Island prison.

The twenties was also the decade of Eugene O'Neill. *Anna Christie* opened in late 1921, *The Hairy Ape* came to Broadway in 1922, *Desire Under the Elms* was presented by the Provincetown Players in 1924, *The Great God Brown* opened in 1926, and *Strange Interlude* in 1928. If Erwin began his movie career at a time when the image of the American male was being redefined, he also began his stage career during a period of transition in the theater; even Eugene O'Neill received mixed reviews from his contemporaries for the innovative, daring form and content of his plays.

Not only were the plays themselves outstanding at this time, but they were also so numerous that the Broadway audience had over one hundred to choose from on any given night during the decade. For instance, during the 1920–21 season, 157 productions could be seen in New York. By 1923–24, the number had jumped to almost 200. The 1924–25 season offered 230, and by 1927–28, an all-time high of 280 was reached. Out of this total, two hundred productions were new plays. Furthermore, a list of names of the new playwrights of the twenties will sound familiar to any student in a beginning course in American theater history: Zoe Adkins, Maxwell Anderson, Philip Barry, S. N. Behrman, Marc Connelly, Zona Gale, Susan Glaspell, Sidney Howard, George S. Kaufman, George Kelly, Eugene O'Neill, Elmer Rice, and Robert E. Sherwood. It was also a decade of growth for the repertory theater. In 1926, Eva Le Gallienne opened her Civic Repertory Theatre on 14th Street in New York, which presented outstanding plays at an affordable price.

By the same token, smaller community theaters were spreading throughout the country; cities such as Cleveland, Chicago, Dallas, Kansas City, and Pasadena were among the most notable for the quality of their productions. Professional acting schools proliferated around the country, as did drama departments at colleges and universities. Although motion pictures provided competition to the stage, attendance at and participation in live productions remained high.

Following his acting debut in *White Collars*, Erwin continued to work in community and repertory theater until 1928. For one whole year, he played five roles in *The Open Gate* at the Morosco Theater in Los Angeles. He also worked in various capacities backstage, willing to take on any job asked of him. He would carry this professional attitude over into his film performances, for he often took minor roles, even after he had become an established star. Nor did his work in the theater always go smoothly. In an interview he gave in 1937, Erwin told a story about a theatrical producer he had worked for in the twenties, a gentleman whom Erwin graciously avoided naming. This individual refused to allow Erwin to act in his plays. "You know," Erwin recalled in the interview, "that guy would let me stage manage all his shows, handle the money and the business, ferry the company up and down between Los Angeles and San Francisco, but he *wouldn't* let me play in them." Erwin was typically to the point and candid about himself, unafraid to reveal the criticism made of his acting, as he resumed his tale of the producer: "He said he didn't like my type of work and I should be kept behind the scenery and not in front where cash customers could get a load of me. He stuck to his guns, too, and he never did let me play a single role the whole time I was with him!"[10]

But Erwin was not to remain behind the scenes forever. He ultimately went to work for Edward Everett Horton's stock company in Los Angeles, appearing in such contemporary, popular plays as *Beggar on Horseback* and *Women Go On Forever*. The former had premiered on Broadway in 1924, the latter in 1927 with Mary Boland and featuring James Cagney in a small role. One evening, while he was appearing as the lead in *Women Go On Forever*, Erwin was seen by some talent scouts for Fox, who happened to be in the audience that night. They were so impressed by his performance that he subsequently received a movie contract offer from Fox, and in 1928, he made his first film, *Mother Knows Best*. What is extraordinary about Erwin's good fortune in this instance is that, prior to this particular evening, he had been the stage manager as well as the understudy to the lead in *Women Go On Forever*. On this night, however, the leading man got sick, enabling Erwin to go on stage.[11] Such is the stuff of formula fiction and films, but here the facts indeed take precedence over the fantasy.

Moreover, unlike some other stage actors of the twenties who later went into movies, Erwin loved the stage and would continually return to it, occasionally on Broadway, sometimes in summer stock in New England. In November of 1942, he appeared in a play for the Theatre Guild, an oddly charming fantasy called *Mr. Sycamore*. Then, in 1943 he traveled to Chicago to costar with Skeets Gallagher at the Blackstone Theatre in the play *Good*

Night, Ladies, which ran from August 1943 till March 1944. Claudia Cassidy, drama editor of the *Chicago Tribune*, called *Good Night, Ladies* "astounding," and reported that "this was the show every stranger who hit town made a beeline to see, then went away saying, 'It's what Chicago likes.' Whoever liked it, 'Good Night, Ladies' left town in the face of capacity business."[12]

Seven years later, Erwin returned to Broadway to appear with Vivienne Segal in *Great to be Alive*. Not nearly as successful as *Good Night, Ladies*, *Great to be Alive* was a musical, which opened on March 23, 1950, and closed on May 13 of that year. It was produced by Vinton Freedley, who financed his own productions and who clearly lost on this one. An elaborate, handsome, and expensive show, *Great to be Alive* ended after fifty-two costly performances. Like *Mr. Sycamore*, it was a fantasy, with the kind of preposterous story that Erwin typically handled with aplomb. It concerned one Mrs. Leslie Butterfield (Vivienne Segal) who buys an old haunted mansion from Woodrow Twigg (Erwin). What is unusual about this dwelling is that the ghosts, all of whom are former residents, can be seen and heard only by virgins. Finally, these ghosts succeed in chasing all of the living residents from the house. Apparently, each and every one of these routed inhabitants meets the correct sexual standards for recognizing the ghosts. The premise is absurd, but with definite comic possibilities; such a vast number of sexual innocents as this play suggests, however, does seem a bit unrealistic, even for 1950.

Mr. Sycamore had an even briefer run of only nineteen performances, although a fairly good critical reception, with Erwin cited as being particularly noteworthy in the title role. (It is interesting that in both *Mr. Sycamore* as well as *Great to be Alive*, Erwin's sylvan name suggests that he is a natural character, one with no pretensions whatsoever.) In *Mr. Sycamore*, Erwin played a postman who becomes disillusioned with the woes of the world, so he finally decides to become a tree. David Burnham, writing in *Commonweal* in 1942, gave an entertaining synopsis of the play, which was based on a short fable by Robert Ayre and adapted for the stage by Ketti Frings:

> One fine spring morning, John Gwilt decides that twenty years of delivering mail to his small-souled neighbors are enough. He dumps the contents of his sack in the middle of the road, retires to his own back yard, digs a hole there, removes his shoes and socks and proceeds to plant himself. Naturally, his wife and neighbors think him demented. But their tune changes when his toes begin to put out roots, bark covers his legs, leaves sprout from his fingers. By the last curtain, John is a full-grown sycamore tree: stately, placid, benevolent: blissfully detached from the worries and bickerings and hypocrisies of humankind.[13]

On the surface, the plot sounds foolish; the actions of the title character resembling those of a game that a young boy would play with other children in the backyard. Yet Stuart Erwin was always able to make such purity of heart convincing. This quality of artlessness is noted by Burnham, as he continues with high praise for Erwin in his creation of John Gwilt: "To play the postman, the Guild recruited Stuart Erwin from Hollywood, and it's a happy choice. Mr. Erwin's John Gwilt is human, natural, modest and altogether lovable."[14]

Rosamond Gilder in her January 1943 *Theatre Arts* review agreed with Burnham's assessment, although she did offer a reason for the play's failure "to catch the imagination of critics or public." Referring to the mood of the World War II audience, Gilder suggested that "the ultra-isolationist attitude of Mr. John Gwilt . . . did not appeal at a moment when action is the order of the day. Mr. Gwilt's desire to plant his feet in the ground and raise his arms to heaven in perpetual contemplation seemed too oriental for the western mind. . . . Stuart Erwin, happily abstracted from Hollywood by the Guild to play the man-tree, gave a remarkably touching and dignified performance. His simple attack, his quiet, forthright honesty lent full value to what there was of poetry and honest imagination in the play."[15] However, by the time Gilder's favorable review of Erwin was published, *Mr. Sycamore* had already closed, with its last performance on November 28, 1942.

Then, in 1944, Erwin thought that he had been given a tremendous opportunity to further his reputation as a Broadway star. Mary Chase, a Denver native who had previously written one unsuccessful Broadway play, wrote *Harvey* with Erwin in mind as the lead. As she later told him, she never envisioned any other actor in the role of Elwood P. Dowd. In fact, she had even "heard" his speech rhythms as she composed the lines to be spoken by Dowd. But the studio that Erwin was under contract to at this time refused to release him to do the play. No matter how much Erwin and his agent argued with the studio bosses, they remained adamant; they had him in mind for a couple of forgettable pictures.[16] So the part went instead to vaudevillian Frank Fay in a comeback role. Fay had been a popular, influential comedian in the twenties and had enjoyed some success in films in the thirties. In fact, James Cagney admired Fay so much that he later recalled imitating Fay's "pleasantly acidic view of life" in his own performances.[17] However, Fay had suffered so from alcohol addiction that, by the late thirties, his career had faltered. Yet *Harvey* revived Fay's reputation: he received good notices for his performance as Elwood P. Dowd; Mary Chase received the Pulitzer Prize for her play; and Stuart Erwin received one of the greatest disappointments of his career.

Although many of the New York drama critics expressed their belief that Erwin would be a welcome addition to the Broadway theater any time he chose to return to the stage, it was as a movie actor that Stuart Erwin built his reputation. In his first three years in motion pictures, from 1928 through 1930, he appeared in twenty-one movies. One is tempted to wonder when or if he had time for a private life. However, in 1931, such private life as he was enjoying would undergo a permanent change.

JUNE COLLYER

In December of 1929, movie fans could browse through their latest issue of *Photoplay* magazine, for which they had paid 25 cents, and see articles on such diverse subjects as actress Olive Borden (*The story of a girl who learned to be natural*); the appearance of a new type of film called Grandeur Film, which was twice the width of the old-fashioned film, which required a wide camera lens and a new type of projector, and which was thrown on a screen forty feet wide and twenty feet high, "or one about twice as wide as the sheet we know." They could also read about what it took to be a girl in Hollywood who wanted to be an "extra" in movies. (*She Must Dance! She Must Sing! She's Pretty and Pert, and So's Her Old Adagio!*)

These 1929 readers might also have found entertaining the article about how to seat various movie stars at the table of a fancy dinner party. The seating arrangement had to be just perfect, of course, because the hostess wouldn't dare to seat two people next to one another who might be inclined to quarrel. So, continued the article, if you are careful, all will go well and your party will be a success. But wait! Our reader of seventy-one years ago is cautioned: "What's this, what's this? Mary Brian on one side and June Collyer on the other side of Buddy Rogers? I'll bet you worried your pretty head trying to separate Mary and June, but the joke's on you, for Buddy goes with them both and Mary and June get along fine." Well, what a relief it is for our 1929 readers to learn that Mary Brian and June Collyer refuse to bicker over Buddy Rogers. They also need to know that any Hollywood hostess would be glad to welcome June Collyer into her home, for Miss Collyer is "a nice young person."

This issue of *Photoplay* also contained many photographs of popular actresses posing in fashions which were doubtless the envy of budget-conscious women all over America. For instance, they could look longingly at the picture of June Collyer modeling a long-sleeved, modestly-cut V-neckline, ankle-length dress. She stands in three-quarter profile, one hand on her hip, and looks dreamily off into the distance. The caption gives the reader this tidbit about Miss Collyer and her attire: "No, no, June Collyer is not playing in a costume picture. This is the Greer creation she wears when she sips tea with Buddy Rogers. Not a solitary panel relieves the severe ankle length of the gown, which is form fitting and generously flared." It is good to know that what the elegant Miss Collyer is drinking is nothing stronger than *tea*, since we are still in the Prohibition era.

Our envious housewife, perhaps living in an Iowa farmhouse with no electricity or running water, and with an income of around $100 a year, now turns a few more pages, where she finds another photo of June Collyer. This time, Miss Collyer has had her skirt shortened, although her knees are still covered. She is also wearing high-heeled shoes, increasing her height about three inches and calling attention to her well-proportioned calves. Furthermore, the caption tells our reader that "concealed pleats make this sports frock the last rave." And oh yes. We also need to remind our unseen audience that this latest "rave" is another Howard Greer creation.

As the editors of this 1929 *Photoplay* were very much aware, June Collyer was a popular, well-known actress, immediately recognizable to their readers; in addition, she possessed a charming, dimpled smile; a tall, slender figure which showed off designer clothing as the designers intended it to be shown; and a pleasingly refined air. She carried herself as though she were completely satisfied with herself, at home in her own body. She had appeared in her first film in 1927, so with nearly three years' experience as a movie ingenue, she was a natural choice to be featured in movie magazines in the last year of the roaring twenties. Further, if readers of 1929 wanted to see with what film studio Miss Collyer was currently affiliated, they had only to read in *Photoplay* the long lists of players mentioned under each studio heading to find that Miss Collyer could be contacted through Paramount.

Now let's return to our Iowa housewife, browsing through her *Photoplay*, looking for the titles of new pictures; she might even find a title that looks promising, one that might be playing in the local town. Maybe she has recently become a Stuart Erwin fan, having seen him the previous year in his first movie, *Mother Knows Best*. Or perhaps she has already seen a few of his eleven films released in 1929. So she looks through the cast lists for current releases and finds his name once: in the cast of *Sweetie*. However, she would not find his name in the casts and reviews of the following movies, all of which are mentioned in her 1929 *Photoplay*, because Stuart Erwin, the invisible man who appears in all of these films, is not listed among the actors: *The Trespasser*, *The Sophomore*, *Thru Different Eyes*, *The Exalted Flapper*, *Dangerous Curves*, and *The Cock-Eyed World*. Moreover, in the last two of these, Erwin has a fairly large role, with at least two or three scenes as a featured player, with dialogue of enough significance to propel the plot forward. So, having seen one or both of these movies and having been impressed with his brief but memorable appearances, perhaps our rural housewife wants to write Erwin a fan letter. Consequently, she consults the lists of players under their appropriate movie studio affiliation in order to see where to send her letter. But, alas, Erwin will never receive her letter, for his name does not appear on any of these lists.

On the other hand, the photogenic June Collyer, who had debuted in silent movies, is prominently featured in several places throughout the magazine. Much better known in 1929 than Stuart Erwin and from a socially noteworthy family, Miss Collyer was considered at that time to be far more appealing copy to movie fans around the country than he was.

June Collyer, the woman who was to be Stuart Erwin's wife for nearly four decades, was born Dorothea Heermance in New York City on August 19, 1906. Her father, Clayton Heermance, was quite wealthy (he was sometimes referred to as a member of the New York 400) and June would become a much sought-after debutante. But she appears to have grown up with a graceful sense of noblesse oblige that translated itself into charitable work she did throughout most of her life, including contributions to the Actors' Fund. Besides her work with organized charities, she reportedly was generous, privately and anonymously, in her offering time and money to fellow actors who were down on their luck. She sometimes worked with the Hollywood Women's Press Club to give benefit parties for those in the profession who were having financial difficulties.

When she met Stuart Erwin in 1931, she was still the popular ingenue that she had been in 1929—and she was still being featured in fan magazines, often interviewed about her views on topics of the day, such as changing fashions for women or New Year's resolutions—the sorts of things movie magazine editors thought would interest their female readers. In addition, in typical Hollywood publicity style, she was reported to be romantically involved with any number of handsome leading men, among them Buddy Rogers.

Then in 1931 she was cast in a routine, forgettable Paramount picture, *Dude Ranch*. Also cast in the movie was Stuart Erwin, who had already established a reputation as a light and a light-headed comedian. They seemed an odd pairing: she, born into a wealthy family on the East Coast; he, born into a ranching family on the West Coast; she, demure and sophisticated; he, shy and awkward; she, the darling of the fan magazines; he, barely recognized at all in these movie magazines. His successful courtship of her surprised a good many people. One interviewer in 1935 even had the temerity to ask Erwin how he ever happened "to win pretty June Collyer, who had plenty of admirers on both sides of the continent."

Erwin's response was typically modest and understated as he explained, "Well, we were both working in a picture called *Dude Ranch*. We had such putrid parts and felt so sorry for each other that we got right sentimental about it. So finally we just got married."[18]

Somewhat later, June Collyer had a different, much warmer, more sentimental perspective on why she married Stu Erwin. In an interview she gave in 1936, she recalled her first impression of him. If her recollection sounds unrealistic—like overly romantic hyperbole—it also sounds plausible in light of the overall sense felt by others concerning the kind of man Erwin was. As June Erwin told the story: "Stu is so real. That's why I fell in love with him, you know. I fell in love with him the very first time I ever talked to him. I'd seen him about the studio quite a bit and we were working together in *Dude Ranch* and I thought he was nice. But the very first day he ever asked me out to lunch I knew that—well, that it was love—and so real and so satisfying that everything and everyone else in the world seemed unimportant."[19]

Both June Collyer and Stuart Erwin apparently knew what they wanted; their courtship did not last long. They were married on July 22, 1931, the same year in which the fateful *Dude Ranch* was released. They also made up their minds to be married quietly, without telling any of their friends. "We wanted to get married and do the explaining later," they recalled. Because California had a three-day notification law, they decided against being married in Los Angeles, so, accompanied by June's two brothers, Dick and Bud Heermance, they drove all night to Yuma, Arizona—a difficult auto trip in the early 1930s—where they were married by a judge the following morning.[20]

Bud served as best man at his sister's wedding while June's other brother, Dick, kidded himself about being the "bridesmaid," as the four of them stood in the sweltering 108 degree Arizona heat, waiting for the judge to perform the ceremony. According to one account, the Erwins' wedding did not remain secret for long, as the wire services were soon alerted to the marriage of these two celebrities. But, as usual, June Collyer was the one to receive the recognition, for the Hollywood newspaper headlines announced, JUNE COLLYER ELOPES. Once again, her husband remained relatively invisible and in the background.[21] A further illustration of the relative fame of the newlyweds could be seen in a photograph published on July 24, 1931. The photo shows June and Stuart posing in front of a motion picture theater shortly before their marriage. The caption under the photo once again gives top billing to June Collyer: "FILM BEAUTY MARRIES COMEDIAN. June Collyer, motion picture actress and sometimes called the 'most beautiful woman in pictures,' and Stuart Erwin, motion picture comedian, were married at Yuma, Arizona, on July 22nd."

What June's parents thought of this marriage between their daughter and a mere movie comedian from a Squaw Valley ranch remains a question. However, shortly after the wedding took place, they did put in a call to Yuma to their daughter and new son-in-law, a call which took an hour to get through from the Heermances' location in Chicago. It does appear that Erwin got along relatively well with June's parents, for during the thirties when he and June traveled to New York, they usually stayed with the Heermances in their Park Avenue apartment. In fact, early in 1932, when the newlyweds visited New York, Clayton Heermance was asked where the "children" were "stopping" while they were in the city; he reportedly chuckled and replied that, in light of the fact that both of these children were Scottish, the answer to that question would be obvious. Although June would continue to bring her husband with her to New York when she visited her parents, the city was a place that Erwin admitted he never could adjust to. It usually gave him a headache, he once told an interviewer. Nor did he like the late hours kept by New Yorkers. As a California boy, he preferred the climate and the atmosphere of his native state.

Meanwhile, in the years immediately following her marriage, June Collyer continued to be featured and interviewed in fan magazines. The February 1932 issue of *ScreenBook* magazine (10 cents a copy, with a color photo of Greta Garbo on the cover) carried an article, "The Stars' Hopes for 1932" or *What Hollywood favorites wish for more than anything else on the dawn of a new year.* And June Collyer, one of these Hollywood favorites, cogently expressed what she wished for: "A little love nest with Stu Erwin—my husband." No one asked that question of her husband.

It is perhaps interesting to note at this point that, while Stuart Erwin made five movies in 1932, two of which were extremely popular and gave him good, important parts—*The Big Broadcast*, in which he received top billing over Bing Crosby, and *Make Me a Star*—his wife appeared in none that year. Further, although June made only one movie in 1933, *Revenge at Monte Carlo*, her husband made ten movies in that same year. By 1934, the Erwins were the parents of one child (a son, Stuart Jr., born in 1932), and June appeared in four films that year. The best of these is the clever, offbeat, witty mystery *The Ghost Walks*. Both she and the movie received good reviews. Also well received were her two last feature-length movies, *Murder by Television* (1935) and *Face in the Fog* (1936). In all three of these films she managed to make her stock character, a young damsel-in-distress, charming. But despite her continuing popularity and the good notices that she was receiving, June found it more and more difficult after their son was born to concentrate on her work at the studio, especially if she had reason to worry about her baby at home. As a case in point, on the occasions when she had to leave her ailing child at home in order to report to the studio, she could not wait to finish shooting for the day, feeling that her life was becoming increasingly fragmented.

Finally, when she gave birth to their second child (a daughter, Judy) in 1935, she decided to retire from acting in order to devote herself full time to her growing family. It appears to have been a decision that she was comfortable with and one that she did not regret. It was also one that she evidently made on her own, something that was not demanded of her. It was not a requirement that a person of Stuart Erwin's temperament would have imposed. Speaking of June's determination to quit her career, Erwin told an interviewer in 1936: "I had always hoped that June would give up the screen. Of course, I wouldn't have tried to force her—"[22]

And by 1936, Erwin had indeed finally become the better-known actor; in point of fact, 1936 was the year in which Erwin received his only Academy Award nomination—for Best Supporting Actor in *Pigskin Parade*. On the other hand, by the mid-thirties, June Collyer was receiving little notice by the fan magazines, except as the wife of Stuart Erwin. By that time, publicity photographs taken of June included her husband: they were pictured at the racetrack, dining out at a Hollywood nightspot such as the Trocadero, or dancing together. Often she was seen at home with him and their children.

For her part, June also spoke publicly in 1936 about her resolve to stay home with her children. She told an interviewer, "Why shouldn't I give up any idea of working? Perhaps our life would seem quiet and uneventful to many people. But Stu makes every little thing so joyous and important. The baby's new tooth, Stuart Junior's first swimming lesson, the dinners we cook together on cook's night out. He has such a faculty for making daily living vivid and real and fun that I don't need a career—I've got one!"[23] The following year, she offered another interviewer further insights into her feelings about the life she had willingly chosen: "You see, after Stu and I were married, I decided there needn't be more than one career in the family, at least one professional career. So I quit pictures and have made Stu's career mine. It's so much safer and ever so much more fun this way."[24]

But fourteen years later, June Erwin would return to the screen via television, when she played herself, the wife of Stu Erwin, in *Trouble with Father*. The series premiered in October of 1950 and continued until April of 1955. She was his perfect television foil—unruffled but wary, with occasionally snappy remarks when she saw that he was about to embark on a project for which he was mechanically and temperamentally ill-suited, such as installing a TV antenna by climbing on the roof or putting in a burglar alarm system. In the first instance, when his shoes fly off the roof and crash through a neighbor's window, she calmly removes the glass from the shoes' insides and hands them back to him. In the second, when he switches on the alarm system, thus precipitating the movement of her vacuum cleaner, as it starts up and begins easing itself slowly across the room as though by remote control, she looks completely unperturbed and not at all surprised. So too, she appears totally at ease with him, comfortable with him, as does he with her. Moreover, even into his fifties, Erwin here in *Trouble with Father* retains the boyishly confused affability that had been one of his most appealing qualities from his beginnings in films.

A few years after the series began, Erwin maintained that he and June simply played themselves on the show, and that they even built many of the stories around actual events that had occurred in their own lives. Though it is difficult to judge the nature and quality of any marriage—even friends and family often do not know what truly goes on in a couple's private moments—June and Stuart Erwin appear to have had a good, easy relationship and a contented life together for thirty-six years, until his death from a heart attack in the early morning of December 21, 1967.

In the summer of 1932, June Collyer had told an interviewer, "I am looking forward to the time for growing old."[25] On March 16, 1968, June Collyer died of bronchial pneumonia, outliving her husband by less than three months. She was 61.

A STUART ERWIN CAREER OVERVIEW

Because I examine many of Erwin's movies at length in this book, I will give here just a brief summary of some of his lesser-known accomplishments during his five decades in film. His first movie was the part-talking Fox picture *Mother Knows Best* (1928). In the late twenties and early thirties he made a series of movies, primarily at Fox and Paramount, which vary in quality. Some are part-talking, such as the excellent John Ford film *Men Without Women*, the only movie he made from 1930 onward that had silent sequences. Some of these earliest pictures are completely silent, such as *Thru Different Eyes* (1929). Erwin has only a walk-on as a reporter in this latter picture, which is of interest chiefly because it explores in flashbacks a murder; this murder is told from different points of view, until the real murderer is finally disclosed. It is a narrative technique that would be repeated many times in other films, but it is well handled and fairly suspenseful here. At this time, Erwin also starred with Edgar Kennedy in the silent two-reeler, *A Pair of Tights* (1929). The picture was directed by Hal Yates, who directed many of Edgar Kennedy's later two-reel comedies.

Erwin made ten movies in 1930; some of them are discussed at length in subsequent chapters. In addition to those which I examine later, his other 1930 movies of more than passing interest are *Love Among the Millionaires* and *Playboy of Paris*. Both look satirically at the world of the rich, a view taken by many films of this early depression era. In *Love Among the Millionaires*, Clara Bow is the daughter of a coffee shop owner; she waits on the customers, and generally helps out her father (Charles Sellon). When she falls in love with the son of a railroad magnate and wants to marry above her class, she finds herself blackballed by the snobbish father. All turns out happily for the couple, however, when the father comes to his senses about Clara's intrinsic worth and proves to be a human guy after all, even though he is wealthy.

Erwin teams with Skeets Gallagher to provide the comedy in *Love Among the Millionaires*: a running gag involves a car that the two own jointly and which they constantly quarrel over, each asserting that when something goes wrong with their jalopy, the problem is on the other fellow's side. And something is indeed always going wrong. On one of their outings with Bow's father, the old man declares that they have endured a total of nine blowouts to the car's four tires. At one point in the nonsensical story, Erwin and Gallagher become so irate and territorial about which half of the car belongs to which one of them, that each systematically begins to dismantle various essential body parts from the others' half; in this routine they resemble a less frantic version of Laurel and Hardy. Erwin and Gallagher also sing exuberantly, if not particularly melodiously, the movie's title song, obviously not taking too seriously either *love* or *millionaires*. They also do some funny bits with the talented, precocious child actress Mitzi Green.

Playboy of Paris is the other 1930 movie that provides some inspired, entertaining moments. The title character is not played by Erwin, but by Maurice Chevalier. Both are working class, however, and both struggle to get by. Erwin is a dishwasher in a Paris café in which Chevalier works as a waiter. Complications ensue when Chevalier inherits a lot of money and his employer tries to hide the fact from him. There is a funny bit at the film's end when Chevalier is challenged to fight a duel, and his unlikely tutor is portly Eugene Pallette, appearing thinner than he would ten years later, but also sounding even less like a Frenchman than Stuart Erwin does. Erwin and Pallette helpfully volunteer to act as Chevalier's seconds for this duel, but since none of these silly men, who all together look like a parody of the Three Musketeers, knows what he is doing, it is fortunate that the duel is cancelled at the last minute. When Chevalier's potential rival and likely killer discovers that Chevalier is not of the upper class, the duel is naturally called off.

Although Erwin is not given much to do, the movie does display the comic talents of Chevalier, who had the ability to laugh at himself. Especially in his earliest films, he refused to take himself too seriously. Further, Stuart Erwin demonstrates here his skill in playing a good buddy to the leading man, in subordinating himself to the star of the picture. It is a talent which Erwin developed quite well, and which we will explore later when we examine some of Erwin's "good pal" roles in more detail.

One other significant Erwin film of 1930 is *Young Eagles*. Roger Dooley describes the picture as the "first '30s espionage film involving World War I." It is "a bizarre tale that mixed flying with spying. [Buddy] Rogers and his sidekick, Stuart Erwin, are set up by their superiors in an elaborate plot in which they are apparently duped by a German spy (Paul Lukas) who escapes with his accomplice (Jean Arthur). The girl turns out to be a double agent, merely using the German to get behind enemy lines. Surprisingly, her dresses and those of other women in a party scene in Paris are authentic to the war period—most unusual in 1930."[26] The years 1931 through 1933 were busy ones for Erwin. In addition to the films mentioned in later chapters, his most notable movies of this period were *No Limit* (1931), *Dude Ranch* (1931), *Misleading Lady* (1932), *Day of Reckoning* (1933), and *Before Dawn* (1933). He has small, off-center roles in *No Limit* and *Misleading Lady*. In the first, he appears only briefly at the beginning and the end of the movie: he is the man who loans his apartment to a group of people who, unbeknownst to Erwin, turn it into a popular gambling establishment. In *Misleading Lady* he plays a truly odd part in a movie with a distasteful premise. The picture's star, Edmund Lowe, kidnaps Claudette Colbert and keeps her prisoner in his country home in retaliation for a joke she had played earlier on him. There are some unmistakably threatening sexual innuendoes permeating this movie. (These sexual implications are especially intriguing in light of later revelations that both Lowe and Colbert were real-life homosexuals.) But Erwin is not involved directly with the tensions between the two stars. Rather, he crashes the picture toward the finish, as a crazed escapee from a nearby asylum. He intrudes upon the odd Claudette Colbert/Edmund Lowe love nest, bearing approximately one significant word of dialogue, "Waterloo," which he repeats with various intonations from time to time, until he is recaptured and sent back to the asylum, doubtless grateful to be escaping from this movie.

Although Erwin dismissed another interesting movie of 1931, *Dude Ranch*, when he discussed it with an interviewer who had asked him about his courtship of June Collyer, the movie was fairly well received. *Photoplay* reviewed it in the issue of July 1931 with the following endorsement: "Jack Oakie woos and wins June Collyer in this hilarious comedy on a dude ranch, *locale* of many complications. Not a dull moment."

However, a much better film is *Before Dawn* (1933), a Gothic murder mystery in which Erwin plays a police investigator who gets involved with mysticism and the spirit world, and falls in love with exotic, dark-haired Dorothy Wilson, the intense, psychic lady who helps solve the murder of Jane Darwell. *Day of Reckoning* (1933) is also a good picture, albeit melodramatic. Erwin is not given much of a role: he plays a milkman who courts Una Merkel. These two constitute the subplot of a picture which traces the misfortunes of an embezzling husband (Richard Dix) who has a good heart but a greedy will and consequently goes to prison for a stretch, leaving his wife and two children behind.

Two of Erwin's best movies of 1934 are discussed later—*Viva Villa!* and *Palooka*. He made only two feature films in 1935—*Ceiling Zero* and *After Office Hours*. The former movie, which I have considered in the introduction, is one of the best of Howard Hawks's pictures of the thirties. Its fine cast includes James Cagney, Pat O'Brien, Erwin, Isabel Jewell as Erwin's possessive, hysterical wife, and a young newcomer, June Travis, as Cagney's would-be romantic conquest. Cagney plays one of the most blatantly seductive roles of his career, but he looks unusually tired, with dark circles under his eyes, appearing much older than his thirty-six years. Erwin's other 1935 picture, *After Office Hours*, is another murder mystery, this one starring Clark Gable and Constance Bennett. Erwin had already played a secondary role to Gable in *Hold Your Man* (1933); in *After Office Hours*, though, he has more screen time. Gable is a tough-talking reporter who enlists the help of his fellow newsman-photographer Erwin in solving a murder. In his efforts to find out who was responsible for a woman's death, Gable puts his sidekick Erwin in a number of ridiculous situations, which Erwin handles gracefully and comically, often taking the focus off Gable, the romantic lead, in the scenes where they appear together.

In the same year, Erwin appeared as himself in a one-reel picture for Paramount, part of a series called "Hollywood on Parade." One of the first in the series, it is generally considered to be one of the best. Erwin is the host, introducing a number of Paramount stars who do their stuff. The movie uses a format similar to the one utilized in the earlier revue *Paramount on Parade*, which also featured Erwin. Leonard Maltin, in his book *The*

Great Movie Shorts, has an entertaining synopsis of this particular entry in the series:

> It opens with Bing Crosby singing "Auf Wiedersehn." Then Bing intro-
> duces his friend, George Burns, and asks if he might meet his partner.
> George brings out Gracie Allen and says, "Gracie, this is—" She inter-
> rupts. "Oh, Morton Downey!" "No," says Bing with a touch of amuse-
> ment, "I'm Rudy Vallee." "Well," says Gracie, "if you're going to keep
> changing your name, *nobody* will know you!"[27]

The following year, Erwin received his only Academy Award nomination, for Best Supporting Actor in *Pigskin Parade*. However, both Erwin as well as fourteen-year-old Judy Garland, in her feature-film debut, are seriously mis-cast as Arkansas hicks. The only time Garland looks comfortable is when she is singing, and is thereby finally allowed to use good, standard English; the only time Erwin looks comfortable is when he is dancing with some college coeds and at last fittingly dressed in a suit and tie. He comes off much better that same year in *Women Are Trouble*, one of his many cynical reporter roles. Both of these 1936 movies are analyzed in more depth in later chapters.

Small Town Boy (1937) sounds like a title for a quintessential Stuart Erwin picture, and it does indeed contains some funny moments as well as a prem-ise with some promising possibilities for the kind of lunacy that Erwin was so adept at developing. In this one, Erwin finds a thousand dollar bill and, being the honest, upright, if naïve, citizen that he is, he spends a good deal of the movie trying to find the rightful owner. Not till the end of the movie does he discover that the bill is counterfeit. By then, however, the joke about the unworldly young man's honesty has worn thin. Erwin tries hard, but the weak script works against his best efforts. The picture does have an inspired, mani-acal scene featuring the blissfully demented character actor George Chandler, who shows off his car by taking Erwin on a hair-standing-upright ride down a circuitous incline.

Despite the advance publicity for this movie when it premiered in 1937—it was actually touted as being Erwin's first starring role, which it wasn't—the picture misfires. It was Erwin's first picture for the low-budget Grand National; his second and last picture for the studio was the much bet-ter *Mr. Boggs Steps Out* (1937). Although he had been under contract to M-G-M since replacing Lee Tracy in *Viva Villa!*, by 1937, Erwin and M-G-M had agreed to part, whereupon he signed with Grand National. When an in-terviewer in 1937 asked him about what had occurred between Erwin and the studio for which he had worked a number of years, Erwin was typically reticent about revealing any displeasure and resentment he might have felt.

Nor does he name the individual involved in the controversy, a pattern that he would follow each time he was forced to say anything which might be construed as the least bit negative with respect to a friend or colleague. As he explained: "There's a producer at the studio who doesn't seem to like my work. He's a good friend, but every time I thought I was set in a role, I found I wasn't. So I went to the studio and we agreed quite amicably to disagree about signing another contract with them."[28]

In the meantime, when he was not appearing in films and when his studio contract allowed him to take on other work, Erwin did many radio shows, especially during the thirties and forties. He loved radio and enjoyed performing with good friends such as Burns and Allen and Jack Benny and his wife Mary Livingstone. (Both Erwin and Benny were born on Valentine's Day and often celebrated their birthdays together.) In addition to appearances on *Burns and Allen* and *The Jack Benny Show*, Erwin was a regular on several other half-hour comedy/variety shows. In the summer of 1945, he starred in his own half-hour show, *Phone Again, Finnegan*. In addition, Erwin did some dramatic radio shows, including the popular drama anthology, *Suspense*. He was also featured on *Lux Radio Theater* in a reenactment of the movie *Ceiling Zero* with his movie costars James Cagney and Pat O'Brien.[29]

Although he enjoyed working in radio, Erwin would always return to films. By 1938 he was working at 20th Century Fox; in 1939, he appeared in *Hollywood Cavalcade* for Fox. Filmed in Technicolor, this movie provides a sentimental, nostalgic look at the days of silent filmmaking. Erwin has another of his "good pal" roles as the buddy of Don Ameche; he has little to do except play the loyal cameraman who follows the fortunes and misfortunes of silent film director Ameche, who loses and finally wins leading lady Alice Faye. Then, in that same year, Erwin returned to Paramount to make *Back Door to Heaven*, originally titled *Frankie*, a picture that he filmed in New York. In a 1939 interview, Erwin himself gave a neat synopsis of the story: "The story begins when we're all kids. . . . Then five years later—movie time—Wally Ford comes in and after getting in plenty dutch is shipped to the reformatory. Another five years later, the scene is Leavenworth, and we're just getting out from a stretch. Things happen and we're no sooner out of cold storage than back we go again. I'm always around to get into messes even though I don't commit the deed. I guess I'm just too dumb to clear out once the cops head our way."[30]

Back Door to Heaven has more to recommend it than Erwin's brief summary would suggest. The abrasive realism of the opening scene reminds us of the naturalistic settings of Warner Bros. movies of this decade, as we are introduced to the Wallace Ford character as a young boy. The sparsely furnished rooms in which he lives with his parents—the father an alcoholic, the mother a wasted, exhausted woman with nothing left but empty time—introduce a major motif of the picture: that there will never be a way out of this life for any of the characters.

Erwin enters the film as a prison buddy of the boy who grows up to be Wallace Ford. When Erwin, Ford, and Bert Frohman as Bert, the third prison pal, are released from prison for the first time, they head immediately for a diner to eat some real food. Nicely, formally dressed in business suits, they sit at the counter, scooping steak into their mouths, delighting in their freedom to enjoy something so obviously edible. As they are relishing their meal, the cook behind the counter inadvertently ignites grease on the griddle, which immediately begins a fire directly in front of the three ex-convicts. Not wanting to miss a bite of their interrupted supper, they rise from the counter, walk calmly out of the diner and down the street, still carrying their plates of food. Looking for a place to sit, they wander into a nearby mission hall, where an organist is playing a ponderous tune, and where an audience of worn out looking men have gathered in order to be uplifted by a preacher's sermon. Although clearly Erwin and company have no particular desire to be uplifted, they nonetheless remove their hats as they sit with their plates of food, and resume eating. They do not appear especially impressed by the preacher's intoning: "Gentlemen. I should speak to you tonight of success. I have no patience with people who quarrel with their lot in life."[31] Following this homely bit of wisdom, the three ex-convicts emerge from the mission with their plates scraped; their only quarrel at this point is with one another over who is going to wash the plates. Since no one wants this responsibility, they carry the plates and utensils down the street to a local nightspot, where they leave them as a sort of donation. The absurdity of the scene makes it memorable, with the three actors playing it perfectly straight as they move calmly from their stools in the fiery diner to the benches of the mission.

The prison scenes for this movie were shot on Rikers Island in New York, where the actors were put into the real thing. Erwin told an amusing story about his escapades during the filming on the Island. He began by asking his interviewer if he had ever visited the prison on Rikers Island. When he got a negative response, Erwin observed wryly, "Just as well! We had some outside stuff to do there the other day and I'm still not sure whether it was I or the red tape that got us in a jam." One of the early episodes in the movie shows Erwin, still incarcerated at this time, watching a ball game played among the prisoners in the recreation yard. As Erwin related the events that occurred after the actors completed their scene: "When the sequence was over and we asked to get out, the guard took one look at me, shouldered his gun and marched off in the opposite direction! Try as we might we couldn't get an inch nearer to freedom than the big gate. . . . I've got a very sensitive skin, so by five I looked like a broiled lobster. . . . About five-thirty, when the rest of the inmates were taken in, they herded us into the main hall and, luckily, found no place for us. After much ado, the authorities let us go home, and not a minute too soon."

At this point, Erwin's wife interrupted his story with an addition of her own: "I think Stuart would still be there . . . if I hadn't gotten worried and telephoned, when he didn't come in. Even then it took an hour to locate them! He won't have any trouble making people believe he's a graduate of any local jail." Erwin agreed that he was going to be pretty convincing as a convict (which indeed he is), but he also added at this point that he wasn't entirely sure whether or not the whole incident was a practical joke played on the cast by the prison authorities. He concluded the tale with the following self-deprecating aside: "But the funny part is, I still don't know whether it was on the level or whether it was a gag. I wonder if they think I'm dumb enough to fall for a thing like that?"[32]

Another 1939 Erwin picture worth mentioning is *It Could Happen to You*. The reviewer for *Photoplay* gave the following capsule analysis: "Have you ever imagined yourself in the position of an innocent person accused of murder? That's the fix Stuart Erwin's in when he finds a body in his car. He's held in jail but his wife, Gloria Stuart, comes to his rescue. Good suspense."[33] In her autobiography, *I Just Kept Hoping*, Ms. Stuart makes no mention of this picture. She does recall that in 1943 she made a B movie with Erwin entitled *Here Comes Elmer*: an interesting recollection since Erwin was not in this movie with her.

By the 1940s, Erwin was making fewer and fewer movie appearances. Nevertheless, he began the decade with one of his best-known roles, as the milkman in *Our Town* (1940). The movie was well received, although Thornton Wilder, who collaborated on the screenplay with Harry Chandlee and Frank Craven, reportedly was not pleased with the happy ending that the filmmakers insisted on giving to his play. Furthermore, Martha Scott and William Holden were too old by 1940 to be believable as adolescents. As for Stuart Erwin, all that was required of him was that he look congenial and take up some space in the background. Yet he received good notices for his performance, possibly because critics expected to see him as he was here: an unpretentious, lovable, early twentieth-century character dispensing wisdom during a simpler age.

He is also given little to do in two other movies from 1940: *When the Daltons Rode* and *Sandy Gets Her Man*. He plays Ben Dalton in the former, and does die rather well when he is shot halfway through the movie. *Sandy Gets*

Her Man reunites him with Una Merkel, whom he admired as a comedienne. The movie contains some silly goings-on, with Erwin and Jack Carson vying for the matrimonial attention of Merkel, the mother of two-year-old Baby Sandy, a cute infant with a vocabulary of about four words, who made a series of pictures for Universal. It is Erwin who finally wins the love of Merkel when he rescues Baby Sandy from a burning building. We never do learn who Baby Sandy's father was; the casually written script doesn't concern itself with such trivia. Carson and Erwin made effective foils, but they worked to better advantage the following year in *The Bride Came C.O.D.*, which wasn't a particularly good picture either, but did give this duo more clever dialogue, allowing them to trade some good barbs with one another. Erwin's other 1941 movie, *Cracked Nuts*, which I examine later, is entertaining in an offbeat way.

Erwin made another quirky movie in 1942, *Drums of the Congo*. In this one, he plays an adventurer who lands in Africa, working as an assistant to a woman physician and getting involved in a murder. Another 1942 movie, *The Adventures of Martin Eden*, is really a starring vehicle for Glenn Ford, who is the lawyer trying to defend Erwin on charges of mutiny. Evelyn Keyes as Ford's girl and Claire Trevor as Erwin's anxious sister provide the feminine touch to what is basically a tale of the sea. Once again, Erwin does not do much except worry about his ultimate fate, although he capably handles what little he is given to do. When I wrote to Evelyn Keyes to see if she had any memories of working with Erwin, she replied that she could not even remember ever meeting him. Apparently, his part was so minimal that he and Keyes, although their names appear among the cast members of the same picture, never had any direct contact.

Nor did the movie receive good reviews. According to *The Encyclopedia of Novels into Film*, the picture turned the Jack London novel "into an adventure story about a young seaman's literary exposure of brutal conditions, his love affairs with two girls of different classes, his rise as a writer, his role in seeing justice done, and a Hollywood happy ending where he chooses the girl of his own class." This compendium of reviews has a one-sentence mention of Erwin's role, yet fails to mention him by name. He is the "shipmate" referred to in the following line: "The plot centers on Eden's attempts to prove the justice of a shipmate's mutiny." Yet, the encyclopedia summary of the film's reviews points out a positive aspect among all of the critical carping: "Tony Thomas notes, however, that the film does try to convey [Jack] London's socialism—a bold move in 1940s Hollywood—even though it does sacrifice accuracy for high-seas adventure."[34]

Another 1942 Erwin movie, which does *not* represent a bold move for 1940s Hollywood, is *Blondie for Victory*. The picture was one in a long series of popular comedies based on the comic strip and featuring Penny Single-ton as Blondie and Arthur Lake as Dagwood. This particular patriotic World War II entry has as its basic theme the need for an all-out effort on the part of both men and women to win the war. Erwin appears briefly toward the movie's end as a soldier on leave from a military base where, he complains, he is tired of being kissed by sexy movie actresses because he looks so lonely. At one point, Arthur Lake as Dagwood appropriates Erwin's uniform for himself so he can fool Blondie into thinking that he has enlisted. Much taller than Erwin, Lake looks duly ridiculous in his ill-fitting attire. Not so ridiculous is the unexplored consequence of all this tomfoolery with military apparel: in real life, both Erwin and Lake would have found themselves in a load of trouble had the military authorities discovered the efforts at deception on the part of these two "soldiers."

From 1943 till 1950, Erwin made only eight theatrical movies, quite a change from the dozens he made in the early thirties. In only one of these, *Killer Dill* (1947), does he demonstrate some of the sharp, incisive, boyish delight in life that he had shown as a young actor. While *The Great Mike* (1944) pairs him with Carl "Alfalfa" Switzer, who had already lost his childhood cuteness from his days in the Our Gang comedies, and gives him a sympathetic, fatherly role as a horse trainer, its appeal is probably solely for parents looking for a good "family" picture for their children, and for diehard horseracing fans.

In 1947, Erwin shifted his career focus slightly by appearing in *Doctor Jim*, an industrial film made in conjunction with the John Deere Tractor Company. Running only fifty minutes, the movie traces the career of a kindly country doctor, Dr. James Gateson (Erwin), who sacrifices his own private needs in order to serve his patients. What little conflict there is in the picture arises from the appearance in town of a young doctor (William Wright), who poses a threat to the old-fashioned, but wise and effective methods of Erwin. But the movie ends happily, with Erwin as the aging doctor feted at a testimonial dinner, and the grateful townsfolk sending their beloved doctor and Mrs. Gateson (Barbara Wooddell) on a "honeymoon" to Niagara Falls: a trip that had been delayed when the outbreak of World War I some thirty years earlier had cancelled the Gatesons's original plans.

William Schallert, appearing here in his second movie[35] as a young farmer whose sick wife is treated by Erwin, recalled that Stuart Erwin was "Will Rogers without the edge."[36] His observation coincides with the assessment of Erwin's character given by various film reviewers in the mid-thirties, shortly after Rogers's death in a plane crash. Some saw him as a successor to the folksy humorist and social commentator. One interviewer, writing in 1937, presented the following insightful observation: "As to Erwin's histrionics, we can safely predict a long and prosperous future for him. Gifted with a sympathy-inducing physiognomy [face, to us] and a self-deprecative style of acting, he is the typical small-town character in search of an author. There is a real homespun quality about Stu and, in a modest but highly efficient manner, he carries on much in the Will Rogers manner, which is traditional for portraying 'just folks' on the screen. Though youthful, Stuart Erwin seems the logical successor to the late Will Rogers and can fill his shoes as well as anyone could ever hope to do."[37]

Indeed, ten years after this reviewer offered his opinion, Stuart Erwin as Doctor Jim comes as close as he ever did in voice and manner to Will Rogers, especially in the later scenes in which he portrays Dr. Gateson as an elderly man. In the first few flashback episodes, however, Erwin is a reflection of his earlier self: the shy, uncertain, gentle boy of the early thirties.

So too, William Schallert's assessment of Erwin's similarity to Will Rogers was one that was shared by Warner Bros. Throughout the forties, the studio had been trying to develop a screenplay based on the life of the fabled cowboy-philosopher-humorist. Moreover, the studio announced that its choice for the role was Stuart Erwin. Indeed, Warners maintained that Erwin was the only actor who would even be considered for the part. In their columns, Hedda Hopper and Louella Parsons kept reminding their readers that Stuart Erwin was set to play Will Rogers.

But then, Rogers's widow intruded with some demands of her own. When Warners finally had a shooting script ready, she declared that she would allow the movie to be made only if her son, Will Rogers Jr., played his father. Studio executives could not believe this ultimatum. Will Jr. was a newspaper publisher with no acting experience whatsoever, but with definite acting aspirations. Yet Warners acceded to Mrs. Rogers's demand, and the picture was made in 1950 with young Will as his father. *The Story of Will Rogers* was a critical and box office failure, as well as a bitter disappointment to Stuart Erwin.[38]

So Erwin's first movie of the next decade was not *The Story of Will Rogers* but *Father Is a Bachelor* (1950) in which he has a very minor part as the mustached sheriff of a small town. More significantly, however, he appears to be about fifty pounds overweight and looks worn out and somehow defeated, as though all of his energy has been used up. The movie itself has a plodding story, with William Holden as the bachelor father of the title. Holden does demonstrate a little of the sardonic humor that he would master much more skillfully by the mid-fifties, but Erwin once again has what amounts to a walk-on part as a sheriff who sympathizes with the outcast

Holden. *Father Is a Bachelor* is not the movie that *The Story of Will Rogers* could have been under happier circumstances, and Erwin plays his role as the sheriff in this minor picture as if he were painfully aware of that fact.

Another painful reminder of a missed career opportunity also resurfaced to haunt Erwin in 1950. That was the year in which Universal filmed *Harvey*: this time the role of Elwood P. Dowd went to James Stewart. This disappointment must have been somewhat assuaged by the fact that, in the summer of 1950, Erwin finally got to do the part which had been written with him in mind. He traveled throughout New England that summer, playing Elwood P. Dowd in summer stock.[39]

Furthermore, by the latter part of 1950, Erwin had found a new life in television. His series *Trouble with Father* (a.k.a. *The Stu Erwin Show*) provided him with an excellent, different outlet for his type of wry humor. For almost six years he played Stu Erwin, a high school principal living in a small town in Middle America. And the presence of his wife, June Collyer, playing herself, completed the circle that had begun some nineteen years earlier when they had met while appearing together in another comedy, *Dude Ranch* (1931). When the series ended, Erwin wisely stayed in television, making guest appearances through the 1950s on *Kids and Company*, *Bonanza*, *Gunsmoke*, *Perry Mason*, *Wagon Train*, and *The Untouchables*. In addition, Erwin was proud of the fact that his television appearances in the fifties and early sixties included a number of distinguished studio dramas such as *Playhouse 90*, *Studio One*, *Armstrong Circle Theater*, *U.S. Steel Hour*, and *The Defenders*. In one *Playhouse 90* episode, June Collyer was featured with him in a cast that also included Dana Andrews, Anne Baxter, and Leslie Nielsen.[40] Many of these shows provided Erwin with an opportunity to demonstrate his skill as a dramatic actor. These were parts that he felt offered him a welcome contrast to his role as the frequently frazzled father and high school principal in *Trouble with Father*.

Then, in the late 1950s, he returned to the stage to appear in *Three Men on a Horse* in Traverse City, Michigan, and other summer theaters in the Great Lakes area. He continued his stage work for the next few years. According to Stuart Erwin Jr., "In the summer of 1961, Dad had the lead in a two week run in Seattle. I don't remember the play. He often kidded that he wanted to reveal some of his experiences in a book, *Summer Theaters and Some Are Not*. I wish he had."[41]

Although Erwin loved the theater and often told his son that it was his favorite way to work, film commitments frequently kept him from appearing on stage. And he also found television rewarding, continuing his work there well into the sixties, appearing as a guest on *The Andy Griffith Show*,

The Big Valley, The Bing Crosby Show, and *Green Acres.* So too, he appeared in the initial 1967 episode of the series *Gentle Ben.* He was also a regular on the series *The Greatest Show on Earth,* which ran for one season on ABC, from September 1963 to September 1964. During this decade, he also appeared in three theatrical movies—*For the Love of Mike* (1960), *Son of Flubber* (1963), and *Misadventures of Merlin Jones* (1964). His final appearance was in the made-for-TV movie *Shadow Over Elveron,* which was released in 1968, after Erwin's death, and forty years after he made his first movie.

The novelist Charles Dickens once wrote, "I want to die, doing." Stuart Erwin did that very thing; for most of his adult life, he entertained audiences. And his earliest films deserve some close attention, for even in these we can see his sensitivity, his humor, his versatility, and his ability to make us believe in him.

NOTES

1. *Screen Album* (winter 1939): 39.

2. Kay Proctor, "How to be a Howling Social Success," *Hollywood* (December 1937): 59.

3. Stuart Erwin, "My kids won't let me!" *American Magazine* 153 (June 1952): 92.

4. Stuart Erwin Jr., letter to author, 26 November 2000.

5. F. Scott Fitzgerald, *The Great Gatsby,* with foreword and study guide (New York: Charles Scribner's Sons, 1961), 228.

6. Fitzgerald, *Gatsby,* 228.

7. Martha Kerr, "Women Are Trouble," *Modern Screen* (November 1936): 93.

8. Erwin, "My kids won't let me!" 18.

9. Kerr, "Women Are Trouble," 93.

10. Robert H. McIlwaine, "Small Town Boy," *Modern Screen* (July 1937): 14.

11. Stuart Erwin Jr., letter to author, 16 October 2000.

12. "The Season in Chicago," *The Best Plays of 1943–1944,* ed. Burns Mantle (New York: Dodd, Mead and Company, 1944), 19.

13. David Burnham, "Mr. Sycamore," *The Commonweal* 37 (November 17, 1942): 144.

14. Burnham, "Mr. Sycamore," 144.

15. Rosamond Gilder, "Mr. Sycamore," *Theatre Arts* 27 (January 1943): 20.

16. Stuart Erwin Jr., letter to author, 16 October 2000.

17. John McCabe, *Cagney* (New York: Alfred A. Knopf, 1997), 52.

18. William P. Gaines, "Just A Little Bit Timid," *Shadoplay Magazine* (January 1935): 73.

19. Kerr, "Women Are Trouble," 94.

20. Brother Bud later joined his sister in changing his last name to their mother's birth name of *Collyer.* Under the name Bud Collyer, he became a well-known tele-

vision quiz show host in the fifties and sixties; two of his most notable programs were *To Tell the Truth* (Climactic line: "Will the *real* _____please stand up?) and the truly nonsensical *Beat the Clock*. In the latter program, a contestant had a limited amount of time—sixty seconds or so—to perform some odd, impractical, grotesque feat, such as using a bamboo pole held between his teeth to try to hit a golf ball from off a table and make the ball land in a wicker basket ten feet away, all the while he was balancing on one leg. If the contestant failed to succeed in his ridiculous endeavor during the brief time allotted, Collyer would shake his head and say mournfully, "Oh, I'm *so sorry!* You *didn't* beat the clock. The clock beat *you!*"

21. "How Hollywood Entertains," *The New Movie Magazine* (November 1931): 109.

22. Kerr, "Women Are Trouble," 94.

23. Kerr, "Women Are Trouble," 94.

24. McIlwaine, "Small Town Boy," 12.

25. Ted Cook, "Cook-Coo Gossip," *The New Movie Magazine* 6 (July 1932): 33.

26. Roger Dooley, *From Scarface to Scarlett* (New York: Harcourt Brace Jovanovich, 1981), 99.

27. Leonard Maltin, *The Great Movie Shorts* (New York: Crown Publishers, 1972), 189.

28. McIlwaine, "Small Town Boy," 14.

29. Stuart Erwin Jr., letter to author, 26 November 2000. Stuart Jr. also recalled listening to this *Ceiling Zero* broadcast when he was seven or eight years old and breaking into tears when his father's character dies as he crashes his plane into an airport hangar.

30. Robert H. McIlwaine, "Homespun Hero," *Modern Screen* (March 1939): 80.

31. *Back Door to Heaven*. Dir. William K. Howard. Paramount, 1939.

32. McIlwaine, "Homespun Hero," 80.

33. "It Could Happen to You," *Photoplay* 53 (October 1939): 8.

34. John C. Tibbetts and James M. Welsh, eds. *The Encyclopedia of Novels into Film* (New York: Facts on File, 1998), 268.

35. Schallert's first movie was *The Foxes of Harrow*, made early in 1947, in which he played a bank messenger. Letter to author, 5 November 2000.

36. William Schallert, letter to author, 6 July 2000.

37. McIlwaine, "Small Town Boy," 12.

38. Stuart Erwin Jr., letter to author, 16 October 2000.

39. Stuart Erwin Jr., letter to author, 26 November 2000.

40. Stuart Erwin Jr., letter to author, 16 October 2000.

41. Stuart Erwin Jr., letter to author, 26 November 2000.

2

THE EARLY FILMS

"He's a man way out there in the blue, riding on a smile and a shoeshine. And when they start not smiling back—that's an earthquake."

— Arthur Miller, *Death of a Salesman* (1949)

GOOFY STUFF

One has to stay awake and to look closely in order to spot Stuart Erwin in some of his early movies. For instance, in *Thru Different Eyes* (1929), a Fox silent, he can be seen briefly as one among a pool of reporters covering a murder trial. He has no dialogue and remains in the background, appearing early in the film with the reporters who are leaving the courtroom. Then he vanishes until the movie's last few minutes, when the reporters reenter for the reading of the jury's verdict. In another 1929 picture, *The Cock-Eyed World*, a sound sequel to the silent *What Price Glory?*, he does have some dialogue. However, he appears only at the beginning of the movie. By the time the battling Sergeants Flagg and Quirt (Victor McLaglen and Edmund Lowe, respectively, reprising their roles in *What Price Glory?*) lead their troops to the tropics, Erwin has indeed become invisible. He also appears briefly with Clara Bow in *Dangerous Curves* (1929). In this one, he is billed simply as a "Rotarian." He and a fellow traveling Rotarian (Jack Luden) ogle circus performers Clara Bow and Joyce Compton. Seated in the stands under the circus tent, Erwin makes some lecherous remarks about the two women who are displaying their charms in the ring. Later, these two uncouth Romeos take the girls out to eat at a fancy restaurant, where Erwin makes an absolute ass of himself by pretending to understand French and by telling cornball jokes, laughing loudly to cover his self-consciousness. Meanwhile, the girls sit squirming at the table, wishing they were somewhere, anywhere else.

While Erwin's onscreen time is brief, he makes the most of a very unattractive role, showing us a man trying so hard to be liked that his every move rings false. He is the kind of character we can imagine Arthur Miller's Willy Loman would have been in his younger days on the road: during those days that he reminisces about to his sons in *Death of a Salesman*, all the while pretending that he had at one time been an exceedingly popular guy, well-liked by all his clients, bringing home substantial sums of money.

Erwin has an even briefer screen appearance in *Happy Days* (1930), a Fox revue containing some pretty good specialty acts as well as a comedy routine featuring the aging prizefighter James J. "Gentlemen Jim" Corbett. In this movie, a spectacled Erwin pops into the film and speaks one line. In another, more entertaining, more sophisticated revue, *Paramount on Parade* (1930), Erwin is one of the Paramount stars who briefly appear, this time in a serious sketch as a veteran of the Great War listening to Ruth Chatterton sing a mournful song about her dead soldier. In *Up Pops the Devil* (1931), he is billed second, but his role is quite inexplicable. He plays an inebriated stranger dressed in formal attire, who keeps crashing the parties of the major stars of the picture and using the phone to call someone whom we never see. He slurs his way through about ten lines, while the other characters question one another about who he is. No one seems to have the answer, nor does anyone appear to care, and about half way through the picture he just disappears from the screen entirely. Perhaps he owed Paramount a movie that year. Moreover, in many of those early films in which he does have a substantial role, the character he plays is indeed the sort of foolish bungler with whom he would be unfairly associated till he died.

For example, in *Sweetie* (1929), he plays Axel Bronstrup, a constantly baffled but well-meaning college student who can tackle superbly for his football team, but who has trouble passing English literacy tests. Nonetheless, Helen Kane, one of the classmates who seems to be only slightly less intelligent than Axel, has her sights set on him—literally—as she pursues him with a shotgun through much of the movie. A running gag in this early Paramount talkie involves Kane aiming her weapon at Erwin's rear, once while he is sunbathing in the nude, and never missing her target. And Erwin, for his part, looks confused—pained but flattered by her attention—so we assume that they will live happily ever after.

The movie itself is dated, although, as with so many early Paramount comedies, it does have its clever moments, particularly some entertaining slapstick: the movie ends with a satirical observation on the importance of college football via a deranged game played on what looks like a farmer's field with goalposts made from any handy material. A similar scene would be echoed in the Marx Brothers' *Horse Feathers* (1932) and in Erwin's own *Pigskin Parade* (1936). All three movies end with games containing so many rule violations that the NCAA would have barred every one of these colleges from football forever. And *Sweetie*, the earliest of these three college football spoofs, is hampered by the crude sound reproduction, a frequent liability in the early days of talking movies. Notably hard on the ears was Helen Kane, whose broad Bronx accent and high-pitched voice did not record well and made her lines hard to understand, especially when she sang. Also difficult to take was her tendency to try for comedy through shrieking. Coming off much better vocally were Erwin, Jack Oakie, and Nancy Carroll.

COLD COMFORT LOVE

Helen Kane would look and sound more appealing the following year with Erwin in another Paramount comedy, *Dangerous Nan McGrew* (1930), in which she plays the title character. There are some sublimely crazy moments in this movie which, in addition to Erwin, features such versatile actors as Frank Morgan, Victor Moore, and Louise Closser Hale. The movie is vaguely set somewhere in Canada, and the unimportant plot revolves around Kane and Doc Foster, played by Moore, who travel by horse and wagon through snowdrifts, selling patent medicine—nostrums that will cure anything—and perform a two-person carnival type show. These two become entangled with Muldoon (a.k.a. "Blossom"), played by Frank Morgan, who is wanted by the Mounties for killing a man because, as Morgan tells one of his accomplices in crime, the man kicked him in the shins.

Stuart Erwin is one of the inhabitants of this scenic, snow-covered spot. Through much of the movie he is clad in a long fur coat, a fur hat, oversized snowshoes that hamper his movements, and a saxophone which he carries with him everywhere. He lives with a wealthy aunt, Mrs. Benson (Louise Closser Hale), who will not let him play his instrument in the house. And his playing is indeed truly horrendous. The sounds that emanate from his sax when he studiously blows into it resemble those made by a forlorn moose looking for a mate.

Erwin quickly becomes acquainted with Dangerous Nan McGrew (Kane) when she and Moore set up their show for the local town of about sixty residents, and she calls him up from the audience to help her prove her sharpshooting prowess. Moore amiably places a metal headband around Erwin's forehead; attached to this band are ornaments that are suspended like large earrings or perhaps Christmas tree decorations. Erwin looks like a crowned head of state, a Roman Emperor: Julius Caesar transplanted to the Frozen North and wearing a fur coat, fur hat, and thick mittens. Moreover, he and Kane look as though they are dressed for two different climates, with Kane skimpily attired in a cowgirl outfit, complete with boots and a short, fringed skirt stopping above her knees. This apparel makes the diminutive Kane look like a little girl all dressed up to play cowboys and Indians—or maybe Annie Oakley. And Kane demonstrates that she does indeed have much in common with Annie Oakley. She displays her lovable shooting expertise by turning her back on the anxious Erwin and by skillfully breaking the ornaments that are nestled up against his skull. After this wondrous display of talent, Erwin impulsively develops a childlike, even somewhat touching, tenderness for Kane.

But shortly after meeting Erwin, Kane develops a toothache. Unaware of her predicament and knowing that Kane and Moore have very little money and that Christmas is but a few days away, Erwin takes Kane a gift: a box of candy. When she tells him about her toothache, he is naturally concerned, so he tells her that there is a dentist just across the street. However, Kane is afraid of dentists. Hearing this, the ever-solicitous Erwin offers to make her forget her pain by playing a tune for her on his saxophone. Kane has already heard the painful squawks which come forth whenever Erwin tries to get some sort of noise out of the instrument, so she declines his offer, saying that she'd rather have her tooth pulled.

Yet Erwin takes no offense at this commentary on his musical ability, so they make their way to the dentist's office. What follows is a glorious scene, comparable to the one W. C. Fields enacted two years later in his short film, *The Dentist* (1932). Although the scene does not have the lascivious quality found in the Fields movie, in which patient and dentist apparently achieve sexual fulfillment at the point where Fields manages to extract the tooth, Kane and Erwin generate enough silly passion to make the scene quite funny. As Erwin and the moaning Kane enter the office—Erwin still in fur coat, cap, and with the saxophone hanging from his neck—they observe that there is no dentist around, though the examining room looks as if it is just waiting to accept patients. First, Kane insists that Erwin help her off with her snow boots and cap. This he does, in spite of the fact that Kane never sits down but hops toward the dentist chair, allowing Erwin to take off her boots in between bounces. Next, Kane plops herself into the chair, at which point the chair gradually lowers itself a few inches. As he watches Kane and chair propelled downward, Erwin muses quizzically, more to himself than to anyone else, "Gee, you're heavier than I thought you were."[1]

Kane does not appear at all fazed by Erwin's comment on her weight, however, because she is in such pain that she demands that he pull her tooth at once. Erwin is willing to save his beloved from suffering but has no notion of what to do. He does make a helpful comment, only half of which is accurate, when he offers, "I'm a musician, not a dentist, but I'll try." Turning away from her in order to locate an instrument that might look vaguely familiar, he grabs a couple of items that look like kitchen utensils. Holding one in each hand, he turns back, asking, "What do you use for pulling teeth, anyway? Do you know?"[2] At this, Kane looks more pained than ever; she is possibly considering that Erwin's saxophone playing might have been a not-so-awful alternative to his tooth pulling.

Nonetheless, we realize that Erwin does not want her to suffer inordinately, because he looks around for a way to make his proposed treatment painless. He sees a small canister suspended near the chair in which Kane is still nervously seated. Now he has an idea, as he reads to her "Gas. Makes pain a pleasure." From this point on, they get even sillier: he lets her get a whiff of the gas, then he tries some himself. Soon, both are giggling hysterically. While Kane's toothache remains in its original location, she tells Erwin that it has also spread to her ear, but she no longer cares. Nor does he, because he is feeling pretty good himself. She takes a mallet and bangs herself on the head; then she hits Erwin especially hard on his hand. Pulling away from her and chortling, he responds irrelevantly but drunkenly, "Oh, thank you—awful. I'm gonna pull your tooth for that."[3]

And this he does. First he grabs a convenient pair of pliers in his right hand and puts his left arm all the way around her head, so that he is cupping her chin with his left hand. Then he proceeds to yank the offending tooth, only he naturally gets the wrong one—a mistake that Kane makes him cognizant of, all the while she is laughing hysterically and waving the gas canister at him. In addition, he is still restrained by his fur coat and saxophone, an instrument which he continues to wear like a bulky sword. We might even assume that Kane's laughter is exacerbated by the ticklish effect of Erwin's fur as he not so tenderly embraces her head. The scene is particularly ridiculous and mirth provoking, due largely to the unselfconscious nuttiness of the two stars; both Erwin and Kane are full of adolescent silliness that is contagious. The more one of them giggles over the plight of Kane's tooth, the more the other one follows.

Yet Erwin was always skilled at turning from farce to sentiment and at making the shift in tone believable. He does this a little later at a party given

by his aunt to which he has invited Kane and Moore as performers. Knowing that they need money and that they will not accept charity, he is paying
them to entertain at this elegant gathering. Now he is dressed formally in a
dark suit and bow tie; in keeping with his more distinguished appearance, he
has abandoned the loopy demeanor of his earlier scenes. Furthermore, his intense attempts to propose to Kane are moving; he is hesitating, nervous, unsure of her response, so he leads up to it by mentioning that he has wanted to
ask her something for a long time. Kane's eyes open even wider than usual;
she is eager to hear what he has to say. Finally, Erwin manages to stutter: "Do
you like cucumbers?" Taken aback, Kane nonetheless wants to encourage further conversation, so she says, "Cucumbers? Oh no, I hate cucumbers."
Agreeably, Erwin adds, "I don't like 'em either." Then he incoherently observes, "It's a beautiful moon, isn't it?" He inches even closer to her, his nose
almost touching hers. Still thinking of certain kinds of food as substitutes for
what is really on his mind, he continues in the same vein: "Do you like bananas?" Kane's response, "Yea, I like bananas" sends Erwin into a tizzy; he
turns away, rubbing his head in his hand, then turns back to her with an inspiration: "Well, we both like the same vegetables. That's a start, isn't it?"[4]

Kane agrees that it is indeed and, wanting to encourage her stuttering
beau, adds, "Start? What's the finish?" Erwin rubs his head even more furi-
ously, as though such a gesture will give him courage. "Oh dear, whenever I
try to tell you, everything goes black."

"Why?" Kane wants to know.

Erwin confesses, "Oh, I'm frightened, I guess."

Here, Kane pulls her ever-ready gun on her reluctant suitor, cautioning
him not to be frightened of anything ever again. The sight of her gun forces
Erwin to gather himself together enough to say a few words, although these
words come out very slowly and painfully: "Maybe I can tell you—I mean
ask you—" Discerning that Erwin at last has some momentum, Kane tries
to bolster him, "Go on!" But ever the roundabout lover, Erwin can manage
only a sputtering, "Could you ever care for me? Oh, I don't mean right
away, but if you would just try to get used to the idea, why—"[5] Instead of a
direct answer, Kane responds by singing Erwin a love song.

The remainder of the movie involves some crazy business with Victor
Moore and Frank Morgan at a masquerade party, both of them dressed iden-
tically like Buster Brown, and both looking like they belong in the chorus
of a Victor Herbert operetta. And, of course, by the final scene, Erwin manages to complete his marriage proposal to Kane, having taken most of the
seventy-three minutes of the film to finish this one sentence. Kane is so delighted by the audacity he at last demonstrates that she even allows him to

play a tune for her on his saxophone. Thus, to the accompaniment of Erwin's awe-inspiring rendering of "Heart and Soul," they are officially betrothed.

ON THE TRAIL OF THE CULPRITS

In the same year, Erwin had an equally nutty part in *Only Saps Work* (1930), a movie that was considerably superior to *Sweetie* and as good as *Dangerous Nan McGrew*. This one has a plot of sorts involving Leon Errol as a con man par excellence. Errol is particularly adept at lifting money from others, pretending it's his, and using it to pay people to whom he owes money, such as his landlady. Errol gets hooked up with Richard Arlen, who drives the getaway car after Errol has robbed a bank. Except Arlen is unaware that Errol has robbed a bank; he just sees Errol carrying a large suitcase and casually walking out of the financial institution. Nonetheless, both of them become suspects and consequent fugitives from justice, finally landing at the Jasper Health Farm, a health spa and resort hotel where Arlen has been guaranteed a job as a busboy in the pantry and where Erwin is working as a bellboy. The name of the farm sounds totally unglamorous, as though the spa guests were going there to meet a stockbroker rather than to have their constitutions revitalized. And the crafty Errol, whose own collapsible constitution always appeared in need of refurbishing, sees the wide-eyed, slow-talking Erwin as the ideal patsy; the upshot of Errol's chicanery is that Erwin is led to believe that Errol is an incognito detective on the bank robbery case. When Errol realizes that the naïve Erwin dreams of becoming a part of the romantic life of big city cops, Errol makes him his second in charge and drops red herrings his way, causing Erwin to suspect that the most innocuous guests are dangerous criminals.

Errol's first clue that he has a real sucker in Erwin's Otis, the bellboy, comes as Errol is trying to bluff his way past the clerk at the registration desk. Erwin shows Errol the newspaper headlines about the recent bank robbery, solemnly declaring, "I wish I was a detective. I'd solve it in a minute, I would." At this, inspiration hits Errol, who suddenly metamorphoses into Sergeant Wilson of the Winkerton Detective Bureau. (A name sounding like it came from the imagination of W. C. Fields or Groucho Marx.) Now truly impressed with this new hotel guest, Erwin has noticed that Errol is very protective of his valise, so he earnestly asks Errol if his disguises are in the suitcase. Errol is caught off guard by the inquiry, so his reply is equivocal, "Why, even my own mother hasn't recognized me since I was two years of age." More awestruck than ever, Erwin observes quite seriously, "My goodness, but you must have been a detective a long, long time."

Errol has some funny bits in the film, many of which look like set pieces from his days as a performer in the Ziegfeld Follies: a procedure also followed by other stage comedians and vaudevillians who had transferred to the screen, notably W. C. Fields, Burns and Allen, and the Marx Brothers. In one scene he prepares waffles for the hotel guests by throwing in such inappropriate ingredients as Worcestershire sauce, chili sauce, Tabasco sauce, eggshells, and sleigh bells. He also tosses olives at various pans hanging on the wall, seemingly delighted at the musical melody he plays as the olives bounce tunefully off the pans.

Likewise, Erwin and Errol engage in some banter that comes straight from vaudeville. When Erwin as Otis the bellboy first takes the "detective" to his room at the Jasper Health Farm, he initiates the following dialogue with Errol:

ERWIN: Do you know *what*?

ERROL: What's his first name?

ERWIN (ignoring the bad play on words): All my life, I've wanted to be a detective. And now that I've seen a real one . . .

ERROL (taken off guard, looking around the room): Where is he?

ERWIN (oblivious to Errol's previous line): Listen—

ERROL: To what?

ERWIN: Will you give me lessons on how to be a detective?[6]

At first, our clever con artist is reluctant to have this blockhead remain in the room, especially since Errol wants privacy so that he might open the suitcase and admire his loot. However, when Erwin offers to pay him for detective lessons, Errol decides that the wannabe dick isn't such a nuisance after all. After giving this strange bellboy advice on the detecting business and seeing how thickheaded his pupil is, Errol finally sighs, "You know, you shouldn't be a bellboy here. You should be a *patient*."[7]

Only Saps Work ends on a satisfactory note, with Richard Arlen winning the affection of leading lady Mary Brian, with Errol going off to jail for his misdeeds, and with Erwin, having fingered the wrong suspects, going back to work as bellboy. In this one, as frequently happens, Erwin doesn't get a girl.

TRAPPED UNDER THE SEA

On the other hand, Stuart Erwin does have a larger, weightier, far more serious role in the part-talking *Men Without Women* (1930), directed by John

Ford, in which he plays the radio operator on a submarine stranded under the China Sea. *Men Without Women* is a visually impressive movie containing excellent cinematography, with particularly effective tracking shots in the early portion, set in a Shanghai bar. Although Scott Eyman dismisses *Men Without Women* fairly quickly in his biography of John Ford, observing that the film "is very much a patchy early talkie,"[8] the movie has much about it that is fascinating to watch.

For instance, despite the fact that the movie at first appears to be divided into two disjointed parts, with the Shanghai portions fitting loosely up against the scenes on the submarine, the movie retains an impressionistic, seamless quality to it. Especially well done is the integration of the sound with the silent portions, which flow together easily. True, the second part is the more suspenseful, for we see comrades, who are left helplessly adrift 90 feet down, begin to turn on each other as their cabin air turns more and more deadly.

The movie opens in Shanghai with sailors on leave, eager to visit "the longest bar in the world."[9] A convention of the genre that has come to be known as the "disaster" picture is, first, to introduce us to all of the major characters, who will later find their lives in peril. Screenwriter Dudley Nichols does this fairly successfully in these opening scenes, although the emphasis throughout much of the film is on these young sailors as a group. From the beginning, we see their youthful, brightly lit, open faces as the focal point of the mise-en-scènes created by director Ford and cinematographer Joseph August. Nonetheless, they do evince some distinct characteristics at the outset. At the beginning of the film, while we are still on shore in Shanghai, we see that one of the sailors named Dutch (Harry Tenbrook) has acquired what looks like a very large, very valuable Ming vase (but probably isn't) and is trudging along with it in front of him as he passes through the saloon. Erwin as Jenkins, the radioman, teasingly suggests to Dutch—his words are seen as intertitles—"Bring that mug inside . . . and we'll fill it up for you."[10]

There is a cut to some of the sailors looking at picture postcards; we assume that these are not scenic views of the Grand Canyon. An officer tells one of these men, "Don't waste your dough on these pictures, Pollock. . . . I'll show you something better in the flesh."[11] And indeed, the smoke-filled Shanghai bar contains about two prostitutes for every sailor. When they are not casting come-play-with-me glances at the sailors, they appear to be relishing drug-induced pleasures, chiefly the result of opium, whereas the drug-induced pleasures of the sailors are largely the result of alcohol. As the sailors line up at the bar, Erwin urgently gives them the tongue-in-cheek reminder that they have only two hours in which to get drunk.

Throughout these early scenes, the camera is fluid, with constantly moving tracking shots taking us around the saloon, moving in for close-ups of both officers and enlisted men, then backing away to carry us to another spot. So too, the film editors Walter Thompson and Paul Weatherwax use many jump cuts to shift us from one character's perspective to another. The total effect is disorienting; the cinematography gives us a feel of the place; we are as off balance and on edge as the sailors, who are becoming increasingly drunk and increasingly uneasy as the time comes for them to return to their submarine. There are also a number of humorous but further disconcerting close-ups, such as the face of one of the officers at the bar when he tries to focus a fuzzy gaze on his glass and sees a fishing swimming in it.

Moreover, the fine cinematography emphasizes the mood of uneasiness by way of recurring shots that look as though they had been filmed through a translucent inky veil. The indoor scenes of Shanghai appear to us through the haze of cigarette and opium smoke. The scenes outside the bar as the sailors move from the saloon toward the submarine dock appear through fog. Then, when we are on the China Sea, the camera photographs the outdoor scenes from the perspective of the horizon, as though we were sitting on top of the water. Thus, when the waves lash at us, seeming to hit directly on the camera lens, we feel the suffocating helplessness of drowning, similar to the sensation that the lookout sailors on the submarine deck are experiencing.

Further, the sound portions are integrated well with the photography. For instance, while we are still in the bar with the sailors, we hear appropriate musical background accompaniment as well as song and dance numbers that fit the dark, dusky nightclub atmosphere. To illustrate, one of the inebriated sailors sings loudly and off key a very clear rendition of the blues song "Frankie and Johnny." The sailors are also treated to the convolutions of an exotic dancer, clad in something that looks like a skirt left over from a Hawaiian luau and a very fancy bra decorated with bright spangles, perhaps sequins. Her midriff is well proportioned and completely bare. While ogling her motions, one of the sailors gets excited and speaks his dialogue aloud, pretending to be a carnival barker giving his prepared spiel about the attractions of the lady. But Erwin's appreciation of the dancer's obvious physical appeal is disrupted by his comrade's noisy interference, so we hear his voice for the first time when he yells belligerently, "Shut up! Hire a hall!"[12] Then he finds it uproariously funny when the performer climaxes her act by executing a high kick that lands squarely in the "barker's" face.

All of these early scenes perform at least two functions. First, they establish for us the closeness, the camaraderie that exists among these young sailors. Second, they show the rapport evolving between the officers and enlisted men. All of the Navy personnel have developed friendships among themselves and genuinely care for one another. Such intimacy will become especially important when they find themselves lost and floundering in the narrow, doomed confines of their submarine.

And their descent begins when the chief torpedo man Burke enters to say that all men are to report to the submarine at once. Again the camera moves us along with the sailors as they stumble from the bar out into the nighttime fog, Erwin toting a bowl of goldfish that he has acquired from heaven-knows-where. We are back to an evocative silent portion of the movie, where one of his buddies asks Erwin, "Say, Jenkins . . . what are you goin' to do with those goldfish?" Erwin replies wistfully, perhaps thinking of his own impending duties, "I'm going' to take the pretty little things down to the river and set 'em free." However, Erwin doesn't get too far with that goldfish bowl before a prostitute beckons him to come in her direction. We see her squatting behind bamboo bars, coaxing him on. Erwin simply looks at her and shakes his head as he refuses, "Not me, baby, not in a cage . . . I've got *some* modesty left!"[13] Once again, sound now enters the film: somehow, this encounter between Erwin and the teasing girl prompts the rowdy, mischievous sailors to join Erwin in singing "She's Only a Bird in a Gilded Cage."

To the accompaniment of Oriental music, we continue to follow Erwin and his fellow sailors out of the bar—Erwin still with those goldfish. When another prostitute leans over and kisses him, he is so overwhelmed that he places the goldfish bowl in her hands and staggers away, apparently forgetting that his final destination with those fish was to have been the river. And it is clear that the rest of these men on their way to the submarine are in the process of forgetting as well, for all of them are pretty well tanked by the time they reel onto the deck of their submarine.

On the deck we are introduced to Ensign Price (Frank Albertson, who would appear with Erwin again seventeen years later in the satirical *Killer Dill*). Price is another youthful, fresh face, who will prove to be a good, sympathetic leader. But here he is meeting his crew for the first time; one of the officers tells Price through the intertitles that Price has a good crew to work with: "They're a bit rough and boisterous at times, but we overlook it . . . because their duty is so dangerous. As long as they can get up that gangway without help, it's okay . . . understand?"[14] Meanwhile, the silence in this portion underscores the ominous foreshadowing, as the fog and mist envelop the men, who continue to make zigzagging motions as they cut into the darkness and board the ship. One of these men hopefully tells a member of the onboard crew, "I think I can get aboard if you'll give me a shove."[15] Then

the silence is penetrated by a lighter moment: we see a few of the sailors trying to smuggle liquor on board; one succeeds by stuffing a large bottle under
his shirt, all the while the tune "How Dry I Am" plays in the background.

After all are on deck, we see a medium shot of the submarine from the
perspective of those who remain on the dock. We watch with the men on
land as the submarine gradually disappears, obscured by the night, vapor, and
clouds. The next title tells us that we are in the China Sea; the ensuing shot
places us on the sea surface, with waves spraying up over the camera lens.
Through the surges of the sea accompanied by the driving rainstorm, we can
view in the distance the submarine swaying uneasily in the background, the
excellent cinematography emphasizing the fragility of the vessel and the lives
aboard it. Then in a close-up we are shown these waves lapping over the
men on the submarine deck. We are prepared for something tragic to
occur—and it does.

Out of the shadows and fog appears a ship; cutting into the silence is
the plaintive sound of a foghorn. Then we see the collision, as the ship rams
into the submarine and gigantic splays of water emanate from the sides of
both vessels. There is a startling contrast as the camera juxtaposes the shots
of the sea with the scene below deck. The startled crew members appear in-
candescent, suffused with light, their clear, serene faces all the more striking
because they are not yet aware of the extent of their predicament. But they
are about to learn. Chief Burke (Kenneth MacKenna) informs Ensign Price,
"We're struck aft, sir." Price responds with a concerned, "Where's the engine
room crew?" Burke simply shakes his head. "Engine room's flooded, sir!"
Then Price asks a question to which he already knows the all-too-horribly
obvious answer, "Then they're . . . drowned?"[16] At this moment, the crew
members are conscious that they are slowly, inescapably sinking.

Simultaneous with the descent of the submarine are the efforts of the
radio operator on the ship with which the sub has just collided. One officer
on this ship comments, "Poor devils! They went to the bottom like a load
of iron!" Cut back to the interior of the sub, where it continues to drop until
it finally stops at ninety feet. Then the lights go out; all we see are pulsating
flashes, like bolts of lightning on a hot, still, dark summer night. During these
brief seconds of light, we experience the men's terrified faces, now reflected
in stark, parallel contrast to their rowdy expressions in the well-lit indoor
Shanghai scenes.

With Captain Carson (Roy Stewart) and the lookouts on deck washed
over into the sea, Ensign Price is now in command of the crippled vessel.
Focus thus turns to him and to Erwin as Radioman Jenkins, who is trying
frantically to send or receive a message, desperate to make contact with someone—anyone—above the sea's surface. As Erwin's apprehensive face registers

disgust mixed with anticipation, a drunken sailor offers a bit of discouragement: "Aw, I could blow me nose further than you can send with that thing!" Still able to throw out an apt rejoinder, Erwin retorts, "You mean your breath!" Andrew Sarris, writing about this film in *You Ain't Heard Nothin' Yet*, has some perceptive observations about this scene: "The beauty of [John] Ford's direction is that he orchestrates a veritable symphony of fearful expressions without resorting to the showy cross-cutting of anguished angles. We see fear interacting from face to face within a fixed, communal frame. Stuart Erwin's luminously oafish radio operator is particularly memorable as a fixed point of tension in the midst of intermittent flurries of movement and feeling."[17]

Ford does indeed use his camera and his expressive actors to achieve a mood of quiet desperation, as the men face each other in a circle, looking to Ensign Price for direction, all the while the water is seeping higher and higher till, at this point, it covers their knees. When Price, something of an idealist, suggests that they might try to escape through the gun access trunk, Chief Burke, the realist, reminds him that "There isn't one chance in a thousand of being picked up in a storm like this." Ford's screenwriter Dudley Nichols and his title author Otis C. Freeman also allow the men occasional bits of sardonic humor. These lines are frequently given to Erwin, but here another sailor interjects with "I'd sure like to be one of Jenkins' little goldfish just about now!" The light interlude does not last long, though, because our attention shifts to Chief Burke, who is informing Ensign Price that they can last under the sea only a few hours "with luck . . . and sense." From time to time, we focus on Erwin, whose face continues to express frustrated resignation as he fails to communicate with anyone. In answer to Price's equally resigned, negatively worded question, "Nobody calling us yet?" Erwin, with one hand on his radio headphones, as though this gesture will enable him to hear more clearly sounds which never come, simply shakes his head. One joker in the bunch suggests an easier way to make their presence known: "Stick your head out the window and yell!"[18]

Another sailor tries to save them with a more practical, yet difficult—possibly even sacrificial—plan. He climbs up the ladder to see if they might get out through the gun access tank, knowing that if he succeeds in getting out and if there is no ship waiting nearby, he cannot get back inside. Yet he fails to get far, because a barrier of water thrusts him back down the ladder, causing him to choke on that additional part of the sea that he has allowed to enter the submarine. The increasingly distraught sailors learn that "the valve's jammed"; this hoped-for possibility of a way out, then, offers no hope after all. We see the water continue to rise, the small fans in place in their tiny enclosure circulating less and less oxygen-filled air. Their options and their time are running out.

But Chief Burke has another idea, one which might provide them a lane of escape: the torpedo tubes. When he presents this alternative to Ensign Price, we see a fine, glistening close-up of Frank Albertson's youthful, wistful, still innocent face, shining with sweat as the submarine air is gradually being used up. In this film, Albertson demonstrates a subtle propensity for transmitting empathy through his eloquent eyes. His Ensign Price is a striking contrast to many of the boorish, vacant heels that he portrayed in sound films. Perhaps the silent cinema was his true métier. Now Albertson's Price eagerly grasps at the hope symbolized by these torpedo tubes, but he reminds Burke, "We'll have to use them quick . . . the air is getting awfully close!"[19]

Told that only one of the port tubes is undamaged and therefore might be used for evacuation purposes and that the tube can be cleared only from the outside by divers, Price goes back among the circle of his men to think through his ever-diminishing options. The water is inching higher, the air is decreasing, and Erwin's radio operator is still standing, still futilely trying to talk to someone. In answer to Price's unspoken question, Erwin attempts a gamely light-hearted reply, "I'm still calling . . . this thing is worse than a five party line." But such levity never lingers long among these men; a sailor named Pollock (George LeGuere) pleads with Price, "Can't we do something sir?"[20]

It is Chief Burke, an officer as compassionate as Price, who proposes a temporary respite from what increasingly looks like their inevitable deaths. He says that since the air is so dangerously low, he will break out the oxygen. But they have only one tank, enough to postpone death for a few hours, if they ration it. The silent despair of this scene is alone broken by the sounds of men coughing as their lungs strive for oxygen. Thus, when Burke opens the oxygen tank valve, we see close-ups of many of the men, some of whom are now shirtless, as they breathe deeply and gratefully. One sailor remarks, "Gee, I'd sure like to shake hands with the guy who discovered oxygen!" Erwin glances up from his radio and gives a pragmatic retort, "He should have discovered more of it!"[21] Indeed, as their oxygen becomes scarcer, our feeling of claustrophobia intensifies along with the men's. John Ford frames most of the remainder of the picture in a space equaling about seven feet by seven feet, in which nine or ten men are usually seen reacting to one another and to their own increasingly helpless plight.

Furthermore, Ford choreographs the men's movements so that they seem to be performing a danse macabre, with the focus first on one and then on another of the actors. There is even a contrapuntal movement to this dance, as first they fight with one another over the dwindling oxygen supply, followed by the fight's cessation when it is broken up by one of the more composed sailors among them. At one point, Price interferes with a violent altercation by admonishing the sailors that they should at least be prepared to die like *men*. He tells them, "Nobody will ever know how we met the end . . . but let's prove to ourselves that we can meet it like heroes!" When Costello (J. Farrell McDonald) makes fun of this speech by laughing, Erwin, having temporarily suspended his efforts to signal for help and now wearing his headset around his shoulders, turns grave and chastises Costello, "Don't laugh at the kid . . . he's serious!" All the while, we see Erwin in close up, nervously fingering the cords attached to his earphones, afraid of looking directly at Costello, even as he criticizes his friend's mockery of Ensign Price. The exchange between the two sailors is a more sedate reprise of the violent fisticuffs of the quarrel we have just witnessed. Then we see Erwin once again in close up; he has replaced his headset and is listening more attentively than ever for sounds that do not come. His wandering eyes penetrate, knife-like, his surroundings, as they move from side to side, looking for some unseen respondent, someone to hear his pleas for aid. At last, he shakes his head in resignation, saying, "Wrong number."[22]

Costello is no longer worried about summoning anyone now, because he has just sloshed his way through the standing water and come across something that looks like a one-gallon gasoline container; what this discovery does contain is the ship's supply of alcohol. Temporarily oblivious to his previous outburst at Ensign Price's expense, Costello vows generously, "You boys can have the oxygen. I'll take the gin." This silent portion contains only the eerie, pounding beeps of the telegraph keys, as Erwin remains standing at his post, his face growing ever more soaked with sweat, his realization also increasing with each passing second that those SOS signals reverberate only into emptiness, like distinct heartbeats reminding him of his own fragile mortality.

Again sound breaks the silence, providing another effective counterpoint to the mood just created by the stillness in the fetid air. The silence is cracked open by the hysterical outburst of Pollock, who repeats "Save Our Souls! Save Our Souls!" while his fellow sailors try to restrain him as his powerless hands reach out, claws trying to grasp the dead branch from which he is about to tumble. Attention is then once again focused on Erwin's radioman, still listening intently into his headset; we hear the barely audible voices of Albertson and Erwin in the following exchange. Albertson asks "Anything yet?" Aloud, but ever so softly, Erwin responds, "Nothing yet, sir."[23]

Again the point/counterpoint movement occurs, as we are thrust back into another frenetic exchange between Chief Burke, keeper of the oxygen tank, and the men, led by Pollock, who insist on his opening the precious valve once more. Burke offers a kind of pragmatic fatalism in the subsequent lines, "Take it easy! Don't you want to last as long as you can, you fool?"[24]

However, Pollock's frenzy has reached a point beyond which he cannot be stopped, short of desperate means. Standing in the water, soaked by the seepage of the sea and by the oozing of his own sweat, he raises a detonator over his head, threatening to blow them all up and thus quickly end their pathetic efforts at survival. We shift to a close up of many arms raised toward the uplifted arm of Pollock, each hand grabbing at the detonator.

Again the lights go out, and once more the darkness is periodically lifted by quick, bright flashes of light, which serve as a visual parallel to the accompanying sounds of the staccato SOS signals eternally telegraphed by Erwin. When the lights come back on, we see that the water has begun bubbling up from the floor, emitting a lethal gaseous chlorine vapor, incongruously reminding us of the health-giving waters of a spa. The sub interior at this time has the foggy, misty look and feel of the sea. Through this interior haze, Pollock is still out of control, shouting, "Down on your knees, you sinners! Vengeance is mine, saith the Lord! You're going up from the bottom of the ocean in a fiery chariot!"[25]

Suddenly, sound intervenes, and we hear Frank Albertson as Ensign Price yelling, "Stop it! Stop it!" Through the vaporish air, he can be seen pointing a gun at Pollock, trembling, agony reflected in his face. Then he fires, killing Pollock. Stunned by his own desperate act, his gun hanging limply from his hand, his expression revealing awe, horror, and confusion, he calls futilely, desperately, "Pollock! Pollock!" Then the intertitles continue his words, "I . . . I've killed him!" Without a trace of verbal irony, Burke tries to comfort him as we read, "But you've saved your men, sir." Seeing that Price is about to collapse, Burke places his arm around Price's shoulders. As another sailor then leads the weeping Price to a bunk, we hear his voice again, repeating, "I killed him. . . . I killed him."[26]

With the tension increasing, the foul water creeping higher around their legs, the men looking more wasted than ever, a downcast Erwin tells Burke, "Power is gettin' weak, Chief . . . water must be gettin' over the bunks in the battery room!" Suddenly, Erwin's mood shifts; he excitedly reports, "Hey, fellows . . . somebody's calling us!" Grasping both earphones, he holds each one tightly against his ears, so as not to let his invisible contact escape. "It's a British boat!" he announces, all the while waving away the men who quickly surround him, for he is trying to listen carefully to what he has been so long frantic to hear. He even looks heavenward, perhaps as a form of grateful prayer, and resumes his message, "They're right above us now!"[27]

But the poisonous chlorine gas is bubbling faster than ever, coming up through the already fouled water, inexorably rising from the floor of their cabin. At Burke's command, the men slog their way out of the enclosure that has ironically been a kind of refuge, moving slowly toward the torpedo room. As Erwin leaves with the others, he makes a small but telling gesture: he rubs his ears, as though he were trying to get back some circulation after spending so many hours violently pressing the radio phones into his head. Then, in another subtle movement, he turns back to take one final look at his radio receiver.

From this point till the end of the film, the editing and the cinematography are particularly effective. There is much crosscutting between the trapped men in the torpedo room and the Navy divers on the sea above, preparing to rescue as many of the sailors as they can. First, we see the heavily breathing, continually sweating men resting upon the torpedoes—small white whales which look as though they could swim to the surface with the men on their backs. Next, we cut to the sea, now fairly calm, with the sun brightly reflecting off the surface. When we return to the sub, we see two men die, unable to breathe the gaseous air any longer. The first to go is Dutch, still holding the vase we had seen him carrying in Shanghai. The second is Cobb (Walter McGrail) another man we have learned to recognize. A third man loses consciousness and drops from his hand a small wooden boat he had earlier whittled. It falls into the water at his feet; Erwin takes it and holds it gently, like a most precious piece of jewelry; then he carefully places it back into the ghastly water, where it promptly upends, refusing to float properly, becoming a metaphor for the submarine itself.

Again background sounds are used to create mood. The only noises we hear are the creaking sounds of the winches turning the lines, which are lowering the Navy divers into the sea, and the splashing sounds of the sea itself, as we are dropped with the divers into the water and view the descent through their eyes. Then we cut back to the surface and are on board the rescue ship where, if we look closely, we can see John Wayne as Stuart Erwin's counterpart. Wayne is the radio operator relaying information to his superior officer about the status of the stranded men. We never hear Wayne speak, but he tells the officer, through intertitles: "They say there's thirteen men alive, sir . . . they're asking for the port tube to cleared!"[28]

This clearing is done in due course, and the men are stuffed one by one into the tube and thrust upward onto the surface through some sort of pressurized force, much as one would wash out a foreign object from a large garden hose by turning on the water. Then, when each man improbably bobs to the surface—ninety feet upward, no less—he is picked from the water by one of the waiting rowboats, which have been detached from the rescue ship. The photography in this portion, both underwater and on the surface, is stunning; the plot plausibility considerably less so.

All ends happily for everyone but the one man left behind, the one who must remain to work the tube from the inside. Chief Burke does not make it through the tube, but elects instead to stay with the dead submarine and to pay restitution for a shameful episode in his past when, as captain of another vessel, he was the only one to survive the sinking of his ship.

Men Without Women is a well done film in which Stuart Erwin gives us an early glance into the many-faceted character he would continue to create throughout his career: quick-witted yet shy; boisterous yet unruffled; brave yet cautious; and ultimately a hard-working professional, doing his job better than anyone might have ever expected him to do.

NOTES

1. *Dangerous Nan McGrew*. Dir. Malcolm St. Clair. Paramount, 1930.
2. *Dangerous Nan McGrew*, 1930.
3. *Dangerous Nan McGrew*, 1930.
4. *Dangerous Nan McGrew*, 1930.
5. *Dangerous Nan McGrew*, 1930.
6. *Only Saps Work*. Dir. Cyril Gardner and Edwin H. Knopf. Paramount, 1930.
7. *Only Saps Work*, 1930.
8. Scott Eyman, *Print the Legend* (New York: Simon & Schuster, 1999), 123.
9. *Men Without Women*. Dir. John Ford. Fox, 1930.
10. *Men Without Women*, 1930.
11. *Men Without Women*, 1930.
12. *Men Without Women*, 1930.
13. *Men Without Women*, 1930.
14. *Men Without Women*, 1930.
15. *Men Without Women*, 1930.
16. *Men Without Women*, 1930.
17. Andrew Sarris, *"You Ain't Heard Nothin'Yet":The American Talking Film: History and Memory 1927–1949* (New York: Oxford University Press, 1998), 170.
18. *Men Without Women*, 1930.
19. *Men Without Women*, 1930.
20. *Men Without Women*, 1930.
21. *Men Without Women*, 1930.
22. *Men Without Women*, 1930.
23. *Men Without Women*, 1930.
24. *Men Without Women*, 1930.
25. *Men Without Women*, 1930.
26. *Men Without Women*, 1930.
27. *Men Without Women*, 1930.
28. *Men Without Women*, 1930.

3

RESCUED FROM OBSCURITY

I Years had been from Home
And now before the Door
I dared not enter, lest a Face
I never saw before

Stare stolid into mine
And ask my Business there—
"My business but a Life I left
Was such remaining there?"

—Emily Dickinson, *The Complete Poems of Emily Dickinson,*
no. 609 (c. 1872)

"Our sweet illusions are half of them conscious illusions, like
effects of colour that we know to be made up of tinsel, broken glass, and rags."

—George Eliot, *The Lifted Veil* (1878)

"In this business, if it isn't one trick, it's another."

—Director Sam Hardy to movie hopeful Stuart Erwin in
Make Me a Star (1932)

Motion pictures depicting the rise of talented but unknown individuals
have constituted a popular genre for decades. Musicals in particular
lend themselves to this type of narrative. Those "all-talking, all-singing, all-
dancing" movies of the early 1930s established the paradigm that was to be
continued into the 1950s with imaginative biographies of musical performers such as Ruth Etting (*Love Me or Leave Me*, 1955) and Fanny Brice (*Funny
Girl*, 1968). These movies featured the little girl from the chorus, whose flair

for (a) singing, (b) dancing, (c) acting, (d) clowning, or (e) all of the above got her the break that she deserved. What is more, she was always destined to become an overnight sensation—once the harried producer gave her the chance. Indeed, in *Going Hollywood* (1933), a desperate Stuart Erwin gives Marion Davies her big opportunity to star in a movie when his aggressive leading lady Fifi D'Orsay becomes too crazed to handle. A variation of this popular chorus-girl-does-herself-proud genre is one in which a young, inexperienced character is manipulated by an older con man, who subsequently manages his protégé's successful career. Frank Capra's stark, cynical 1931 film *The Miracle Woman*, featuring the rise of a duplicitous evangelist and featuring Barbara Stanwyck and Sam Hardy as the victim and her manager, is an excellent illustration of the type.

In point of fact, the genre would continue to be a favorite for over sixty years. One suspects, however, that the type has finally spent itself with *Boogie Nights* (1997)—part satire and part serious—in which youthful men and women are rescued from jobs as busboys and dishwashers and recruited for porno movies, their talents lying in directions not specifically related to singing, dancing, and acting.

THE BOXING GAME

Stuart Erwin was sometimes the recipient of such machinations on the part of self-seeking promoters, and his abilities were often physical and athletic rather than musical and histrionic. *Palooka* (1934) is one of the best of its type: a mixture of Damon Runyon characters coupled with physical comedy, satire, drama, romantic misunderstandings, and the self-important, puffed-up personality of Jimmy Durante. Erwin plays the title role, the son of prizewinning boxer Pete Palooka (Robert Armstrong), who twenty years earlier had left his wife and infant son so that he might freely enjoy the pursuit of not-so-infant blondes. When fight manager Durante discovers Erwin, he is living in the country with his tough, no-nonsense mother (Marjorie Rambeau, looking too young to be Erwin's mother and, in reality, only fourteen years older than he). Mother and son are living an idyllic existence, selling produce and staying away from the big city corruption that had led the elder Palooka astray. Rambeau is determined that her son not become a copy of his irresponsible father, so she has made him promise that he will never become a prizefighter. He appears content to follow her wishes; in fact, they are comfortable in each other's presence, gently kidding one another, neither trying to assert authority over the other.

Into this rustic setting barges Jimmy Durante. Erwin is on his way to the market with crates of eggs; Durante and his best fighter, Dynamite Wilson, are driving in the opposite direction. When their cars collide, Durante slides under the wheels of Erwin's auto; Dynamite insults Durante, where-upon Erwin punches Dynamite, cleanly decking the champ. Durante wastes no time as he peremptorily brays at Erwin: "You just knocked down my best fighter, and that makes me your manager." When Erwin protests that he must get his crates of eggs to town, Durante pulls out a piece of paper and, bran-dishing it in front of the perplexed Erwin, declares with astounding logic and a peculiar touch of personification: "Sign this contract and you won't ever have to look an egg in the face again."[1] As Erwin continues to object, telling Durante that he doesn't want to break the promise he has made to his mother, he is continually thwarted by Durante, who maintains his nonstop chatter, his head bobbing up and down, a marionette on a string. By the end of the scene, Durante has so rattled the nonplussed Erwin that Erwin signs. As he does so, he utters one of this film's most striking understatements: "Gosh—it was kinda sudden."[2]

Shortly thereafter, Erwin confides the news of his good fortune to his best girl (Mary Carlisle). Apparently unaware of the cosmic irony involved in his decision to follow in his father's mud-spattered, grimy footsteps, he earnestly tells her: "I'm going to be a leather pusher. I'm going to breathe carbon monoxide and gasoline fumes instead of fresh air. I'm going to the city to be a fighter."[3]

So Erwin tags along with the bellicose Durante to the city, but he is faced with more than just the beauties of "carbon monoxide and gasoline fumes." First, Durante robs him of his identity by giving him the name of his former champ (or chump), Dynamite Wilson. Next, while Durante is prais-ing the new Dynamite's boxing ability to a promoter who dislikes the switch of Dynamites, Erwin is busily being battered in his first fight. Finally, in the midst of Durante's ranting about Dynamite's invincibility, Erwin is carried in unconscious, slung between two trainers as though he were a collapsed ham-mock subjected to an excess of weight. Dumbfounded, Durante asks one of the body bearers: "Wha' happened?" "One punch," responds the trainer, holding up one finger, as though to make the situation clearer to Durante.

DURANTE (giving his famous shrug of disgust): Am I haunted by misfor-tune! Me—with an unbroken record of defeats.

ERWIN (awakening both to the world and to the obvious): I lost.

DURANTE: You've been peekin'! Why didn't you fight like I told ya?

ERWIN (defensive): I did. But after we got started, he whispered to me and told me to take it easy on account of his wife and kids—and then—I don't remember anymore.

DURANTE: I might know you'd fall for that old gag.[4]

At this point, Durante is prepared to pay off Erwin in pocket change and send him back to the farm. But while Erwin is out of sight dressing and preparing to leave, another fight promoter corners Durante, telling him that he likes the colorful Erwin because he "tries and he ain't dangerous." This manager's motives are not completely altruistic, however, because he needs a safe set-up for his current barnstorming champion, Al McSwat (Willliam Cagney, in a dreadful burlesque of older brother Jimmy. He had the manner, but lacked the heart.). Naturally, go-get-'em Durante likes this idea, since he knows that he will get a monetary cut of these fights, so he accosts the now thoroughly confused Erwin with the good tidings. Durante finally persuades him of the wisdom of going up against the champion, reminding the soft-hearted Erwin: "But remember—McSwat ain't got no wife and no children either."[5] What Durante neglects to tell Erwin is that he will probably lose against the more experienced McSwat. (The name sounds like one of the modern popular parodies of the fast-food restaurant.)

But Durante is wrong about the outcome: Erwin defeats McSwat—but only because the champ is so drunk that he has trouble standing, never mind accurately punching the lucky challenger. Nevertheless, Durante, ever the pragmatist, now realizes that he will have to do some dodging of his own if he is going to keep Erwin winning. This feat he accomplishes by bribing other fighters to lose more set-ups to Erwin. Consequently, Erwin maintains his champion status for a while by defeating a bunch of thugs who look as though they could be poster boys for Murder, Inc. He also remains happily unaware that his accomplishments are phony. In the interim, however, he collects the trappings of success—an exotic woman (Lupe Velez) who grants him her sexual favors; an expensive wardrobe; a retinue of men and women to attend to his grooming—tailor, manicurist, and barber. This conventional plot prepares the audience for his downfall because the screenplay has developed his character in a predictable way: Nice country boy—something of a boob—goes to the city; nice country boy is taken advantage of by city slickers; nice country boy appears to be corrupted by city slickers; nice country boy follows his better instincts and returns to the country to marry the equally nice girl that he left behind. Film critic/historian Roger Dooley calls *Palooka* "a mediocrity" that nonetheless had a fairly good role for Jimmy Durante, who was given a better part in this United Artists film than those he had been assigned at M-G-M.[6]

But this assessment does not consider what Stuart Erwin was able to do with the title role, for he gives an insightful, complex performance that transcends the clichéd narrative. To begin, he plays the first three-quarters of the picture with whimsical irony, refusing to take either himself or his playful costars (especially Durante and Velez) seriously. Later in the movie, by the time he realizes that he has been cruelly used, Erwin switches his approach to his character by showing Palooka's pain and vulnerability—and by revealing his own shrewd perceptions about what would motivate an individual such as Palooka. Moreover, Erwin depicts Palooka's growing recognition in a gradual way; his character does not suddenly display the cartoon bubble with the light bulb inside. Rather, when Erwin is told by both his mother and Durante that the world is not as accommodating as he has been led to believe, he slowly shifts from willful disbelief to genuine sadness. And Erwin makes this shift believable because he has already portrayed Palooka as too canny, too astute, and too intelligent to lie to himself for very long.

Erwin's dawning realization begins when Durante reveals that all of the "champ's" winning matches have been fixed. Further revelations continue to torment him as Rambeau plants doubts in her son about Lupe Velez' true motives in taking him as her lover. His self-confidence is shattered even more with the reintroduction of the elder Palooka into his life. Erwin's reunion with his father, whom he initially doesn't recognize, is especially poignant. Pete has returned after twenty years, not only to share in the glory of his prizewinning son, but also to try to atone for the much earlier abandonment of his child. Further, Pete reenters his son's life just when Erwin is gamely confronting the two central truths of his present life—facts that he can no longer deny: that he has been defeating goons in fixed fights, and that Lupe Velez hungers for the bodies of only those men who are winners.

As the reunion scene begins, Robert Armstrong as Pete Palooka enters the fancy hotel room where Erwin is seated, head in his hands, facing the camera but with his back to his father. Hearing someone enter but not particularly interested in his visitor's identity, Erwin asks who it is. When Armstrong identifies himself, the camera cuts to Erwin, who turns slowly around and registers astonishment, curiosity, and eagerness. He stands, moves awkwardly toward his father, and, with a shy, tentative smile offers his hand. The scene might have been mawkish, but Erwin finds the right tone when he equivocally tells Armstrong that he has heard a good deal about his father from his mother.

Following Erwin's ambiguous comment, Robert Armstrong (another actor not particularly given to sentiment) quickly changes the subject in order to tell his son that he is proud of his boy becoming the champ: "You're a great fighter." At this undeserved compliment, Erwin winces, replying sadly, "Yea—there seems to be some argument about that." No longer able to face his father but desperate for his approval, Erwin turns away and sits, finally confessing that his manager has said that he doesn't have a chance in this return match against McSwat. Then, reclaiming himself as his father's long-forgotten child, Erwin pleads for his father's help, admitting his love for *the* girl: "I gotta win for her."[7]

When Armstrong offers to train his son, Erwin is thrilled; he has just discovered a missing part of himself in this stranger who has so openly given of his own self. The scene between the long-separated father and son is effective because neither actor allows himself to give free rein to emotion. Like epic battlefield comrades, they define their heroism through restraint.

In spite of Pete Palooka's efforts to prepare his son for his next fight, Erwin loses. And he naturally loses the girl as well. "Come on McSwat!" Velez yells callously, watching excitedly as Erwin begins to succumb to continual battering about his face. "Kill him! Finish him—so we all can go home!"[8]

And go home he does—back to the solid values of the country and to the girl he left behind. And *Palooka* constantly rises above its tired plot because Stuart Erwin skillfully balances the incongruities of its tone and of its narrative structure against the tensions within Joe Palooka and, as a result, gives a coherent portrayal.

ACADEMY AWARD FOLLIES

Two years after he made *Palooka*, Erwin received his only Academy Award nomination—for Best Supporting Actor in *Pigskin Parade* (1936). As in *Palooka*, the plot of *Pigskin Parade* shows him once again being rescued from obscurity, this time in order to play college football. Moreover, the year of this film's release was the first year in which the Academy gave awards for supporting actors, and there is something revealing and intriguing about the fact that Erwin was among the first performers considered in this category. But *Pigskin Parade* was all wrong for an actor of Erwin's sensitivity and talents. Nevertheless, in a shortsighted gesture typical of the movie industry's critical misapprehension of Erwin's entire career, the Academy recognized him for one of his most stereotypical roles—one which, as written, lacks even the depth of many of his B-movie parts.

His rise from obscurity begins when he is discovered by Texas State football coach Winston "Slug" Winters (Jack Haley), his wife Bessie Winters

(Patsy Kelly), and two Texas State students, Laura Watson (Betty Grable) and Chip Carson (Johnny Downs). Erwin plays backwoods Amos Dodd, who, when he is first seen by this unlikely group of talent scouts, is standing in an Arkansas field, pitching melons to his sister Sairy Dodd (the adolescent Judy Garland in her first feature-length movie). Before this movie, Erwin had never dressed as though he were a fugitive from an Erskine Caldwell novel. Although audiences had been accustomed to seeing him in carefully tailored suits, here he looks as though he belongs in *Tobacco Road* or *God's Little Acre*, both published in the early 1930s. Prior to this movie, if he had been required in a film to remove his suit jacket, his shirts were always clean and pressed. In *Pigskin Parade*, however, he first emerges dressed like a scarecrow; in fact, his appearance gives an odd foreshadowing of the later pairing between Judy Garland and Ray Bolger in *The Wizard of Oz*. He has no jacket; his shirt is torn and dirty; his trousers are ragged and contain more holes than his shirt—he is William Faulkner's Abner Snopes without the malignity. In addition, when he runs across the field toward Garland, it is evident that he is having trouble moving with ease, as he is barefoot. Furthermore, he is apparently illiterate—another difference between Amos Dodd and the other characters he had played previously, many of whom were college graduates.

But Coach Jack Haley and his troop of friends ignore the obvious fact that Erwin is not quite ready for the academic rigors of college. Betty Grable sidles up to him, trying to encourage him by referring to a possible subject of interest to him. Erwin tries hard in this exchange, but he seems uncomfortable playing an awkward boob:

GRABLE: You could study agriculture, Amos.

ERWIN: What I want with that? I'm a'gonna be a farmer.

GRABLE (flirting): You could meet some nice girls in college.

ERWIN: Aw shucks.

GARLAND (also uncomfortable as a hayseed): Aw—Amos is scared of girls.

ERWIN: I ain't not.

GRABLE: I could introduce you to a lot of lovely girls.

ERWIN: With shoes on?

KELLY: Sure—and stockings too.[9]

Of course, the obvious problems arise when this quartet of dippy college types haul Erwin back to Texas: Erwin is lacking in a few basic skills that would make him eligible for college. But never mind; Johnny Downs and his buddies concoct a scheme to give Erwin the credentials of an evident egghead, Herbert Terwilliger Van Dyck (Elisha Cook Jr.). These four accomplish their feat to eliminate Cook by setting him up to be arrested for throwing left-wing, anticapitalist pamphlets at a local bank.

When we next see Erwin, he looks more like a college student—at least in his dress. He has lost his scarecrow hat along with his scarecrow appearance. He has on a collegiate sweater, light-color slacks, and what appear to be saddle shoes, which cause him to move as though he were trying to maintain his balance while walking on railroad ties. As he awkwardly ambles across the campus, he at first passes Garland, who is moving toward him. They initially fail to recognize each other because she has also changed her appearance, giving up her ragged dress for a skirt and sweater. (Although still a young teen, Garland fills out her sweater even better than Betty Grable, one of her adult costars here.) But after Erwin and Garland have swirled to face each other in a simultaneous motion of recognition, they seem genuinely pleased to see each other. A close look at this scene reveals both humor as well as some enlightening details about Erwin's apparent concern and protectiveness toward Garland.

As the scene begins, Erwin boasts that his name is no longer Amos. In fact, as in *Palooka*, his handlers have stripped him of his previous identity and given him a new name. Trying hard to remember what it is, he pulls out a piece of paper; but, because he is unable to read what is written there, he hands it to his sister Judy Garland. She looks at the words—HERBERT VAN DYCK—and tells him that his name is now Herbert Van Dick. At this, Erwin remembers both the name and the pronunciation, as he corrects her by repeating clearly: "Van *Dike*."[10] The scene is humorous because of the earnestness of Garland's attempts to be helpful and because of her youthful naiveté; she possibly misses the sexual innuendo here. And Erwin, who probably does not miss it at all, lets the moment pass.

What is really fascinating about this scene, however, involves something that goes beyond the script, beyond the crude, forced jokes. When Erwin first admires Garland's new clothes, he reaches out to her gently, tentatively, patting her on the shoulder and on the arm, as though to reassure her that she looks fine and that everything is going to be all right.

He maintains this supportive attitude in their scenes together throughout the movie, not so much in what he says but in the subtle gestures he makes toward her. For instance, when he first arrives on campus and meets coach Jack Haley, he pretends to be afraid of the much more sophisticated Haley (sophisticated insofar as Haley's clothes appear at least to be properly stitched together). For protection, then, Erwin "hides" behind Garland, but in so doing, he places his hands on her shoulders in a gesture of reassurance rather than one of alarm at meeting his new rescuers.

The sad facts of Judy Garland's life have been chronicled at length in numerous books and articles; however, in 1936, the year of *Pigskin Parade*, the year in which Garland had her fourteenth birthday, her troubled history was just beginning. But there is recent evidence which reveals that by this time she was already addicted to drugs and living on the edge of disaster, her emotions swinging between giddiness and dejection. Writing about Garland in his book *The Hollywood Musical*, Ethan Mordden observes that in this movie, Garland, on loan to 20th Century Fox from M-G-M, "which didn't know what to do with her," exudes "wonderful, raw exuberance. . . . *Pigskin Parade* didn't break any house records, but it told M-G-M what to do with Judy Garland."[11] But M-G-M didn't *really* know what to do with Judy Garland, except to exploit her fragility. And Stuart Erwin isn't quite sure what to do with her either, except to treat her with gentle, supportive humor. In any event, Erwin, supposedly an unlettered, uncultured hick who cannot even read his own bogus name, once again as in *Palooka* transcends his trite material. He does this by showing—maybe unwittingly, maybe not—how awkward he is as a country bumpkin; and by revealing—perhaps subconsciously, perhaps not—his desire to comfort Garland. He also does his best with a poor script. Unlike *Palooka*, which at least had some good, sharp, witty dialogue, *Pigskin Parade*, despite its talented performers, never achieves the absurdly sublime moments that can occasionally be seen in *Palooka*.

In addition, *Pigskin Parade* exemplifies Erwin's distrust of anything that does not seem authentic, that seems forced and fake. For example, when the script finally allows him to put on a proper suit and to look more like himself, he is plainly more at ease than he had been when he had been dressed in clothes doubtless rejected by the Salvation Army.

Another difference between this movie and the earlier *Palooka* can be seen in the endings of the two. Whereas in *Palooka* Erwin loses his rematch and goes back to his previous life, where he indeed belongs, in *Pigskin Parade*, he enables Texas State to win its game against Yale by running a last-minute touchdown in his bare feet in blizzard conditions. And this is where the movie ends. The audience is left to wonder about Erwin's future. What will become of him and Judy Garland when they return to the life they left behind in Arkansas? Will they be tossed back into that melon field? Will Garland find a job singing in some dreary rural roadhouse? Will she marry the boy next door and become a battered wife? Or will she and her brother continue to live in poverty until they die? No one seems to care, least of all Jack Haley, Patsy Kelly, et al., and the scriptwriters. But this was Stuart

Erwin's only Academy Award nomination. That he was given recognition for his acting in a part that so unquestionably ill-suited him must have given him pause, at least in his more private, contemplative moments.

What he had to say publicly about his work, however, provides at least a partial clue to the reasons for his being associated in his viewers' minds with ignorant hillbillies. In the 1930s, he told an interviewer: "Put me down as a guy who loves being loony. And I mean it! Give me a nice goofy part anytime. I've found that a dumb character requires much more thought and study than a conventional one, and, therefore, is more interesting and stimulating. Suckers may be born every minute, according to Mr. Barnum, but I'd like to add that there are a thousand different ways of playing one."[12] This self-appraisal is disingenuous; in fact, Stuart Erwin seems more uncomfortable in the role of "dumb" Amos Dodd than he does in any other part he ever played. The only scenes where he appears somewhat at ease are those in which he dresses formally and dances with some college coeds, and those where he tries to give some reassurance and confidence to Judy Garland.

THE UNKINDEST CUT OF ALL

One film for which Erwin *did* deserve the Academy Award—for Best Actor—is one that contains perhaps his most fully realized performance, one that is probably the closest he ever came to exposing his private self. It is also one that probes as well as any film ever did the nature of comedy itself and the immense difficulties inherent in playing comedy. The movie is *Make Me A Star* (1932), which was a remake of the silent *Merton of the Movies* (1924), and which would subsequently be filmed again in 1947 with Red Skelton. The Erwin version, however, is generally considered to be the best. Although film historians have often referred to the movie as a comedy, I suspect that they were not really paying attention, perhaps taking short naps as they watched it, for the film is *not* a comedy by any stretch of the definition. In fact, Erwin's poignant performance as the small town boy who is duped by the vulgar Hollywood moviemakers into thinking that he is making a serious western, all the while he is being made the butt of their jokes, is unbearably painful to watch. Erwin is so heartrending in his depiction of a lonely, gentle man who is ultimately annihilated by the studio system that we continue to hurt for him long after the movie is over.

And the film is all the more distressing because Erwin catches us off balance. His performance at the beginning, before he leaves for Hollywood, is full of comic business; we think that this is going to be a satire on one of those unknown-performer-rises-to-fame stories. However, the tale quickly turns sad and bitter when Erwin travels to Hollywood and is exposed to the fraudulent craftiness of the movie establishment, its representatives battering at his integrity, nearly destroying every decent human impulse he possesses. Moreover, by the end of the film, when he learns the truth, when he learns that he has been tricked, when he finally allows himself to cry as he confronts Joan Blondell, whom he sees as his most perfidious betrayer because he has loved and trusted her so much, we cry with him. And we cry because we know that his tears come not from self-pity, but from his awful realization that he has unwittingly bargained with the Mephistophelian forces of the movie industry, and that he has paid with his soul.

Make Me a Star begins cheerily enough, with the jaunty "California, Here I Come" played under the opening credits. Likewise, the opening scenes are humorous. For instance, before we even see Erwin, we learn that he is an absent-minded delivery boy for Gashwiler's Emporium in the small midwestern town of Simsbury. But even this early in the film, we catch an undercurrent of sadness, for we soon discover that Erwin is pretty much alone in the world, having been yanked from an orphan asylum by Mr. Gashwiler, the owner of the Emporium, and his wife. Moreover, he is something of a charity case, living with the Gashwilers only so long as he can be a useful employee. And we also note that Erwin is already living a precarious existence, for in the film's opening scene we are introduced to his carelessness by ZaSu Pitts as Mrs. Scudder, who is complaining to Mr. Gashwiler about a sack of turnips that Erwin has mistakenly delivered to her.

Charles Sellon, who had played the same part in the 1924 silent version, *Merton of the Movies*, is Gashwiler. Sellon was a clever actor with a sardonic edge; he always looked on the verge of exasperation with the idiots of this world. He would also appear briefly but memorably as the destructive blind and deaf man Mr. Muckle in W. C. Fields's *It's a Gift* (1934). Here, he is listening to Mrs. Scudder complain about her turnips, when she had ordered eggs so that she could make cake frosting. "Can you make frosting with *turnips*?"[13] she challenges Gashwiler.

Erwin appears from the back when Gashwiler summons him. From our first glimpse of him, we see that he is shy, timid, stuttering, gentle, soft-spoken, and unutterably forlorn. We are also reminded that the young Stuart Erwin had a good deal of sex appeal, an important fact in light of Merton Gill's later experiences in Hollywood, where the base moviemaking ruffians get laughs by trying to make him seem effeminate. But in her complaint to Gashwiler, Mrs. Scudder is not as concerned with Erwin's physical attractiveness as she is with her missing eggs. She is also puzzled by Erwin's peculiar penchant for talking to himself. She quizzes him about why she had found him muttering about wanting to get to a town called Red Gap; she is curious to know just where this Red Gap is located. Hers is a line of questioning which makes him quite uncomfortable, for Mrs. Scudder has just intruded on his dream world, a world in which he is a famous hero in western movies.

One whom he *has* allowed into his private world is Tessie (Helen Jerome Eddy), for he sees her as a soulmate, one as starstruck in her own way as he, except that Tessie wants to be a screenwriter. When one of her screenplays is repeatedly returned to her, he tries to reassure her; he wants to keep her from being discouraged. But to her suggestion that perhaps the story would sell if she injected some comedy into it, Erwin is horrified. "*Comedy?*" he gasps. So Tessie explains: "Yes. For instance, suppose I give the old Earl—you remember the dignified old Earl—a cross-eyed butler?" Her suggestion goes counter to everything Erwin believes about the role of Art, so now it is his turn to explain: "Oh no, Tessie, no. They might give the part to that cross-eyed fellow who plays in those awful Lodestone Comedies. It's things like that that *debase* a noble art."[14] And indeed this "cross-eyed fellow" (in the person of Ben Turpin, playing himself) will return to gall Erwin.

But Tessie is enchanted with what she sees as Erwin's sensitive insights into the essentials of great Art, so she replies admiringly, "Oh, Merton. I wish I had your wonderful instincts." The line is an important one, for neither Tessie nor the viewer realizes at this moment the extent to which Erwin does have "wonderful instincts"; it is precisely these decent instincts that are going to be shattered, leaving Erwin no choice but to sweep them up and throw them away by the end of the film. But at this point, Erwin lacks such prescience, so he adopts his cowboy hero persona as he recites to Tessie the words of his favorite star: "You mustn't get discouraged, Tessie. Remember what Buck Benson said in his interview. Success comes only after a long ordeal of sacrifice and suffering."[15]

Erwin is so obsessed with Buck Benson that he calls Gashwiler's delivery horse *Pinto*—after Buck's own steed—and talks to "Pinto" when he thinks no one is listening. (In truth, Pinto has the far more prosaic name of Dexter.) The monologue that Erwin has as he stands next to the horse, patting its head and addressing it, has a truly farcical quality to it: "Let's get going Pinto, old pal. We've got to make Red Gap by sundown."[16] Now we know the answer to Mrs. Scudder's earlier question; we know where Red Gap is—in the Never Never Land of the moviemaker's imagination and therefore in Erwin's own private daydreams. Meanwhile, Erwin is gazing across the road at a movie marquee featuring his hero's name in large letters, and at a large picture of Buck Benson on the poster board outside the theater. We also note by this time that the moviemakers have made Benson look suspiciously like Tom Mix. So far, we are prepared to enjoy a satire on filmmakers and on the innocent naiveté of Erwin's Merton Gill.

Further kidding of Erwin's character comes in the next scene at the end of the day when Erwin is helping Mr. Gashwiler close the store. Gashwiler tells Erwin not to forget to put out the light. "I won't, sir," says Erwin, agreeably following Gashwiler's instructions, but flipping the switch immediately, just as Gashwiler is ascending the stairs. We hear a crash, followed by Gashwiler's curses, 1932-style: "Jumpin' Jehoshaphat! Gosh! Doggone it! Can't you wait till I get upstairs?" As Erwin replies, "Yes, sir," Gashwiler nags, "Why don't you, then?"

"Good night," adds Erwin, irrelevantly.

"Ah, shut up," retorts Gashwiler.[17]

As Gashwiler finally succeeds in climbing the stairs, Erwin retreats to his small, sparsely furnished room to continue his study of acting. We see that he has purchased a book and accompanying phonograph records to help him get closer to his career goal. He looks carefully at the recording he is about to play, the label reading National Correspondence Academy of Acting. Lesson No. 4. Western Hero Course. (*Learn a Language at Home in Your Spare Time! Amaze Your Friends When You Sit Down to Play the Piano! Earn Fifty Dollars a Week Writing Screenplays for the Movies!*) Popular newspaper and magazine advertisements of the time carried slogans such as these and preyed upon those depression-era readers who were desperate to be both rich and popular. And Erwin's Merton Gill is very much in the mainstream of this gullible public, convinced that these records represent the first step on the road to his becoming a star. As he places his next lesson on the Victrola, we hear the announcer cheerily advise this unseen would-be actor what scenario he will be acting out in Lesson No. 4.

In the meantime, Erwin's anonymous instructor refers him to the book that has come with these recordings. This book contains numerous numbered facial expressions, many of which Erwin tries to assume according to the mood that he is being instructed to convey. The scene is humorous, largely because Erwin plays it so straight; he is unrelentingly serious about being an actor and unswervingly convinced that his systematic study will quickly land him a job when he gets to Hollywood.

Among his preparations to sell himself as an actor are publicity poses as a cowboy. He hires a photographer and, with a good deal of effort, mounts the patient horse Dexter (a.k.a. Pinto). Complete with cowboy outfit and ten-gallon hat, he looks as much like Buck Benson (Tom Mix?) as it is possible for Stuart Erwin to look. He has also been carefully studying his book of poses, so he tells the photographer the titles of his positions. Unfortunately, the one designated Shooting Back At The Posse calls for him to shoot his gun toward the horse's rear, an action not appreciated by Dexter, who bolts. Erwin does not bolt with Dexter, however, doing a backward somersault and landing ungracefully in the foreground, while Dexter trots happily off, rid of the nuisance of this novice gunman.

Watching Erwin's efforts to pass himself off as a cowboy actor is the loyal Tessie. There is a definite rapport between these two, but the script does not allow the relationship to be pursued. By the conclusion of the film, after Erwin has been virtually shattered, we can only hope that he might return to Simsbury to find peace with Tessie, but we also know that such an unrealistic finish is not to be.

It is from this point on that the film loses its light touch. It is from this moment that Erwin, in essence, reaches down into our emotional centers and never lets go, finally breaking our hearts. The first true note of seriousness occurs when Erwin returns to his room in Gashwiler's house and finds that the old man has gone through his precious possessions and scattered them around the room. His recordings with their attendant acting lessons are fanned out like playing cards on his dresser, his publicity photos strewn on the bed. He expresses to Gashwiler his pain at having his private self intruded upon, but Gashwiler is not impressed, for he cruelly informs Erwin that he is making himself the laughingstock of the whole town. That Gashwiler doesn't give two hoots about Erwin's sensibilities but that he is primarily concerned with his own reputation becomes clear when he reminds his delivery boy-cum-"adopted" son that Erwin is living there only at Gashwiler's pleasure and discretion. He also reminds Erwin that he had been grooming Erwin to become a partner in the Emporium business. Obviously, Gashwiler does not want a partner who continually makes an ass of himself.

Erwin listens patiently to this dressing down; then he tells Gashwiler that his plans don't include Gashwiler's Emporium, but that he *does* figure some day on going to Hollywood, where he will assuredly have a successful career. An exasperated Gashwiler is tired of such ingratitude, so he lets Erwin know that this vague "some day" is closer than he thinks, that he'd better pack and leave on the morning train. And this Erwin does, hopefully heading off to fame and fortune in Hollywood.

One of the first of many errors in judgment that he makes when he gets to California occurs as he arrives at Majestic Studios, home of Buck Benson, thinking that he will automatically be allowed to get past the gate and into the studio. The elderly guard treats him with a sort of bemused tolerance, informing him where he might find the casting office. So Erwin trudges off to central casting, carrying his portfolio of horse and rider pictures under his arm.

The first roadblock he encounters is the casting secretary known as The Countess, played by Ruth Donnelly, a deft actress who specialized in playing off-the-wall, scatterbrained, but nonetheless worldly dames, often at Warners. The Countess cannot believe that Erwin is serious when he shows her his publicity portfolio of pictures taken with Dexter, the horse. Both Donnelly and Joan Blondell, who is playing a featured movie actress known as "Flips" Montague, laugh at Erwin when he is out of hearing range. Blondell tells Donnelly that she has known a lot of actors and that she consequently cannot believe that Erwin is not putting them on. But when Blondell meets Erwin, she also knows a gullible person when she sees one. And although she will eventually learn to love him and will be broken by this love, she is not as yet affected by his earnestness, his seriousness of purpose. That will come later and will torture her forever.

But at this moment, Erwin is still idealistic, eager to talk about his ambitions, about his overwhelming desire to be a movie actor. Thus, he overcomes his shyness and speaks to both of these tough, worldly women about his extensive training in preparation for stardom. As he tells them in his slow, deliberate, dignified way about his graduation from the National Correspondence Academy of Acting, both women nearly break up with mirth. But Erwin is not funny here. He takes his character so solemnly that not once does Merton Gill descend into farcical caricature. Nor does Erwin treat his character with either condescension or sentimentality; Erwin *is* Merton Gill, the small town boy—polite, neat, tipping his hat to the ladies, genuine in his belief that the world as a good place where good things can happen, if only you work hard enough.

And one of the good things that happens to him here while he is addressing the ladies is that he gets to see his hero Buck Benson (Dink Templeton) in the flesh, as the narcissistic Benson drives up in an ostentatious limousine, enters the office, and acts bored when one of the movie extra hopefuls gushes over him. (One assumes that the name *Buck* is allegedly synonymous with masculinity and toughness—that is, if one defines *masculinity* as crude, egotistical boorishness.) As Buck passes on into the inner office, Erwin turns excitedly to Donnelly and Blondell, enthusing, "I couldda touched him!" Like a young boy seeing in person his favorite sports figure, Erwin cannot believe that he got so close to his hero.

For her part, Blondell still cannot believe that Erwin is for real. And indeed, occasionally he appears to act like a very polite nine-year-old, well-trained in good manners but totally lacking in common sense. However, if we remember that Erwin's Merton Gill is an orphan who has spent most of his life living in a small town with an elderly couple, and if we remember that such towns in the early twentieth century were more isolated than they would be some sixty or seventy years later, then we can better understand Erwin's portrayal of oblivious provinciality.

Of course, at this time neither Donnelly nor Blondell knows anything about Erwin's background, so they continue to poke sly fun at him. As he is about to leave the office, Donnelly reminds him, "Don't forget your pictures, Mr. Barrymore." Naturally, Erwin misses the dig, so he responds, "Not Barrymore. Gill." Then he feels the need to clarify something important: "Merton Gill's my private name." Still in a bantering mood, Blondell asks, "About your *public* name?" Now grateful for her attention and curiosity, he informs her, "Ryder. Whoop Ryder." Furthermore, he tells the astonished ladies that he intends to wait at the studio until his big chance comes. He confidently divulges that he does not want to work as an extra, so he declares that he'll be sitting "right over there,"[18] and he gestures toward a bench in the corner, waiting for his big opportunity, for the moment when he will be discovered by an astute talent scout. By this point, both Donnelly and Blondell are rendered nearly speechless by this extraordinary man.

And so he remains in the outer office: waiting and waiting and waiting. Time passes. The camera cuts to a close-up of a short note in the Simsbury paper, reporting that Merton Gill has been in touch with Tessie and that he is doing very nicely in Hollywood. Then we cut back to the real thing: Erwin sitting on the bed in his boardinghouse room, cutting out pieces of paper to paste into the soles of his shoes, which are so worn that large holes have appeared in them. We also know that he is about to be evicted, because we hear his landlady on the phone in the next room telling her listener that she expects to have a vacancy soon. Next, we cut to a restaurant, where we see Erwin on his way out, having the last hole in his meal ticket punched by the cashier. As she keeps the ticket, she asks him if he needs a new one. Too proud to concede defeat but too honest to lie, he simply equivocates, "I—I'll be back later."[19]

But he refuses to give up. Every day when Donnelly comes in to work, Erwin is sitting on that bench, still expecting a miracle. He is a permanent fixture in the office, much like Herman Melville's tragic Bartleby, the quintessential alienated man who moves into his employer's legal chambers. In spite of herself, Donnelly has begun to look forward to seeing Erwin each morning, so she compliments him in the only way she knows how: "If I ever come in here some morning and you're not here, I'm gonna think I'm in the wrong studio." To this, the increasingly rumpled Erwin tips his hat to her politely, ever the gentleman, albeit a down-and-out one by now. Then, calling on all his inner strength, he tells her, "If any extra work should come up, I'd take it—please." But Donnelly cuts him off, saying that there is nothing available—not even extra work. Both, of course, recall that Erwin had earlier disdained such work. Neither of them alludes to this fact, however; Erwin just looks heartbreakingly downcast at Donnelly's words as he politely responds, "Well, thank you."[20]

Blondell, who has heard this exchange, knows how much courage it has required for Erwin to make his request. After Erwin leaves, she asks a question of Donnelly to which she already knows the answer, "Isn't that the yap that wanted to be a star or nothin'?" Donnelly's answer is characteristically flippant: "Yea, the barnyard actor."[21] Unlike Donnelly, Blondell can no longer be as "flip" as her nickname ("Flips" Montague) implies; she arranges with one of the studio bosses who owes her a favor to have Erwin hired as an extra—in a Buck Benson picture, no less. When Erwin is told about his lucky break, he is as excited as a schoolboy who has just received a good grade on a test. He chatters on and on to Blondell about his good fortune, unaware that she has arranged it. For her part, Blondell remains discreet, never wanting to wound his pride, his fragile sense of self.

On the set of the Buck Benson western, we glimpse some fascinating details connected with the early days of sound pictures. For example, the camera is encased in what looks like a very large, very bulky cabinet, which was a necessity for soundproofing camera noise. We also see that an actor's voice quality could either make or break an individual, once the movies began to talk. To illustrate, the director asks one of the extras on this movie to recite a one-line piece of dialogue while he holds a piece of paper, purportedly a letter. After this minor player reveals a very heavy Yiddish accent—plainly unsuitable for a western—and the director hears Erwin say the same sentence, he decides to give the line to Erwin instead. Erwin apologizes to the Jewish actor, "I'm sorry." Then, excitedly and repeatedly practicing his one line with various inflections, he exits through a prop door and prepares to make his entrance into the world of stardom.

But what a time he has with what he had hoped would be his big break. First, he can't remember which hand is supposed to hold the letter. Then, after he gets that problem resolved, he flubs the line multiple times, sometimes forgetting it altogether. Although the line is a simple one—all he is required to say is "Hey boys, here's something funny"—he can never get it right. And each time he fails, he becomes more and more flustered. One suspects that his efforts in this scene come close to echoing the early acting attempts of the real Stuart Erwin: the shy country boy who had worked double shifts one summer, crating cantaloupes in the hot California sun, so that he might have enough money to go to drama school.

At this point, the director of the fictional Erwin as Merton Gill finally gives up on him entirely and calls a lunch break. Then, after everyone leaves, Erwin stands on the set and recites the line perfectly. But he says it to an empty stage. It is one of the many scenes emphasizing a major motif of the film: the isolation and loneliness of Erwin's character.

The bitterness of his isolation is emphasized in the following scene as well. We see Erwin late at night on the darkened sound stage, carrying his pitiful stack of photos. Having been evicted, he has sneaked back onto the set in search of a place to sleep. He settles down on a bed, which is part of the set of a miner's cabin; the set itself resembles the one in Chaplin's *The Gold Rush* (1925). The allusion might be deliberate, as Chaplin's gold prospector was also starving and lonely. Unlike Chaplin in that film, however, Erwin is not yet so hungry that he has to eat his shoelaces. Instead, he finds a pot of beans that have been congealing all night; he proceeds to scrape these into a dirty plate. We are spared the sight of his eating this stomach-turning goop by the arrival of the movie's cast and crew to begin another day's shooting. Not wanting to be seen, Erwin hastily leaves his makeshift dwelling.

Nor does he want to be seen at the casting office anymore. Both Donnelly and Blondell note that Erwin has disappeared from his usual spot on the bench outside the casting office inner door. Blondell hints to Donnelly that Erwin had really blown it as the extra on the Benson movie when he had been unable to get his lines out. Retorts Donnelly, "It must have been funny."

"Maybe," ruminates Blondell, "to anyone who can laugh at an explosion in a coal mine."[22]

From this point on, Erwin will so touch Blondell's heart that their scenes together become truly, unbearably sad. The next time Blondell sees him, he is sitting in profile, but with his back turned slightly, so that neither the audience nor Blondell can see his face. In addition, we watch him in a medium shot from Blondell's point of view, enabling us to see his surroundings as well. He is sitting next to a garbage can, poking through a stack of nearly empty boxes. He is hunched over—defeated, used up. The silence of his body language is eloquent and pathetic. As Blondell approaches him from the back, we see that he has been digging into discarded box lunches, one of the few perks given to extra players. He is trying to salvage something to eat from the leavings of these extras. Blondell tries to assume a cheerful air. "Hello, trooper," she greets him.

Although weak from hunger, he stands and tips his hat to her. "I was lookin' for somethin'. I mean, I lost somethin'. I can't find it anywhere. Aw, it's all right. It wasn't anything much." Blondell's expression says much; it reflects doubt, disbelief, and grief. She looks like a mother who is listening to her son give flimsy alibis for bad behavior. Erwin, however, continues with his transparent bluff. He says that he looks this way because "I'm playing a character part—sort of an outcast." When he realizes that she knows he is lying, he politely changes the subject: "You look awfully nice today." But Blondell won't be put off. "Now wait a minute," she interrupts, "how long since you've eaten anything?"

"I don't remember," Erwin admits. At this, he sways backward, almost collapsing, but still clutching his package of photos, as though it were a fragile infant in need of nurturing. Knowing the pride that he has always taken in his appearance, and understanding the extent to which this pride is being trampled, she puts her arm around his shoulders, assuring him that no one will ever know and inviting him to get something to eat.

"I'm all right," he protests. Here Blondell rejoins with an ironic, "All *right*. Hmmm. You're darn near perfect, you are."[23] As the crumpled Erwin wobbles off, supported by Blondell, he draws his elbows and arms inward, like a prizefighter protecting himself from repeated punches to the stomach.

Erwin seems even more vulnerable in the restaurant, as he opens himself up to Blondell, telling her his troubles of recent days. But he is no less determined to keep plugging away. His confession here is remarkable. It is the sort of speech which could have very easily descended into parody, but Erwin is too honest and forthright an actor to satirize his characters, to make them appear outrageously artificial. Therefore, when he speaks to her in perfect seriousness, we feel as helpless as Blondell, who is beginning to fear that he is beyond saving.

He begins by confessing that he should never have left the lot because he had a pretty good place to sleep, "not the miner's cabin—they took the blankets away from there—the same day they took away the beans. I never did find that table again. But they probably got moldy right away. And you shouldn't eat moldy beans—that's bad, isn't it?"[24] At this moment, the waitress brings his coffee. He tries to drink it, but his hand shakes so badly that he finds the cup impossible to hold, so he steadies it with both hands, lifting it to his mouth and looking so grateful that Blondell appears about to cry. Instead, she tries to knock some sense into him by arguing that he does not have a chance in the movie business, that what he is doing is all wrong.

But Erwin's rebuttal is an attempt to try to explain the creative impulse; it is an explanation that probably came close to the heart of Stuart Erwin himself. "It isn't the money," he avows, "it's kinda hard to explain. It's something inside like—like—like wanting to write a book or paint pictures. I mean, well, a fella wants to do something except sweep out a store. You can't spend your whole life arguing about eggs and turnips, can you?" He adamantly refuses her offer to buy him a ticket back to Simsbury. By this time, Blondell is really confused and exasperated, her nerves so frayed and exposed by Erwin's artlessness that she cannot stay at their table much longer. But she does ask him why he still won't go home. There is no question in his mind why: "I *couldn't*. Not the way I feel about pictures. I mean—just think—making millions of people happy every day, the way Buck Benson does, even trying to do it. That's worth sacrificing and suffering for it, isn't it?"[25]

About to give up, Blondell sighs, "I don't know whether it's sublime courage or supreme dumbness." Already she has decided that the answer lies on the side of *courage*; as a result, she gives him money as she leaves, enough for the meal and for cleaning himself up. "And when you're all through," she concludes, finding it more and more difficult to maintain her customary flippant air, "come on over and I'll have St. Peter pass you in at the gate." Erwin further softens her hard-boiled center as he gently responds, "Aw gee. That's the nicest thing you could do."[26]

But Blondell is not content to stop there. Her last meeting with Erwin has given her an idea. She goes to her friend Jeff Baird (Sam Hardy), the producer/director of Lodestone Comedies, those low class films that are Erwin's bête noire. She persuades Baird to make a burlesque of a western, with Erwin in the starring role. Playing Baird is Sam Hardy, who specialized in treacherous manipulators, all bombast but no moral compunction. In *Make Me a Star* he plays the type quite well, although he is not as absolutely evil in this film as he had been the year before when he played Barbara Stanwyck's lecherous manager in Frank Capra's *The Miracle Woman*. In this latter film, Hardy had even been responsible for a murder, for which he had gone unpunished. However, in *Make Me a Star*, he is a churlish egotist, a typical representative of the Hollywood establishment, but not a killer. Blondell knows that Hardy wants only to make money from his movies, so she tells him that Erwin will produce a hit, that he will be humorous in a western satire because he is so serious that he will not realize he is burlesquing the genre.

Hardy asks her, "Doesn't he know he's funny?"[27] Blondell's response is the result of her recent close contact with the unfortunate Erwin: "He don't think anything in the world is funny." What the jaded Blondell does not realize is that Erwin's Merton Gill, the alienated, lonely small-town orphan, has blocked from his consciousness the world's hardness, its cruelty. The world is too real, so he has retreated into his sadly deluded fantasies. Nor does she realize that only when we can face the world's brutality, only when we can get past the ugly truths of human indifference and avarice and savagery—only then can we cultivate the absurd, ironic perspective that we must have before we can find things to be funny. She does not yet know the extent of this solitary young man's idealistic yearning, nor is she able to foresee the horrible fate that awaits him when he is no longer able to hide from the truth. The narrow circumstances of his cheerless life have given him no chance to find that protective shield of humor and cynicism, so that he is finally crushed by his own trusting goodness.

As a result of her lack of understanding, Blondell makes a decision that will torment her forever; she takes advantage of Erwin's seriousness by pretending that the Hollywood establishment is on the level about making a thoughtful western with Erwin as the star. She also persuades him that Sam Hardy's Jeff Baird has quit making "those awful cross-eyed comedies"; that he is now ready to make a noble, uplifting western with Erwin.

Erwin's horrible tryout for Hardy is painful to watch. Erwin makes Merton Gill try so hard to be a regular cowboy that we wish he had been alone in the room, practicing before a mirror, instead of making a fool of himself in front of these hardened movie veterans. After Erwin effusively thanks Hardy for being so kind as to let him audition and then leaves Hardy and Blondell alone, Hardy enjoys a good laugh. "*Sold!*" he bellows at Blondell. Which is just what they are about to do to Erwin. One recalls here an interview given by Arthur Miller in connection with his Pulitzer Prize-winning *Death of a Salesman*. Miller was asked by the interviewer just what it was that his protagonist Willy Loman sold, since we are never provided this information in the course of the play. To this question, Miller replied, "He sold himself." Miller's deliberately equivocal answer deserves some comment at this point. Both Willy Loman and Erwin's Merton Gill must sell themselves through their personal appeal if they are to succeed—one as a salesman and the other as an actor—but both ultimately sell themselves out to the system.

The destruction of Merton Gill begins in the next scene, as Erwin is about to make his starring debut, just like his western hero, Buck Benson. He is somewhat taken aback when he sees that Ben Turpin (playing Ben Turpin) is going to be in the picture. Apparently, Turpin's well-known (and real-life) disability has provided the label for those "cross-eyed westerns" which Erwin so loathes. Thinking fast, not wanting to mess up anything so early, Hardy assures Erwin that Turpin is making the picture only so that he might earn enough money to have his eyes straightened. This explanation satisfies the sensitive Erwin; moreover, at this point, we are reminded that one of the prime reasons Erwin has always believed comedy to be debasing is that he has often heard people laugh at things which he feels are too disquieting to be laughed at.

And indeed, unknown to Erwin, all the members of the cast and crew of this picture are now laughing at *him*. In fact, Hardy warns his employees that Gill believes he is making a serious picture and that the first one who laughs will be fired. Thus, the selling of Merton Gill continues. For instance, the technicians utilize a mechanism that will distort his voice, rendering it high-pitched. They also persuade him to sit down and powder his nose—an action that will make him look even more inane and effeminate in the final print. All the while, cast and crew continue to mock him.

One who no longer wants to make fun of him, however, is Joan Blondell. She watches as he does a scene in which he bids farewell to his horse, and she sees his genuine tears after the scene is over. He is embarrassed but admits that he has trouble turning off emotion, perhaps because the forsaken character of Merton Gill has never been given a chance to feel emotion for anyone or anything. After he stumbles off the set, still wiping his eyes, Hardy observes enthusiastically, "Oh boy, will that scene kill 'em. It'll lay 'em right in the aisles."[28] Blondell now realizes that they are indeed killing someone, but it is not the audience.

The movie finally completed, Erwin approaches Blondell to ask her for a date. He, uncomfortably shy and stuttering, stands next to her, turning his oversized cowboy hat in his hands, trying to tell her how much she has meant to him; she, hurting as though her skin has just been cut away, accepts. But Erwin is not through delivering his grateful and graceful gestures. He turns to Hardy, saying, "You couldn't 'a been nicer to me if you'd been my own father."[29] Once more, we are reminded of just how alone Erwin's Merton Gill truly is, of how he has known neither parent. Even the crude Hardy is touched.

The day of the movie's first screening arrives, and Blondell has made herself physically ill as she thinks of the revelation awaiting Erwin that evening. Nor does he make her predicament any easier when he visits her apartment earlier in the day, disclosing his excitement about the upcoming preview. His only qualm, he admits, involves the cross-eyed actor; Erwin doesn't want anyone to laugh at the man's deformity. When she tells him that she is too sick to go with him that evening, he offers her something he had been planning to surprise her with later; he ever-so-gently gives her a box containing a watch with a small, delicate face—the perfect present for a perfect lady, or so he thinks. As she gazes on it, growing ever more helpless to contain her pain, he unknowingly twists the stiletto further into her heart when he says, "It isn't much, after all you've done for me. Like the time you found me on the lot and introduced me to Mr. Baird. It's only a little token of my esteem and . . ." Here he breaks off, stumbling over his feelings, trying to regain his emotional balance, and deliberately ending on a prosaic note, "it's guaranteed."[30]

Blondell's response appears anticlimactic, but it is all she can manage, paralyzed as she is by love, grief, pity, and fear: "You're a sweet kid. Awfully sweet." Encouraged, Erwin uses less formal language than he had in his previous speech, "I guess you kinda know now how I feel about you, too."[31] This is all she can bear, so she pushes the watch back at him, telling him that if he still wants to give it to her *after* the preview, she would love to keep it.

The preview, which Erwin attends all alone, is a horror. At first he is excited, thrilled with seeing all the famous stars come out to participate in his big night. But his exhilaration swiftly metamorphoses into sorrow and heartache—emotions all the more distressing because they are juxtaposed against the hysterical laughter of the audience members, all of whom are thoroughly relishing this burlesque of the western, especially the performance of Whoop Ryder (a.k.a. Merton Gill). We share in Erwin's heartache because he has worked so hard, has believed in his goals so thoroughly, and has never played false to anyone. And because he has been deliberately, mercilessly betrayed by those whom he trusted and believed in the most, we are forced to agree with the medieval Italian poet Dante, who placed the betrayers in one of the deepest pits of his Inferno.

At last, Erwin has had enough: when he sees himself on screen reciting in an awful falsetto voice his tearful farewell to his horse, to the accompaniment of the tears of bystander Ben Turpin, whose crossed eyes have been made through special effects to look like two faucets from which water is pouring forth, he rises, trying to make himself as inconspicuous as possible. In a gesture which parallels his earlier movements when he had cradled his photos under his arm, he places his large hat under his jacket, folds his arms inward toward his chest, and hastens in humiliation out of the theater.

When he arrives at his boardinghouse, he is met by the other residents, all of whom are still laughing over his great performance in such a hilarious movie and who are full of congratulations for their new star. One even tells him that he is "funnier than the cross-eyed man."[32] He rebuffs their praises and hurries to his room. Once again, he is alone in a stark, shabby environment. He looks at his reflection in the bureau mirror, as if trying to recognize someone familiar, looking for something that he had lost. Then he looks at the pictures he has lined up in front of the mirror, publicity photos from the movie, and in a fit of desperation he angrily sweeps them off, also knocking down the box containing Blondell's gift. He picks it up, along with one of Blondell's photos, and sits on the bed, staring in shock from the watch to the picture. Rarely has a movie shown a man so totally bewildered and defeated.

In the next scene, he is seated at a restaurant, going over the train timetables, planning his return to Simsbury. Then he overhears two men seated nearby; they are discussing his wonderful performance of the previous evening; in addition, they argue over the nature of comedy. Referring to the newspaper review which touts Whoop Ryder as a new comedy sensation, one of them sneers that Erwin *has* to get laughs "with that low comedy face of his." While this dialogue is taking place, the camera focuses almost exclusively on Erwin's reactions. When he hears the reference to his "low comedy face" he winces. But the other man's reply also catches his attention. In fact, the screenwriters George S. Kaufman and Marc Connelly give the second man more of a speech than a response. And what he says bears repeating, for it is a perceptive analysis of the nature of comedy itself. It is also a discerning analysis of Stuart Erwin, the shrewd comedian, if not of Merton Gill, the dejected, deluded failure.

So the second man observes that, "low comedy face" or not, Whoop Ryder has comic talent: "In the first place, real comedy demands tremendous sincerity on the part of an actor—the same sincerity he needs to play Hamlet. And do audiences love a sincere artist. They always have. Where can you get a clown that can turn on the pathos with the wave of the hand? When you can turn on pathos, especially in farce, and make it stick—that takes genius, my boy. There isn't one person in a hundred who really knows himself. It's a relief to find somebody that's perfectly satisfied to be exactly what heaven meant him to be. That's being smart—smart as the devil. He'll probably make a million dollars at it. Clown or no clown."[33]

Throughout this scene, we see Erwin's dismayed expression. He has succeeded in becoming an overnight star, but at the price of his dignity. When we next see him, he has just gotten out of a taxi in front of Blondell's building. Having decided to go "home" to Simsbury, he is on his way to the train station, but he tells the taxi to wait. He has gathered his courage to face her one more time. When she answers the door, he is standing with a shy, cheery, but forced smile on his face. The scene that follows is the most heartrending in the film, if not one of the most heartbreaking in film history. Erwin holds out the watch he has bought for her. He can't let go—not yet, so he smiles gallantly, "Here's your watch. I almost forgot it. I was just . . . just passing by. Well—so long."[34] He tries to keep the watch at arm's length as he hands it to her, afraid to get any closer. Blondell is puzzled, so she asks if he really wants her to keep it.

Still determined to seem light-hearted, he replies, "Sure—why not? It may not keep very good time. I—I dropped it on the floor. But you can have it fixed. Well—so long." He starts to leave, but Blondell refuses to give him up. She says that she can't let him go like that, that she has to talk to him. So she grabs his lapels and pulls him through the door. Once inside, he is at first afraid to face her, but she insists, "Merton, look at me."[35] He turns toward her, fearful of what is coming next. What is coming next is her challenge. She wants him to talk to her, to shoot at her whatever it is that she knows she has coming to her. And so he talks, and what he says reflects the pain of years of rejection, of self-doubt, of utter abandonment. It is a remarkable performance on Erwin's part, the more so because he refuses to allow it to become sticky or cloying.

He responds to Blondell's request with an attempt to save what little is left of his feeling of self-worth, but his words tumble out, incoherent, as he tries to remember the praise he had heard in the restaurant, as he tries to recall what the man had said about the genius required to be a comic actor. All of his defensive words remain jumbled, perhaps because he is trying so hard to justify himself to Blondell, yet not appear weak and helpless. He still loves her so much that he cannot work through his feelings; but she has hurt him so badly that he wants to strike back by showing her she can no longer hurt him. Therefore, everything which comes out is all terribly, terribly wrong: "Oh, you mean about the *comedy* last night. There's nothing to say about it, except I—I hope you didn't think I was surprised." Here he forces a laugh. "Not me. You and Mr. Baird must've thought I was awful dumb to think that . . . I mean . . . about being serious. Especially the cross-eyed man— I was funnier than *he* was."[36] Through all of this, Blondell stares at him, uncomprehending.

Now that he has started, he is so afraid to stop talking that his words become even more and more tangled, his sentences mixed, illogical, strange. And the more mixed up he becomes, the faster he talks. Erwin's graceful hands also contribute to our feelings about his mood, as he rubs them together in anguish, thrusts them in back of him as though to hide his growing self-consciousness, or simply throws them into the air, his extended fingers punctuation marks emphasizing the ache he cannot assuage.

He continues his gallant effort to seem cavalier about his accomplishment on screen as he tries gamely to recall the overheard restaurant conversation: "Yea, and *pathos*. Like when I said goodbye to the horse. I've got *pathos*. And *farce*. Especially *farce*. Just by waving my hand"—here he gestures feebly, his hand flailing in the air—"I'm a clown. But when you turn it on and—I made it stick too and when you make it stick that's—that's *genius*, my girl."[37] On this line, he raises his voice, shakes his hand at Blondell as though he were lecturing her, and walks away from her. He has never shown such aggression before, but his anger comes from his fear of her rejection, not from his desire to harm her in turn.

Now he turns back, vaguely recalling another important point he is driven to make: "And—and Hamlet. For instance, Hamlet. Audiences *love* me." His voice is beginning to break. He has gone on too long, but he knows that it's too late to stop. "And you know why—I'll tell you why audiences love me—I'm . . . I'm . . . I'm *sincere*. I'm sincere as the devil, I am." With the tears beginning to come, he hesitates. As he does so, Blondell gently touches his shoulder, "Merton, please." He pulls away, cringing, unaware that pity is often an important part of every woman's love. "Leave me alone," he pleads. But he can't stop. His voice breaks as he becomes more desperate; his spoken words clutching to what little remains of his pride, his unspoken words beseeching her to help him—he wants her to make him stop hurting: "I'm *smart*. I'm gonna make a million dollars. Smart enough to be exactly what heaven—what heaven—" Here he can no longer maintain any emotional control whatsoever, for now he remembers the most savage comment of all of those he had overheard, "what else *could* I be with this low comedy face of mine? I . . ."[38] He turns away from her, sobbing.

"Merton," she comforts him, putting her arms around his shoulders. And he finally lets her into his suffering. Still sobbing, he sits down, saying, "I knew I shouldn't have come here." But he embraces her, his head buried in her chest.

"Easy, trooper," continues Blondell, as she cradles him against her breast, "you sure had mother guessing for a minute."

Then, in a reprise of their conversation after she had found him going through the garbage, Erwin reassures her, "I'm all right." And this time, her answer is no longer tinged with verbal irony. She means it when she answers, "All *right*? You're damn near perfect, you are." Suddenly, Erwin looks up, as though he has just remembered something. "What's the matter, dear?" questions Blondell. To which Erwin replies, "Nothing. Only—do taxicabs charge for just standing still?" Blondell affirms that they do indeed. "Why?" she wants to know. Clutching her more tightly, still sobbing on her breast, Erwin concludes, "Well, it's worth it."[39]

Here the movie ends on an uncertain note. We don't know if Erwin will soon leave Blondell, pick up his waiting taxi, and go back to Simsbury. Or perhaps he will stay, marry her, and make that million dollars. What is clear from the screenplay is that Erwin has been relentlessly battered and wounded, a wound from which he will probably never truly recover. And we are left with a feeling of emptiness and deep sorrow for his loss.

Not only is the movie one which leaves us feeling incredibly sad, but it is also one which bears analysis on a more cerebral, symbolic level as well. To begin, Erwin's inconceivable isolation and loneliness is emphasized throughout the film by effective use of *setting*. For instance, we usually see Erwin existing in small, cramped quarters where he spends much of his time protecting himself from the outside world. These quarters are both his escape and his prison, his fantasy and his reality. They reinforce the feeling of claustrophobia and impotence that permeate this fine movie. We see him in Simsbury in his tiny room, the only space allotted to him by his guardian, Gashwiler. It is in this room that he practices posing as a western star, playing those wretched recordings. Yet it is also in this room that he discovers the way in which Gashwiler has invaded his private world: by going through his belongings, desecrating everything that he holds valuable.

Later, when he arrives in Hollywood, we see him in another small room, cutting out paper to place in the bottoms of his shoes. Then, after he loses that living space, he moves into an even smaller spot on the movie lot, his world dwindling by the minute, his life becoming more and more circumscribed, even as he is trying to escape from his environment by breaking into the movies.

The last two enclosures that constrict him make their appearance after he has witnessed his preview. The first is his room in the boardinghouse, where he shoves from off his bureau all reminders of his relationship to the Hollywood establishment. The second enclosure is a cage into which he does not want to go—Blondell's apartment. It is in this final place of confinement that he finds himself both physically and emotionally trapped. But it is the only time in the movie in which he shares his imprisonment with someone else. And the closeness to another is important at this point, for Blondell is as trapped by her feelings and by her past actions as Erwin is.

So too, Erwin's body language throughout is remarkably subtle, even as it contributes to the melancholy tone of the film. In the scenes in which he is optimistic about his chances for success, his gestures are open and expansive, his shoulders held high. In the scenes in which he is beaten down by the harsh realities of the Hollywood system, he folds his arms inward, drawing together his shoulders, as though he had just received a hard blow to the stomach.

Two other prominent symbols occur throughout the film. Both are representative of Erwin's illusory hopes. The first is his portfolio of pictures, those photos that he takes so much pride in, the ones taken before he left Simsbury. He carries them carefully, as one would a newborn, fearful that harm will come to his child. He is still holding these cherished items as he accompanies Blondell out of the garbage dump. The other is his white, ten-gallon cowboy hat: the symbol, first, of his yearning to be a western star like his hero Buck Benson. Then it becomes the symbol of his successful completion of the movie. Finally, it represents his mortification as he furtively places it under his jacket and leaves the preview, all the while the audience is laughing at his onscreen antics. Significantly, he carries the hat with him when he goes to Blondell's apartment to tell her goodbye; of further interest is the fact that she takes the hat from his hand when she forces him into her home to talk to her. In essence, she removes his shell, his protection, when she appropriates the hat.

Another thought-provoking aspect of *Make Me a Star* is the film's attempt to probe the nature of comedy, to define what it is that we find funny and what it takes to be funny. Erwin's portrayal of Merton Gill suggests that Merton is always so serious, so earnest, because he has never allowed himself to look at the world squarely enough to develop the objectivity needed to see humor in people and in their circumstances. Moreover, Erwin shows us that we need to be selective in those things we laugh at; we should not laugh, for instance, at people who have the misfortune to be cross-eyed. It is also significant that Erwin as Merton finally weeps at the point where he confesses to Blondell one of his deepest insecurities: his feelings about what he sees as his own physical misfortune, his "low comedy face." Furthermore, we are also reminded in this film that, in order to play comedy well, one must be "sincere." Although Erwin demonstrates that Merton is so anguished he cannot make sense of the overheard allusion to *sincerity*, we know that both Stuart Erwin and Merton Gill are indeed "sincere as the devil." In point of fact, Merton's sincerity is his weakness; Erwin's sincerity as an actor is his great strength.

Make Me a Star is a many-layered movie, one of the best of the decade. It has a splendid cast, many of them veterans of silent films; in addition, it contains excellent cinematography, judicious editing, and a literate screenplay. It is also leads one to wonder just how close the film comes to probing Erwin's own psychological makeup, just how close it cuts to the bone. The answer to such a question is naturally impossible to determine, but one thing is clear: *Make Me a Star* demonstrates Erwin's versatility. To truly appreciate his range, we have only to compare his performance as Bing Crosby's goofy pal in another 1932 film—the silly, farcical, "low comedy" but very popular movie *The Big Broadcast*—with his crafting of the character of the kind-hearted Merton Gill.

Finally, the film also contains an excellent performance by Joan Blondell, a gifted actress who specialized in playing tough dames, women who did not suffer fools easily. In every scene that they share, she and Erwin establish a unique, unforgettable rapport, demonstrating considerable sensitivity toward one another. In sum, the total emotional impact of *Make Me a Star* is ultimately quite hard to shake.

NOTES

1. *Palooka*. Dir. Benjamin Stoloff. United Artists, 1934.

2. *Palooka*, 1934.

3. *Palooka*, 1934.

4. *Palooka*, 1934.

5. *Palooka*, 1934.

6. Roger Dooley, *From Scarface to Scarlett: American Films in the 1930s* (New York: Harcourt, 1981), 407.

7. *Palooka*, 1934.

8. *Palooka*, 1934.

9. *Pigskin Parade*. Dir. David Butler. 20th Century Fox, 1936.

10. *Pigskin Parade*, 1936.

11. Ethan Mordden, *The Hollywood Musical* (New York: St. Martin's Press, 1981), 94.

12. "Stuart Erwin, the Lovable Yokel of 115 Films and TV, Dies at 64," *New York Times*, 22 December 1967, p. 31.

13. *Make Me a Star*. Dir. William Beaudine. Paramount, 1932.

14. *Make Me a Star*, 1932.

15. *Make Me a Star*, 1932.

16. *Make Me a Star*, 1932.

17. *Make Me a Star*, 1932.

18. *Make Me a Star*, 1932.

19. *Make Me a Star*, 1932.

20. *Make Me a Star*, 1932.

21. *Make Me a Star*, 1932.

22. *Make Me a Star*, 1932.

23. *Make Me a Star*, 1932.

24. *Make Me a Star*, 1932.

25. *Make Me a Star*, 1932.

26. *Make Me a Star*, 1932.

27. *Make Me a Star*, 1932.

28. *Make Me a Star*, 1932.

29. *Make Me a Star*, 1932.

30. *Make Me a Star*, 1932.

31. *Make Me a Star*, 1932.

32. *Make Me a Star*, 1932.

33. *Make Me a Star*, 1932.
34. *Make Me a Star*, 1932.
35. *Make Me a Star*, 1932.
36. *Make Me a Star*, 1932.
37. *Make Me a Star*, 1932.
38. *Make Me a Star*, 1932.
39. *Make Me a Star*, 1932.

4

A GOOD PAL

We never know how high we are
Till we are asked to rise
And then if we are true to plan
Our statures touch the skies—

—Emily Dickinson, *The Complete Poems of Emily Dickinson*,
no. 1176 (c. 1870)

It is a tribute to Erwin's versatility that throughout his career he slipped easily from leading roles to supporting parts, and that he did so without a hint of jealousy, with no desire to steal scenes from the leading players. Among those for whom he proved a capable foil were Bing Crosby, Charles "Buddy" Rogers, and Ralph Bellamy. With each of these actors, he established a rapport that was both humorous and appealing in its earnestness, as well as generous in its urge to please.

WHERE THE BLUE OF THE NIGHT MEETS MR. FRISBEE

In *The Big Broadcast* (1932), Erwin appeared on film for the first time with Bing Crosby, a man with whom he would work the following year in *Going Hollywood* and then much later on television in the 1960s. In this movie, Bing Crosby plays—surprise!—Bing Crosby, a famous radio star, beloved of all his many female fans. And, oddly enough, Erwin receives billing over Crosby in this one. But as the plot of *The Big Broadcast* reveals, it is Crosby whose well-known face and voice make him much in demand and therefore the real star of the movie.

As a matter of fact, the character Crosby plays here (who bears a definite resemblance to the real Bing Crosby) has so many women chasing him through the streets that he is chronically late for his broadcasts. However, when we first meet him, he has eyes for only one woman, his fiancée Mona Low. The echo in her name to the famous jazz age blues song "Moanin' Low" is probably not accidental. It was a popular song of the day, with its story of the woman who sexually betrays her lover and is in turn strangled by him. The dark-haired, sensual, catlike child-woman Libby Holman, a gifted blues singer with a trembling, plaintive style, had introduced the song on Broadway in 1929 in *The Little Show*; it also became her theme song. Additionally, Holman was not the type of woman, either on stage or off, that a young man would have been glad to take home to meet his mother. So 1932 audiences were likely to make the connection between the melancholy two-timing woman of "Moanin' Low" and the dilemma that Crosby ultimately faces with his own Mona, who will soon marry another man. The song's refrain, which declares that the singer knows what kind of tempting woman her man really needs, neatly condenses the on-off-on-again relationship Crosby has with Miss Low in the course of the film. At the beginning of the movie, however, Bing is unaware of what lies ahead for him and Mona; indeed, he has been spending so much time with her that he gets fired by the radio station's sponsor, a man with the ungraceful and possibly symbolic name of Clapsaddle.

Yet Bing wastes little time in mourning his unemployed state, even here in one of the worst years of the depression. He celebrates his freedom by going alone to a speakeasy, where we first encounter Erwin in a close up, sitting at a table with a series of empty beer glasses lined up before him. He seems to be viewing these glasses as though they are prizes he has won at a fair as a result of his target shooting skill. As the waiter brings him a full glass of beer to add to his collection, we see that Erwin is pleasantly drunk and crying. We also learn that he is a rich Texas oilman named Leslie McWhinney, who is at present "moanin'" over a tragedy which has recently befallen him. As he later tells Crosby, he has just lost $100,000 to a woman in Dallas. He is also chagrined by the fact that the woman he had been engaged to no longer wants to have anything to do with him. He shows Crosby her picture; she just happens to be Anita Rogers (Leila Hyams) the secretary at the radio station where Crosby has only recently been employed. Anita, incidentally, has a crush on Crosby. Yet the terribly egocentric crooner has trouble placing her, although he concedes to Erwin that she does look vaguely familiar.

Erwin also punctures Crosby's ego when he admits that he does not recognize Crosby's name. In an effort to prod Erwin's recollection, Crosby even tries singing a few bars of his signature song, "Where The Blue Of The

Night Meets The Gold Of The Day," but Erwin remains blissfully unconscious of the song's significance to the man seated next to him. He even
flinches and moves back slightly when Crosby emphasizes his crooning skills
by thrusting his face in Erwin's. This movement might mean one of three
things: Crosby has halitosis, Crosby is singing too loudly for his tipsy hearer,
or Crosby has invaded Erwin's personal space. Or maybe all three. After
Crosby finishes singing his brief solo, Erwin gives him a quizzical look, pats
his arm, and gently comforts him by saying, "It'll be all right. My voice slips
like that too, sometimes. Are you a singer by profession, Mr. Frisbee?" Flab-
bergasted at Erwin's peculiar misunderstanding of his name, Crosby rests his
chin on his hand and muses, "You called me *Frisbee*." Once again missing the
significance of the misnomer he has just planted on Crosby, Erwin replies
drunkenly but ever so reassuringly, "Let me call you *pal*."[1]

Indeed, Crosby is about to discover he truly needs a pal, for when he
goes to the bar to get some more drinks, he sees a newspaper headline proclaiming his fiancée's marriage to another man. As he returns to the table to
join Erwin in bemoaning the duplicity of women, we hear the first strains of
the beautifully haunting song "Here Lies Love." It is sung here in the
speakeasy by accordion-playing Arthur Tracy, the famous Street Singer, and
will be reprised twice: once by Crosby, and once by a ghostly apparition appearing to Erwin and Crosby as the two neglected and rejected suitors attempt a joint suicide.

The idea for the suicide is Crosby's, but he doesn't have to do much convincing to persuade Erwin to go along with the plan. After leaving the
speakeasy, they go to another nightspot, and finally stagger back to Crosby's luxurious apartment, where Crosby gets the idea to die. The inspiration comes
gradually. First, he sings the melancholy song "Here Lies Love," all the while
stacking pictures of the traitorous Mona Low into a pyramid, a House of Cards
that we know is going to tumble momentarily. Meanwhile, Erwin is seated
nearby, energetically sobbing, venting his own overpowering sorrow, and, like a
good nineteenth-century Romantic poet, enjoying his pain. (In the movie
Crime of the Century, made the following year, Erwin seems to be enjoying a private joke as he hums to himself "Here Lies Love" while wandering around a
darkened house, carrying a lighted candelabrum and looking for clues to a murder.) When Crosby ignites the cards, making a strangely small flame burst forth,
the pile crashes, causing a lamp to fall, a fuse to blow, and the lights to fail. At
this apocalyptic moment, the besotted Erwin figures that the loud noise has
been caused by a gunshot, so he jumps up, fearing that his "pal" has shot himself. Now Crosby does in fact get the idea to end it all, and he encourages Erwin
as his companion in self-destruction, an idea that Erwin at first rebels against.

"Oh, *pal*," Erwin weeps lugubriously, even as he considers Crosby's solution. Crosby, in turn, lights some candles, and they gaze at each other in hopeless despair through the darkness, their faces lit only by the eerie flames, Erwin still inappropriately wearing his hat. They look like two characters who have become lost after leaving the speakeasies, and who have then wandered out of a different movie—*Dracula* perhaps—and into this one. Peering over the flame at Erwin, Crosby asks ominously, "I can't face the future. Could you?" To this, Erwin replies quite seriously and thoughtfully, "Well, I did have a five-year plan, but it's not working out." Encouraged by this sign of agreement, Crosby prods, "Are you afraid?" When Erwin responds in the negative, Crosby says, "Then let's do it." Still not entirely conscious of his blurred and ever-darkening surroundings, Erwin agrees, "All right." Further evidence of his obliviousness comes when he ventures to guess about the lethal method. His verb choice in his response suggests that he is still thinking about his booze-filled evening, for he helpfully tells Crosby, "I'll split a gun with you."[2]

But no, Crosby has a better idea. They will turn on the gas in the kitchen and end their sorrows this way. However, they must first prepare. Crosby writes a note to his former sweetheart, places it in an envelope, addresses it, and pins it to his suit. Erwin, in turn, speaks tearful good-byes to his true love's photo. Then Crosby takes Erwin by the hand, an older brother guiding his sibling across a dangerous street, and leads him into the kitchen. He also thoughtfully remembers to bring pillows so that they may be comfortable. He carefully shuts the window and turns on the gas. Meanwhile Erwin, who is already sitting, inquires, as though they were discussing the health benefits of cigarettes, "Tell me, do you inhale?"[3] Finally, they nestle on their pillows, settling down in their evening clothes—preparing to enter the hereafter.

As they breathe deeply, contemplating their brief future on this earth, they look divinely silly: two five-year-olds in kindergarten lying down for their midday nap, one bearing a note pinned on him by his teacher so that he will remember to give it to his parents. Two five-year-olds all dressed up like adults, who just happen to be in the process of killing themselves. And at some unspecified point after he sits on the kitchen floor, Erwin has at least removed his hat. Then, thinking of something important that he has forgotten to mention, he raises up again and addresses Crosby, "Would you object if I open the window about that—about that much?" He gestures with thumb and forefinger. Crosby looks at him in disgust as he orders him to "lie down."[4]

As they lie awaiting the end, there appears to them a spooky spot of light, which materializes into a luminous skull moving toward them like an apparition out of a nightmarish German expressionist movie of the twenties. Then from a puff of smoke appears another vision—this time an undulating Arthur Tracy, the Street Singer from the speakeasy come back to lead them to their celestial reward, complete with accordion, still singing "Here Lies Love"—but at the wrong speed. Looking like Marley's ghost in Dickens's "A Christmas Carol," he thoroughly frightens the two pals, who now huddle together on the floor. The comically spooky mood is reinforced when the beautiful love lyrics now apply to the absurd situation of Crosby and Erwin. Tracy croons in distorted, stentorian tones of the approaching end, of the numbness of his heart, of his disbelief attendant upon the loss of his love, and of the ultimate reality that "Here Lies Love." Then Tracy vanishes in another puff of smoke, a genie returning to his lamp, along with the skull's head that has hung like a memento mori while Tracy and his accordion have been chilling Crosby and Erwin.

Writing about *The Big Broadcast*, film historian Ted Sennett has observed that "Here Lies Love" is "sung in an oddly morbid sequence."[5] Yet that is precisely the point: this ghostly scene is effective because the song's love lyrics fit so nicely the plight of the lovesick and forlorn. Out of the ironic incongruity between the song's haunting, melancholy tune with its pain-filled words and the two silly boys who want literally to die for love arises the mirthful peculiarity of the scene.

Moreover, it is obvious that no one is going to see this odd duo expire. What prevents these two from passing away in an untimely fashion is the curiosity of Leila Hyams as Anita. By a fortuitous coincidence, she knows both Crosby and Erwin: Crosby because she is the secretary at the radio station from which Crosby has just been fired, and Erwin because she is the girl whose picture he has just bid farewell to, the girl whom Crosby didn't quite recognize when Erwin showed him the photo while they were exchanging pleasantries in the speakeasy. We assume that Leila has come seeking Crosby, since it is, after all, his apartment, and since she fancies herself in love with him.

Their rescue almost goes awry, however, because Leila and the porter, who lets her in, light a match in the darkness. Following the explosion, we cut to the next morning, where we see Crosby and Erwin, now dressed in pajamas, sleeping in twin beds. How they were divested of their evening attire and placed in sleeping garb is never made clear. Perhaps Leila, who has also spent the night there, discreetly, in another room, is responsible. Moreover, how the apartment has survived the explosion and remains as neat and intact as it did the night before is not explained either. At any rate, the newly acquainted buddies are thoroughly confused when they awaken. Erwin wakes himself up, sneezing—doubtless from the open windows that have blown away the deadly fumes of the night before. He glances curiously at Crosby, "Mornin'." Crosby looks equally puzzled as he replies, "Mornin'."

Then, with the dawn comes the light, for Erwin suggests, "I've seen you somewhere before." At this, Crosby looks around the room, decides that he recognizes it, and offers helpfully, "This is my bedroom." Then, clearly recognizing the symbolic significance of a bedroom, Erwin asks, with a straight face and without a touch of sarcasm, "Are we married?" Looking disturbed at this thought, Crosby, sitting up in his bed, backs away slightly. Finally, Erwin recalls the climax of their evening, "Oh—I remember—sssssss—GAS!" Now Crosby has his own recollection as he chastises his friend, "But you broke your promise. You got up and turned it off. You see if I invite you next time. You see if I invite you." At this, Erwin protests, "But pal—I *didn't*."[6] Neither of them contemplates the mystery of how they wound up in bed in their pajamas.

While the self-pitying Crosby is thinking about how he will try suicide "next time," Hyams enters the bathroom to take a shower. Crosby, who is unaware that he has one other guest besides Erwin, follows her. Hearing the water running and naturally assuming that the shower is occupied by his pal, he slaps her on the butt through the shower curtain, saying, "Well, pal, I guess you're right. No woman is worth it. Now make it snappy." The camera cuts to Hyams in the process of lathering, her expression registering a good deal of apprehension. When Crosby turns away for a moment in order to wash his hands, Erwin enters, wearing only his pajama bottoms, ready for a good cleansing, as he enthusiastically announces, "Boy, a nice cold shower, and I'll feel fine."[7] Now it is his turn to reach into the shower, turning on the cold water. As he does so, he comes within an inch or so of touching Hyams' very bare shoulder, whereupon she tries to back into the wall and become invisible.

Meanwhile, Crosby has just turned back around, and seeing Erwin out of the shower, misunderstands, as he informs his pal, "Hey—what's wrong with you? You just had a shower." Crosby apparently has not noticed that Erwin is completely dry, a fact which also escapes Erwin as he replies, "I did?" But Crosby has the answer, "Boy, you're still groggy from the gas." To this, Erwin agrees, and for the second time he reaches into the shower, once again barely missing Hyams' shoulder, and turns off the water. He is still not totally convinced, however, as he asks Crosby, who is exiting the bathroom, "Are you *sure* I had a shower?" Here he grabs a garment hanging on the bathroom door and painstakingly pulls it over his head, smoothing it down over his completely dry body. It is not until he looks in the mirror that he realizes something looks awfully funny: he has just put on Hyams' nightgown, which fits snugly across his chest and stretches full length, covering his pajama bottoms, like a tight but flimsy straightjacket.

While he is contemplating his odd reflection in the mirror, Hyams pops her head from between the shower curtains, announcing her presence to the confounded Erwin. She tells him that she has been there all night. "In the shower?" he asks. "No," she replies patiently, "I slept on the divan. The doctor told me to." Still confused, Erwin observes, "What a funny prescription."[8] After she explains that she has been the one to find them in the process of asphyxiating themselves, Erwin mistakenly thinks that she had come there the night before to save *him*. Just like Crosby in the matter of the shower that Erwin never took, Erwin remains unconscious of the obvious; he is oblivious to the fact that he is in *Crosby's* apartment and that his former girlfriend has had no way of knowing that he would be accompanying Crosby there and occupying it for the night.

In addition, Erwin is also unaware that Hyams has a crush on Crosby. Their conversation takes on a surreal quality, as they calmly discuss their respective actions of the night before—Erwin still dressed in his pajama bottoms, which remain ungracefully covered by Hyams' nightgown; Hyams, naked, with her head poking through the opening in the shower curtain, as she scolds him, "You ought to be ashamed of yourself. Getting poor Mr. Crosby drunk. Persuading him to end his life. I'd like to give you a good shaking." Erwin follows this tirade with an inappropriate response, asking the ludicrous question, "Are you dressed?" "No," replies Hyams quite seriously. "Then you'd better not,"[9] concludes Erwin solemnly, deciding that it would be prudent to allow Hyams some privacy so that she might complete whatever it is that she is doing. He then struggles out of her nightgown and joins Crosby with the exciting news that there is a girl in the bathroom whom he wants Crosby to meet. This time it is Erwin who takes Crosby's hand and leads him to see Hyams.

Once they do meet, however, Erwin regrets his earlier enthusiasm, for soon it is Hyams and Crosby who are holding hands. She is more concerned with the good news that Crosby is safe than she is with the importunities of Erwin, who is still proposing to her. One minute after meeting Crosby, who finally remembers her from the radio station, she tells Erwin that she cannot marry him because she is in love with Crosby, who has just been rehired by the sponsor in a fit of pity over Crosby's jilting by Mona Low. But Erwin is still Crosby's pal, so he agrees to accompany Crosby and Hyams to the station, where Crosby, in a fit of generosity, has promised to find something that his buddy can do there.

What the three of them discover when they reach the financially troubled station is that there is no longer anything for *any* of them to do. All of the station fixtures are in the process of being dismantled and Erwin is at first mistaken for a furniture mover ("one dollar an hour" the foreman tells him, after scolding Erwin for being late). Thinking that this is the job Crosby has lined up for him, he obligingly carries a drawer outside, commenting that the pay is pretty good, considering that he has no previous experience. When he realizes why the furniture is being hauled away, Erwin does the logical thing: he buys both the station as well as a national network. Not that he especially wants to be a radio entrepreneur, but he wants to help his pal as well as Anita, his former girlfriend, who has fallen hard for his pal. He even tells Bing that he is going back to Texas, leaving the station management to Bing. He also offers Bing and Anita half interest in the station, "as a wedding present."

Erwin's generosity is matched only by Anita's happiness. When they find themselves alone in the station, she cries because, as she explains to a puzzled Erwin, she is so happy. She also tells him that she wants to kiss him because she loves Bing. Erwin really doesn't want to kiss her or even get close enough to touch her, for he still loves her but has resolved to willingly relinquish her to Crosby, since he wants her to be happy. However, he acquiesces, leans over across the desk and gives her a brotherly kiss. Anita contemplates something for a moment and then observes, "You know, it's funny. There's something about Bing that reminds me of you." To this, Erwin kids himself, "It couldn't be the profile?" "No," responds Anita, "it's that funny little catch in his voice when he sings." Thinking that anything he can do to imitate his rival will be an improvement, Erwin counters with, "I'll have to practice that." But Anita reassures him that practice won't be necessary, "You do it sometimes when you talk." Encouraged that she has at least noticed one of his personal characteristics, Erwin becomes more enthusiastic, "Do I, *really?*"[10]

But he will go only so far with her, for when she tells him how sweet and generous she thinks he is and then stands, as though she were going to kiss him again, he backs away, saying, "I'll see you tonight." He is determined to remain firm in his resolve not to allow her the chance to hurt him anymore.

The "tonight" to which Erwin refers is the "tonight" of The Big Broadcast, with Crosby as the climactic, featured performer on the show. But various plot complications develop to conspire against Erwin and his pal Bing. In the first place, Mona Low, who is in the process of divorcing her rich husband, resurfaces the same day at Bing's apartment, much to Erwin's consternation. Alone in Bing's apartment upon Mona's arrival, Erwin tries to get her out of there before Bing returns. His reasons for wanting to oust her are twofold: first, he doesn't want Bing reunited with his old flame, despite the fact that Bing had earlier displayed his grief by torching pictures of this flame while singing "Here Lies Love." Erwin continues to love Anita enough to let her go, and he doesn't want to see her lose out to the aggressive Miss Low. (Interestingly, Sharon Lynne, who plays Mona, is dark-haired and sultry, and somewhat resembles Libby Holman, the originator of the song "Moanin' Low.") Second, Erwin knows his pal well enough by this time to realize that, once Bing is back in Miss Mona's attractive clutches, his star radio performer will again be so distracted that he misses that evening's performance. This time around, however, Erwin owns the station and is therefore Bing's boss, making him loathe to lose his hefty investment to the dilatory Bing and his egocentric peccadilloes.

But Erwin is too late, for Bing and Mona have already settled themselves on the sofa in a very friendly embrace. Moreover, when Erwin leaves the happy couple to go to another room to answer the phone, Bing and Mona walk out. To further add to Erwin's woes, the person on the phone is Anita, who naturally wants to speak to her idol. Before Erwin has the chance to tell her the name of the woman Bing has just left with, she asks Erwin to relay to Bing the message that she will be listening to his broadcast that evening. Erwin, with a broad Texas accent, draws out his sarcasm exceptionally well when he comes back with, "Isn't that *nice!*" He continues in the same tone, which is lost on Anita, when she asks if he would mind if she listened to the broadcast from his office. To this request, he rebounds facetiously, "*Sure* not. Go right ahead. That's *fine*."[11]

But Erwin is not feeling especially fine at this point. Later that day, still frantic about putting his broadcast together, he breaks in on Mona and Bing; they are in the process of having a fruitful discussion concerning all of the loot Mona is going to scoop up from her ex. As Erwin intrudes, Bing feigns drunkenness, protesting that he is in no condition to perform that evening and that he does not want Anita to see him in such a state. Actually, Bing would like to see Erwin reunited with Anita; furthermore, he fully intends to make the broadcast. But Erwin does not suspect either one of these intentions, as he frantically dashes out, desperate to find a way to salvage Bing's contribution to the show.

The following scenes with Erwin, formally dressed in top hat and tuxedo, are interspersed with variety acts performed for the radio audience. These acts involve such well-known performers of the day as Kate Smith, the Mills brothers, the Boswell sisters, and Cab Calloway. In the meantime, what is fascinating about Erwin's search for a way out of the box into which he thinks Crosby has trapped him is that he plays these next few scenes entirely in pantomime. He had begun his movie career at the very end of the silent era, and he demonstrates here that he is skilled in the art of comedy without words. He strides down the city street, looking somewhat out of the place in his formal attire. Then, from out of a window he hears the song "Please," sung by none other than Crosby. The voice is coming from a phonograph; we follow Erwin's point of view as the camera tracks into the interior of the street-level apartment. Inside we see a middle-aged woman leaning against the phonograph; she is in an ecstatic pose, looking heavenward as though she expected Bing himself to descend and carry her off to great heights of bliss. But her husband does not share this bliss, for he stands, crosses the room, grabs the record, and tosses it out the window, where it lands at Erwin's feet, breaking into several pieces—a fate that frequently awaited 78 rpm records. In fact, the aggrieved husband's throw resembles the pitch that one would use to hurl a Frisbee—Erwin's earlier misnomer for Crosby.

The broken record of "Please" does give Erwin an idea, however. He proceeds on until he comes to a store that sells phonographs, records, and radios. (Who among the generation born after 1980 would even recognize the words *phonograph* and *record*?) Since the store is closed, and since Erwin is frantic to obtain an intact copy of the disk that has just been so unceremoniously unloaded onto the pavement, he rouses through silent gestures the store owner, who is not too thrilled about coming down to street level in his nightshirt. But he soon emerges onto the street, still in his nightshirt, holding a little pajama-clad boy by the hand. While Erwin and the disgruntled owner are trying to unlock the door, the child simply opens it for them and walks in.

Once inside, they begin to look through shelves reaching almost to the ceiling; these are stacked with records, apparently unclassified, for Erwin and the store owner randomly search each shelf for Bing's "Please." Likewise, the shelves are apparently too flimsy to hold piles of these heavy records, as they tumble very nicely when they are ransacked by these night visitors. Soon, these three are buried under an avalanche of broken records. While Erwin is unsuccessfully hunting through these fragments of music, the toddler proudly hands him the prize—Crosby's recording of "Please" on the Famous Record Co. label. The little boy seems to be quite literate for a child of around two years. But Erwin acts not at all surprised at the boy's precocious behavior; he gives the child some money and leaves happily.

His happiness is not to last long, though, because as he is walking out with his treasure, his foot gets caught in the toddler's donkey-shaped pull toy, and he skates his way along the pavement, is airborne, and lands on his back, smashing the record—naturally. Never one to quit, he rises up, returns to the shop, which is once again closed, and is this time rebuffed by the old man and the little boy, who are tired of inflicting damage on merchandise in the middle of the night. Now he has to think of an alternative plan; this he does when he sees another copy of "Please" in the store window. But how to get to it? He plucks a pineapple from a nearby fruit stand and prepares to toss it, although he fails to consider that a piece of fruit is not exactly the most effective tool for breaking glass. Meanwhile, a cop comes into the picture, leading a suspect along. Unfortunately for both Erwin and the cop, Erwin throws the pineapple just as the officer walks by. Of course, he hits the cop in the face, displeasing the lawman, whose attention is now focused on Erwin's explanation. This temporary distraction allows the criminal to escape and dash around the corner. From this position, he is able to get a good aim at the window himself. But the lawbreaker has had more practice than Erwin, so he succeeds in helping Erwin by smashing the glass with a rock, whereupon the cop resumes his chase and Erwin resumes his efforts to obtain another copy of Crosby's voice.

At first, he thinks that all of his hard work has come to nothing. The first record he sees is Crosby's—another broken one. But then he sees one that is, surprisingly, not smashed, so, realizing that here is his last chance to retrieve Bing and get him to the broadcast on time, he carefully slips his hand in over the shattered glass and pulls out his precious find. Then, cradling it like a baby, he hastens down the street and stops at a public phone to call the station director to tell him that he, Leslie McWhinney, has Bing Crosby and to stall the show until he can arrive. As Erwin hastens into the lobby, he is threatened again with disaster, for he places the record on the floor as he bends to tie his shoe and has to push away a passerby who nearly steps on it.

Finally, in a fitting touch of cosmic irony, he puts the record on top of a humidor, where it rests against a cigar lighter. By the time he retrieves it a few seconds later from its position of safety, it is neatly warped. However, because Erwin is in such a hurry and is so distracted by the realization that the time for Bing's song is quickly approaching, he fails to notice that his cherished record has assumed a grotesque shape—that is, until he positions it on the turntable and hears the dreadfully distorted voice coming out for the radio listeners to puzzle over. Now truly desperate, he stops the record and tries singing the song himself. His uninspiring efforts reveal why Crosby was the singer and Erwin the comedian.

But his valiant attempts are not lost on Anita, who comes out of Erwin's office to find out what is happening. She has only to look at Erwin to figure out the situation—and to understand the sacrifice Erwin is making. It is at this point that we know she has fallen back in love with Erwin;

it is also at this point that Crosby enters to shore up the ruins by singing "Please" the way it was written, with the proper pitch and at the proper speed. As he looks at Erwin and Anita, he sings to them, watching with delight as they embrace and kiss. On this musical note, *The Big Broadcast* ends.

As with *International House* made the following year and also featuring Stuart Erwin, *The Big Broadcast* showcases many talented performers while it builds a sort of plot around the musical and the comedy routines. Likewise, both are cleverly scripted, with absurdly funny situations holding together these routines. So too, many of the performers in *The Big Broadcast* would return in *International House* to repeat their stuff: Burns and Allen, Cab Calloway, and Stuart Erwin himself. Moreover, in both movies, Erwin gets the girl whom he had wanted all along. In *The Big Broadcast* he wins back Anita. In the final scene of *International House* he flies off in W. C. Fields's airborne contraption, taking with him on their way to be married his long-suffering betrothed Carol Fortesque (Sari Maritza), who for two years has put up with Erwin postponing their wedding each time he catches a childhood disease. However, *The Big Broadcast* allows him a better part; his Leslie McWhinney is an ideal foil to Crosby. They worked well together, Erwin's edgy anxiety a neat counterpoint to Crosby's laid back attitude.

Moreover, Erwin and Crosby were as compatible in real life as they were onscreen. They met when they worked on *The Big Broadcast* and subsequently developed a close friendship. In fact, the Erwin and Crosby families would later spend some time together in Del Mar during the summers, along with the family of Pat O'Brien,[12] another good pal and Erwin's costar in *Ceiling Zero* (1935).

THE NEARSIGHTED AMBROSE

Erwin has another goofy "good pal" part in the early talkie *Along Came Youth* (1930). As he does in *The Big Broadcast*, he offers himself in contrast to a smooth, polished leading man: in this case the extremely handsome Charles "Buddy" Rogers as Larry Brooks. In truth, Erwin was himself nice looking, but he often subordinated his vulnerable boyish attractiveness in the service of comedy—much as Chaplin did. In this one, he plays the nearsighted Ambrose, wearing large glasses and a dumbfounded expression throughout much of the movie.

Along Came Youth puts Erwin and this pal together in London; Buddy Rogers is a formerly wealthy man-about-town who owns a racehorse with an aversion to water. Erwin is the horse trainer, but not a very successful one;

the horse and Erwin actively dislike each other. We are told that these two have been forced to remain in London since their equine's ignominious defeat at the Grand National race, when he sat down at the first water jump. Rogers feels that he needs to ride his own horse in order to have a chance at winning, so he observes to Erwin: "One race, and I'd be sitting pretty." Erwin's sharp retort reveals that his mind is much sharper than his silly expression suggests: "One race, and you'd never sit again."[13]

When we first see Erwin and Rogers, they are outside a swanky London café, and we quickly learn what they are now obligated to do in order to make up for the losses incurred by Rogers's horse. Both are dressed in evening clothes, but we cannot see Erwin's attire quite as well because he is sporting something over his formal evening dress: two large sandwich boards which completely cover him and which are tied at his neck in order to hold them in place, one on either side of him. He is pacing along the sidewalk, accompanied by friend Rogers, who is waving a cane and flourishing his outer cape with great, sweeping motions, pointing both the cane and cape in Erwin's direction. What passersby are supposed to notice is the message on Erwin's board: *I am wearing an evening outfit by Adkins the Tailor Beautiful.* Rogers looks more like Dracula about to crawl down the outside of the nearest building than an elegant man out for a formal evening; Erwin looks like an exhibit from a carnival sideshow. Throughout the movie, Erwin as the nearsighted Ambrose maintains the stupefied expression one often sees on people who refuse to wear needed glasses and so must constantly squint in order to put the world into focus. Erwin takes this characteristic of the nearsighted one step further and demonstrates how such people, even when they condescend to wear their glasses, often continue from habit to look at the world as though it were invisible.

A few moments after Erwin and his sandwich board appear, Adkins the Tailor Beautiful himself shows up (Arthur Hoyt) and berates Erwin for not being prompt in getting to his job. Poor spectacled Erwin explains that he was late because he lost his eyeglasses so, as a result, "I had to sit down and wait till somebody found them. I used to try to find them myself, and you've no idea what strange things I'd pick up."[14]

By this point in the narrative, ladies' man Rogers has already picked up something himself: an exquisite beauty named Elinor Farrington (Frances Dee), who is in London with her overbearing aunt, Lady Prunella (Evelyn Hall)—a pushy, nose-in-the-air lady trying to find a millionaire for her niece to marry. Up to the present, Elinor informs her elderly mentor, all the eligible men who have been shoved her way have had the looks and feel of "poached eggs." But Elinor is immediately attracted to Rogers, who she assumes is rich, because he looks nothing like the dilettantes her aunt has been so fond of pushing in her direction. As the young Frances Dee portrays her character, she demonstrates that she wisely knows she is considered nothing more than a commodity on the marriage market, as bait dangled in front of rich gentleman, one of whom will grab at it and carry off his prize.

Yet as the nearsighted Ambrose dutifully marches along with both his sandwich board and his pal Rogers, who is benignly smiling and waving at Ambrose's side, Erwin berates his handsome pal for pursuing another woman. According to the miffed Erwin, each time Rogers goes after a lady, they wind up losing their jobs. And this fate is what occurs to them on this occasion as well.

We first hear of it after Rogers returns to the apartment he shares with Erwin; he has just escorted Frances Dee home, and he opens the door to a disaster: friend Erwin has lost his glasses. He is on his hands and knees in the middle of what appears to be a burglary in which the whole place was ransacked. Or perhaps the bedroom of the average teenager. Drawers have been pulled out, clothes strewn everywhere, furniture moved and upended. Erwin has the puzzled look of a small boy who has lost his favorite stuffed bear. Hearing Rogers enter, he looks up, vaguely pointing his gaze in the direction of the noise, and accuses his roommate: "I should think you'd be ashamed to look at me. You lost our jobs again."

Rogers chooses to ignore Erwin's indictment; instead he asks, "What happened?" Erwin's reply is the obvious, "I lost my glasses."

"*Again?*" is the impatient response. Erwin continues his boyish reprimand: "Yes, and you were gone so long I had to try to find them myself. Had to move everything. But I'll put it all back." Throughout this scene, Erwin reminds us of that later cartoon character Mr. Magoo. And, like Magoo, he is funny because he is so serious in his efforts to muddle through a landscape which he cannot see; and, because he is so convinced he can cope, he remains happily unaware of the havoc he is causing with his blindness. When Rogers looks around at the disarray, he tries to be a pal by offering, "I'll help you, Ambrose." Still peeved at Rogers's desertion of him that evening, Erwin, now off the floor and on his feet, rebuffs the proposal: "Oh, no, you won't, either. I got along this far without you, and I can finish without you."[15] As he says this, he peers off into the distance, his back to Rogers.

Then, as if to show how well he can get along without help, he busies himself while Rogers is in another room. He begins by picking up from the floor a drawer filled with clothes, intending to put it back in its proper place in the correct piece of furniture. He very carefully lifts it, so as not to spill any clothes, carries it to a window that is open only a few inches, enough space to fit in the drawer, places it in this narrow opening—and tosses the clothes-filled drawer out the window. Hearing the crash, Erwin turns in Rogers's general direction in the next room, admonishing him: "Hey, you better be careful in there!" Rogers responds with a curious, "Did you drop something?" To this, an indignant Erwin replies, "Certainly not. I'm putting everything back in place."[16]

Erwin continues his methodical, studious endeavors to put "everything back in place" as he tries to return some fruit to a serving bowl. He does this by first putting the glass serving bowl over a lamp; then he takes the glass fixture which should cover the lamp and drops pieces of fruit into the fixture, whereby they immediately slide through the hole at the bottom and onto the floor. Through all of this, not once does it ever occur to him that he is being anything but extremely thorough, precise, and careful. Nor does his friend Rogers ever notice anything amiss. Finally, Rogers finds Erwin's glasses and consequently saves their apartment from further destruction. In answer to Erwin's question, "Where were they?" Rogers replies, "In the tub." Neither one thinks it odd that Erwin would leave his glasses in the tub. But Erwin is now grateful to his buddy; he offers his thanks: "Gee, it's a good thing I live with you. I wouldn't have found them till Saturday night."[17]

Since the immediate crisis has passed, Rogers delivers more good news: he has found them another job, this one involves cooking for a wealthy South American couple. When Erwin reminds Rogers that neither one of them can cook, Rogers replies that he has taken care of that by hiring Emil, the cook from the ritzy London café, to cook for them. The scheme works so well and the South American gentleman, Señor Cortés (Leo White), thinks they are such wonderful chefs, that he takes them with him to his country place, where Rogers has to find other people to do the cooking. But Rogers is delighted to go, especially when he discovers that Señor Cortéz's country place is near Farrington Hall, home of the beautiful Elinor. Naturally, Erwin tags along.

In point of fact, the character played by Erwin has more common sense than his buddy; his wit is quick, his perception of human nature is sharper; Rogers often plays straight man to Erwin's quips: *viz*, at one point Rogers refers to Elinor, asking rhetorically what he possibly has to offer her. Erwin replies sarcastically: "I think it's a leg of lamb tonight." Then Rogers looks dreamily into the distance and alludes to his visionary romanticism as he asks: "What do you call a fellow who can look at a cottage and make you think it's a castle?" Erwin hastily cracks: "A real estate agent."[18]

But for some unaccountable reason, Erwin is devoted to Rogers's Larry Brooks: model playboy and totally fanciful idealist. Perhaps he stays with Rogers because he needs someone to find his glasses for him; perhaps he admires Rogers's optimistic willingness to take risks. Or perhaps he is just lonely and in need of the companionship Rogers offers. In any event, as with the Erwin-Crosby pairing in *The Big Broadcast*, the twosome of Erwin-Rogers is fortuitous. Erwin's comic antics are a fitting chorus to leading man Rogers's romantic melodies.

Sometimes these antics result in humorous complications. Shortly after Erwin regains his sight, thanks to Rogers, he is sitting outside the gate to the Farrington home, eating an apple. He is waiting for Rogers, who has managed to gain entrance into the lavish gardens of the Farrington estate and who continues to hope that he might further his acquaintance with Elinor Farrington. When prissy Aunt Prunella has Rogers thrown out, Erwin delightedly trudges off with his dejected buddy, who fears that he has lost Elinor forever. As Erwin walks along next to his pal, he blithely tosses his apple core over the wall of the Farrington estate, where it lands unfortuitously in a delicate teacup on a formal dining table set up in the Farrington garden. Aunt Prunella, who has had the misfortune to be standing nearby, accuses the butler of such uncouth behavior. Vigorously denying her insult, the butler claims he saw it flying through midair, "where I took it for a swallow."

"Well, take it for me,"[19] retorts Prunella, handing it over with thumb and forefinger to the butler, who handles it equally cautiously, taking it away to dispose of it. Prunella never discovers who the culprit is, nor does she know the true state of Rogers's finances. At this time, she is under the erroneous impression that Rogers has money. Another Farrington, Eustace (William Austin, an actor specializing in mannered fussiness), has informed her that Rogers is living next door in a sumptuous dwelling. Neither Prunella nor Austin knows that Rogers is the "cook" of sorts at that address.

Were Prunella to see the Erwin/Rogers car, however, her impression about Rogers's wealth would have changed immediately. In the next scene, Erwin and Rogers are trying to make their ancient vehicle get up enough power to tow something attached to a rope in back. The car is of an indeterminate make and vintage, though it does resemble a racing car, circa 1912. Soon there appears in the film frame what it is that they are towing: Señora Cortéz, the wife of their current employer. The señora is a hefty dame, resembling a Kewpie Doll. She looks like a little girl, wearing a ruffled dress, a dainty cloche hat, very popular in the twenties but about three sizes too small; in addition, she is holding a parasol over her head, and she giggles a lot. She is about fifty. Stacked in back of her is a mound of luggage, balancing on the contraption on which the señora is also stacked. This apparatus, which is now attached by a rope to the Erwin/Rogers auto, looks like one of those horseless carriages advertised in Sears catalogs around 1900. Erwin observes to Rogers about this weighty freight they are hauling: "I hear when the señor married her, she was a mere slip of a girl. Now she's a landslide." When Rogers protests that the lady might know enough English to understand Erwin's insensitive, albeit clever, remark, Erwin replies by giving a new twist on a cliché: "She can't even hear. She's deaf as a haddock."[20]

And what a ride the two boys take her on. Erwin, the none-too-cautious chauffeur, wearing a silly-looking derby hat—also three sizes too small—begins their hair-upending journey by tailgating and subsequently rear-ending another car, to which they become coupled by way of the fenders. Through a tidy coincidence, the car now leading this odd procession is being driven by Elinor Farrington, who is accompanied by her airhead girlfriend Sue Long (Betty Boyd); stuffy Aunt Prunella; fastidious, whining Eustace Farrington; and five mischievous little boys: brothers with the very proper, very British, very foolish sounding name of Neetsfoot. With Erwin madly honking to get the girls' attention to the fact that they are now attached to the boys in back, with the girls thinking that they are being harassed by rude tailgaters, and with the terrified, lumpish señora bouncing along behind, trying to stay aboard her makeshift carriage, the scene takes on a marvelously farcical, slapstick quality. It looks much like one of those chase scenes that had been a staple of silent pictures.

And the humor increases as Elinor increases her speed, foot pushed all the way to the floorboard, trying to lose those bothersome tailgaters. The more frantically Erwin honks—the horn sounding like the noise made by a beginning student of the trumpet—the more Elinor is determined to try to lose her pursuers. These three vehicles, Elinor's car coupled to Erwin's car coupled to the wagon toting the señora, look like a miniature train seen at amusement parks; only this train is not on tracks and is completely out of control, a roller coaster gone berserk. Then one of these roller coaster cars breaks loose—of course it is the one carrying the señora—as the pathetically frayed rope, which has been keeping her tied to the auto just ahead, can no longer stand the strain and splits in two. While the oversized Kewpie Doll careens off alone, the two lead cars finally stop, where Elinor and Sue finally get a look at what has been fettered to them. In the meantime, the hysterical señora has long since lost her dopey expression of giggly complacency as she continues madly zooming down the road, nearly flattening two unfortunate bicyclists, who spring off their cycles, like trampoline artists jumping in air and doing somersaults, when the large runaway gadget veers neatly between them.

The cinematography in this chase scene is especially effective, with tracking shots giving us several perspectives on the wild ride. In particular, the luckless señora is photographed close up and with low angle photography, making her appear even larger than she is. So too, the camera fastens on her spread-eagled legs and looks up her bloomers as they billow in the air. The three frilly, laced tiers of her white dress make her look like a huge, three-layered wedding cake. Her appearance is thus both provocative and comical. Here she looks less like a Kewpie Doll and more like Dolly Dingle, the trademark name of a popular, round-cheeked, chubby little doll with corkscrew curls.

As the señora whips past the two stalled cars, traveling at about forty miles per hour, Aunt Prunella inquires loftily, "What was *that*?" Seemingly unconcerned and matter-of-fact, Rogers replies, "The señora." Then, in typically British, understated style, Prunella observes, "What an extraordinary way to travel."[21]

One significant note in this scene is sounded at the point where the señora first breezes by the two cars that have initiated all of this chaos. In order to keep Elinor's friend Sue from being struck by the señora's out of control wheels, Erwin picks her up and carries her to the side of the road, where for a few minutes he holds her up in his arms, as one might hold a child of two or three. The lonely, basically shy Ambrose has found a girl to love.

Meanwhile, here comes the señora rounding the corner, while all of the occupants of the other two cars race after her on foot: Elinor, Sue, Prunella, the Neetsfoot brothers, Eustace Farrington, Erwin, and Rogers. What they find is the splintered ruins of the wagon with its wheels in the air, spinning uselessly, and the lady's scattered luggage. There is no señora in sight. Then one of the Neetsfoot boys yells excitedly that he can hear something moving under the debris. It takes all of the company several minutes to dig through the remains until they find the señora, where she has made a large trench in the ground. She is dirty and disarranged, but not hurt; in fact, she happily waves her arms and legs at her rescuers, like an infant will do in its crib as it tries itself out on the new world.

While the señora is being excavated, Erwin and his newfound love are getting acquainted. Sue asks Erwin if he is all right. Then she adds gratefully, "Do you realize you saved my life a minute ago?" Erwin was always able to slip easily from a comic tone into a more pensive mood; he gracefully manages such a switch when he answers Sue, his voice shaking, "Yea, and I had such a good time doin' it, I'm almost ashamed." In awkward situations like this one, where he faces a girl on whom he has a crush, Erwin was never sure what to do with his hands; as he tries to talk to Sue, he wrings them together, puts them in back of him, and nervously rubs them on the seat of his trousers. Yet Sue does not seem at all fazed by his ineptitude, for she offers her hand, saying, "Well, I'd like to shake your hand." Erwin cringes at this; he doesn't want to be offensive, so he offers a counter suggestion: "Oh no. It's too dirty. I—I'm afraid you'll have to kiss me instead."[22] At this, he lowers his head sheepishly, afraid of looking directly at her.

To his great delight and consternation, Sue obliges by maneuvering her lips around his nose and glasses and kissing him several times directly on the mouth. Laughing, she declares, "You're *wonderful!*" Now truly embarrassed, bashful, and flustered, Erwin reconsiders, telling her, "Maybe you'd better shake hands."[23]

Soon Erwin has to pause in his nascent courtship in order to help the others push and pull the señora into the wagon, which has been miraculously restored in just a few minutes. With a good deal of grunting, they wedge her back in. Moreover, they have apparently appropriated a sign from somewhere along the road, which provides a fitting backdrop to the type of construction work they are engaged in; the sign, which sits in front of this hard-working crew, reads, DANGER: MEN AT WORK.

Once the señora is comfortably ensconced with her husband at her estate, Erwin and Rogers can again concentrate on their pursuit of Sue and Elinor, respectively. Part of Rogers's plan involves retrieving his racehorse, Gangster, and showing off to Elinor by riding him in a race. Erwin, Gangster's trainer, is the one to bring Gangster back. We know that he has retrieved the spooky horse because when he next appears, he is wearing two bandages: a large one covering his left thumb, and multiple, crisscrossed bandages on his right cheek. But Rogers is oblivious to Erwin's obvious injuries; his only concern is the condition of his horse. "How is he, Ambrose?" he asks, vigorously pumping Erwin's good right hand. Without alluding to his wounds, Erwin gives the following heartening assurance: "Oh, *he's* all right. You know, that horse recognized me. How an animal can remember . . ."[24] But at this instant, Erwin is more concerned with finding Sue so that he might propose to her; his interests do not lie with Gangster.

He sets off on his search for his beloved Sue, looking more like a recent accident victim than a dignified suitor. The absurdity of his appearance is heightened by incongruity. Whereas he is dressed well in a double-breasted suit, still wearing his derby, the bandages on his face call even more attention to his thick glasses and to the befuddled expression that is his most constant feature. Similarly, his heavily bandaged thumb inhibits mobility with his left hand, so that when he attempts a gesture, he looks something like a mummy just arisen from his tomb. On the other hand, Erwin's demeanor is sincere and dignified. He makes us want to cheer him on; we want him to win Sue's love.

But before he can do this, he has to get past Eustace, who feels that it is his "duty" to propose to Sue. Erwin finds Eustace, towel in hand, rubbing a prudently clothed statue in the Farrington garden. At first, Erwin does not see the statue, so he asks Eustace, "Uh—have you seen . . . " Then, noting that Eustace is massaging a female form and, mistaking the statue for the real thing, he apologetically removes his hat, holding it in front of him, and looking down discreetly as he expresses his regret: "Oh, pardon me—I guess I'm intruding." Apparently, Erwin's Ambrose does not see too well *with* glasses, either. The prim Eustace quickly corrects him: "Oh, tut, tut, and triple tut. I'm only swabbing a nymph." Erwin reaches out and gingerly feels the nymph, expressing relief when he discovers that it's just a statue. When Eustace tells Erwin that he is also looking for Sue in order to propose to her, Erwin asks, "Do you love her?" Eustace's answer is bluntly realistic: "Oh no. But then, I'm only proposing *marriage*."[25]

This reply seems not at all strange, but instead quite reasonable to the seriously smitten Erwin. In fact, the tone of the whole scene between William Austin as Eustace and Erwin as Ambrose is an odd one. Austin was a prolific actor who had appeared in silent films (notably in 1927 with Clara Bow in *It*) and his was a familiar face, especially to fans of Paramount pictures. He was an actor who played fastidious characters of indefinite sexual orientation, much like Erwin's old stage mentor, Edward Everett Horton. Yet in his exchange with Austin here, Erwin truly believes that this effeminate man is indeed a serious rival for Sue. Accordingly, when Eustace offers to be Erwin's surrogate and propose to Sue in his place, Erwin is boyishly excited about the prospect. He even acts like a child playing hide-and-seek as he cowers behind the now-buffed nymph statue and peers around it, watching Eustace and Sue as Eustace extols Erwin's desirability as a mate. Unimpressed with Eustace's oration, Sue walks away, prompting Erwin to come out of hiding and whisper confidentially to Eustace, "I'd better take over the work," whereupon he removes his glasses and hands them to Eustace. "Here, you hold these. I don't want her to know I'm nearsighted," he requests, even as he turns around, wondering aloud, "Where is she?"[26]

Sue is seated on a bench about one yard away, so Eustace points his forefinger. "Over there," he directs. Able to see the finger in front of his face, Erwin grabs it, tracing it with his own finger so as to be able to "see" the direction it is pointing. But once his finger is no longer attached to Eustace's, Erwin has trouble following his own finger, which is now on its own. Consequently, he points himself toward another statue, about one foot from Sue, trips, and falls into it. Sue rushes to rescue the hopelessly confused Erwin, who is now clutching the statue in an attempt not to fall any further. She grabs him and leads him out of this precarious position. Afraid to ask her the overwhelming question that he wants to ask, he instead ventures obliquely, "Sue, whaddya know that's good?" In reply, she seizes him and kisses him. Poor Ambrose as played by Erwin, who has never before had the self-confidence to approach a girl before (evidenced by the fact that his foolish vanity has prompted him to remove his glasses and thus look even more foolish), is so astonished that he says, "My goodness." Then he offers her his unbandaged hand, shakes it, and adds irrelevantly, "Congratulations."

But Sue is not finished with him, for she tries to kiss him again, exclaiming, "Oh, darling." No longer sure of what to do in this unaccustomed social situation, Erwin backs away, protesting, "No." Then, considering the circumstances, he uses an inappropriate figure of speech with his parting words, "I'll be seeing you." He turns, places his derby back on, strolls off to the edge of a nearby garden precipice, and casually walks off into the air, tumbling over the ledge headfirst. As she sees his legs disappear, Sue screams in dismay, "Oh *Ambrose!*" and rushes to see what shape he is in. It seems that the only thing injured is his dignity, for he is now planted about four feet down in the middle of a tree that has broken his descent. Trying to put the best face on his clumsy antics, he looks up at the woman he has been trying so hard to impress and laughs awkwardly, even as he assumes the most decorous demeanor possible in his situation. "I'm a great kidder," he tells her. Then he carries through with, "Good thing this bush was here to break my fall. I'll step down."[27]

Unfortunately, the step down he takes is about twelve feet from where he started, for he falls out of the tree, landing flat on his stomach to the accompaniment of Sue's frantic screams. Sue and Eustace emerge from the house, Sue convinced that her beloved Ambrose is dead. But Erwin maintains his composure as he stands without their assistance. To Sue's anxious, "Ambrose, are you hurt?" he extends his arms, offering himself to her as he replies, "Oh, not much, Sue." And he blindly embraces Eustace instead. So at this moment, Eustace decides that it would be prudent to return Erwin's discarded glasses. As Erwin presses them back on his nose, Sue gushes, "My *hero!* Are you sure you're all right?"

Whereas the romance between Erwin and Sue is progressing nicely, the love between Rogers and Elinor has turned rocky, particularly after Rogers confesses to Elinor, her friends, and her family that he is in reality a poor man and only an employee at the estate where he lives. Fearful that his confession has harmed Erwin's chances with Sue, Rogers asks Erwin what effect it will have on his buddy's marriage prospects, if poverty will make a difference to Sue. "Oh, no," Erwin assures him. "She's glad. She's always wanted to marry a poor man. Isn't that rich?" Rogers is relieved, "I was afraid she'd think you were unworthy." Erwin quips in his best self-mocking style, "Oh, she does. But she's willing to be big about it."[28]

Although events are moving more smoothly for Erwin at this point than they are for his pal Rogers, Erwin still remains loyal to his friend. When Erwin learns that Rogers is going to ride Gangster in an important race (the horse is now owned by Señor Cortez), Erwin is truly worried. He even remarks to Eustace, "He'll be killed, and he won't let his best friend tell him."[29] But Rogers is not killed; Gangster wins the race; Señora Cortez wins money on the outcome; Elinor doesn't mind marrying a poor man after all; and Erwin and Sue will live together contentedly—as long as Erwin is able to see where she is.

Along Came Youth is one of a series of entertaining Paramount comedies made in the early sound period from 1928 to 1933. Unlike many other major studios such as M-G-M and Warners, Paramount allowed its talented artists a relatively free rein with respect to acting, writing, and directing. It is no accident that such iconoclasts as W. C. Fields, Mae West, and the Marx Brothers did their best work at Paramount. And *Along Came Youth* is one of these satisfactory pictures, with much to recommend it. In addition to imaginative, mood-enhancing cinematography and editing, *Along Came Youth* is ably directed by Lloyd Corrigan and Norman Z. McLeod. The latter continued to work for Paramount into the mid-thirties, directing the Marx Brothers in *Monkey Business* (1931) and *Horse Feathers* (1932) and W. C. Fields in what is considered by many to be his best, most manic film, *It's a Gift* (1934). McLeod stayed active into the fifties, directing his last movie in 1959.

His co-director, Lloyd Corrigan, became better known as an actor, eventually appearing in over one hundred movies. He was a short, rotund, chubby-cheeked man, with a rolling gait when he walked; he specialized in playing businessmen or kindly uncles. But he also wrote the scripts for about twenty pictures and directed around fifteen, including one other Erwin film, the very clever *He Learned About Women* (1933). He would also appear on screen with Erwin many years later in the plodding, mediocre *Father Is a Bachelor* (1950), in which both made only brief appearances.

In both *The Big Broadcast* and *Along Came Youth* Erwin subordinates his own good looks and gives up screen time to two popular, handsome leading men: Bing Crosby and Buddy Rogers. Yet in both of these films, it is Erwin whom we are usually watching closely in the scenes he shares with Crosby and Rogers. Erwin has some of the best lines in both movies (Rogers made a better straight man than Crosby; Crosby had a nice wit of his own), and his ability to use his body effectively for comic purposes easily catches our notice. But the studios ordinarily did not consider Erwin a romantic lead, so he makes efficient use of the material that he is given in both of these movies, and does a superb job as a gauche but amusing sidekick.

OH, WHAT A TANGLED WEB WE WEAVE

Like Stuart Erwin, Ralph Bellamy was a skilled but modest and unassuming actor who often kidded about his inability to win the girl in pictures. Bellamy frequently played the hero's best friend or the man to whom the heroine was at first engaged until she saw someone she preferred—specifically, someone such as Cary Grant. But in *The Magnificent Lie* (1931), Bellamy is in an unusual situation; he is not only the star of the movie but also the man who gets the girl in the end. It is Stuart Erwin, playing Elmer Graham, who has the typical Bellamy part here. It is Erwin who is the pal, the one who has only a brief moment of longing for the lady in question and then devotes the remainder of his energy to ensuring that Bellamy, who loses his sight early in the film, gets everything he desires. Unlike the supporting roles he takes on with Bing Crosby and Buddy Rogers, Erwin has no funny lines in this movie, no quips to trade with the leading man. He is truly a background figure, but he plays his part as expertly and honestly as he does when he has the advantage of capturing our attention through physical and verbal humor.

We know from the opening scene of *The Magnificent Lie* that the focus of the picture will be Ralph Bellamy as Bill. We are taken back to 1918 France where we see that Bellamy is a hospitalized soldier with bandaged eyes. Although he is shell-shocked and has poor vision, we also discover that he is a hero who had saved a comrade in the trenches when his fellow soldier had become trapped on the barbed wire. So our sympathies are with him. Also sympathizing with him is a famous French actress, Rosa Duchene (Françoise Rosay), who has come to the hospital to visit the wounded. She comforts him and holds him when he panics after bombs explode near the hospital.

We now shift to the present: New Orleans, 1931. Bellamy has survived his wartime trauma and is currently the owner of a lumber company, with Erwin working for him. Yet Erwin seems to be more partner than employee. From the outset, we note that they have a close, comfortable relationship and that Erwin acts genuinely concerned about his friend's health, especially

Bellamy's deteriorating eyesight. In this movie, Erwin truly has a supporting part as Bellamy's protector. So when Bellamy hears that Rosa Duchene is in New Orleans to appear on stage in *Camille*, Erwin naturally accompanies him to the theater, where the two of them naively think they can wander past the stage entrance and into Duchene's presence without encountering any opposition.

But they are mistaken. Loitering at the entrance are two Frenchmen, Jacques (Charles Boyer) and Pierre (Tyler Brooke), who are also appearing in the play with Rosa Duchene. Boyer was as yet relatively unknown to American audiences, but even in this early picture he demonstrates the savoir faire that was to become integral to his reputation till the end of his life. In *The Magnificent Lie*, both Jacques and Pierre are full of giggly mischief, two flirtatious schoolboys who love to play pranks. And who better to play a prank on than Erwin and Bellamy, those sober, naïve working men, one of whom has had a crush on Rosa since that day in the French hospital when she embraced him, soothing him as he cowered, terrified by the sound of the bombs. So this fun-loving pair of actors tell the American visitors that Rosa will invite her old friend Bill to supper after she has finished her performance that evening.

What a confusing performance it turns out to be for both Erwin and Bellamy; for Erwin, because the play is in French, a language that he does not recognize at all; for Bellamy, because he is no longer able to see anything by the play's conclusion and must rely on Erwin to help him from the theater. One positive note is sounded, however, before the play begins, when Erwin, seated in the balcony, sees an attractive woman enter the theater and sit below them on the main floor. He informs Bellamy that this lady will be his by the evening's end, even though she has arrived with another man. The woman is a cabaret singer, an American who speaks French, and who will soon complicate Bellamy's life. She is played by Ruth Chatterton, a superb actress and a favorite of moviegoers in the thirties. A native New Yorker, Chatterton had an amusing but hard-edged Yankee practicality about her, yet she never stooped to caricature; she transcended the stoical, tough New England type that she frequently portrayed by never taking herself too seriously, by never resorting to overdone, campy behavior. Chatterton was the kind of intelligent, adroit actress that her fellow Yankee Bette Davis might have been had Davis not forgotten where she parked her sense of humor.

In this movie, Chatterton's French accent so impresses Boyer's Jacques and Tyler Brooke's Pierre, who listen to her singing in the café, that they compliment her on sounding just like Rosa Duchene. Also still interested in Chatterton is Erwin, who, having reluctantly left the now-blind Bellamy at their hotel, has spent the evening getting drunk. He lurches toward the table where Chatterton is seated with Boyer, Brooke, and her employer and wishful suitor, Larry (Sam Hardy). Boyer and Brooke remember Erwin as one of the two dupes whom they had tricked earlier in the evening. And Erwin, despite his plastered condition, remembers them as well, for he tells them that his friend is now blind. At first, the two arrogant Frenchmen assume that Bellamy is only "blind drunk," but Erwin immediately corrects them. After Boyer and Brooke finally comprehend that *blind* has another definition when applied to Bellamy's current state, these two fun-filled fellows hit upon another neat joke. Boyer impishly suggests that Chatterton call poor blind Bill and invite him to her room, which is handily in the same hotel as his. All the while Chatterton will be practicing her superb French accent, pretending that she is Rosa, and Bellamy as Bill will never suspect the truth.

After Tyler Brooke as Pierre leads Bellamy to "Rosa's" room, the three jokesters—Boyer, Brooke, and Chatterton—share much mirth at Bellamy's expense, especially since Bellamy falls for the joke, never suspecting that he is not talking to Rosa Duchene herself. They are particularly amused at Bellamy's sincere devotion to Rosa's memory and to the moment in wartime France when she had comforted him during the bombing raid. But all three soon tire of this fun, so Chatterton offers to take Bellamy back to his room. By this point in the narrative, we know that Chatterton as Poll, the cabaret singer, is not as tough and conscienceless as she at first appears. Earlier, Boyer had offered to show her how much he could be like the romantic character of Armand whom he has just played onstage in *Camille* with the real Rosa Duchene. But as she leaves the room with Bellamy, she clearly rebuffs Boyer's come-hither advances and his transparently sexual proposition to join him later in the evening for further merriment.

Furthermore, she is forthright with Erwin, whom she sees in the hall outside the door of the hotel room he is sharing with Bellamy. When he hears her saying goodnight to Bellamy, having dropped her own eastern accent and adopted Rosa Duchene's inflections, he catches on to what she is doing. And, because he is once again sober, and because he wants nothing more than to ease his friend's pain, we know that he will keep her secret, especially when he sees her make a shushing gesture with her forefinger against her lips and hurry away.

Yet Erwin has more serious problems to worry him than keeping Chatterton's secrets, for in the next scene, he is anxiously watching while a doctor examines Bellamy's eyes. The prognosis is grim: Bellamy's blindness is permanent. After the doctor leaves, Erwin tries to be encouraging, notwithstanding all evidence to the contrary, as he tells Bellamy, "Bill, he might be wrong." Bellamy wants no childish optimism, though. To Erwin's advice that he should forget "Rosa," Bellamy curtly replies, "I don't wanna remember anything at all."[30] Erwin's body language in this scene, although subtle, reveals much about his feelings. Gone are the broad, farcical gestures that he had used as Buddy Rogers' nearsighted and uncoordinated pal in *Along Came Youth*. His purpose here is to show his gentle, caring side—not to be the silly foil for the leading man. So he responds to Bellamy's denial of the world by lightly tugging on Bellamy's sleeves, as if he were trying to pull Bellamy away from his own despair.

But Bellamy reads Erwin's beckoning touch as pity, and shrugs off his pal's offer of help, abruptly avowing, "I'm through with *everything*. Do you hear me? *Everything*." Here Erwin interrupts, "You mean by that . . ." Yet he already knows how to finish his sentence, even before Bellamy continues, "*That's* what I mean by *that*. What's the world got for a blind man? I'm at war *again*, and this time, I'm on the *losing* side. Well, there's a way to end all that and end it *quick*."[31] All through Bellamy's tortured speech, Erwin is absolutely quiet, maintaining a stillness that all the same communicates a good deal. If we pay close attention to Stuart Erwin, the actor content to remain in the background, we can, after all, see in his expression his desire to get to the heart of Bellamy's torment as well as his perception that he can do nothing to prevent Bellamy's unraveling.

Truly afraid that Bellamy will kill himself, Erwin feels that he must try to do something, so he goes to Chatterton's home to plead with her to help his friend, now permanently blind. As he is entering her house, he meets Boyer on his way out. Boyer has just been repulsed once more in his efforts to make love to Chatterton, so he cautions Erwin that Chatterton is not in the mood. Nor is Erwin. If he had been at one time interested in playing with Chatterton himself, now all Erwin wants is help for Bellamy. He begs her to go to Bellamy again, pretend to be Rosa, "and brace him up." Feeling sorry for Bellamy, she accompanies Erwin to the house and one more time puts on her best French accent. This time a very bitter Bellamy rejects her.

But good pal Erwin won't give up. He next tries to get Bellamy out of his self-pitying self-absorption by taking him to the cabaret where Chatterton is singing as herself, where she has not masked her identity. When Bellamy hears her singing "Just One More Chance," he tells Erwin to bring her to his table so that he might buy her a drink.[32] Bellamy, naturally unaware of the dual role that Chatterton has been playing, admonishes Erwin not to tell the singer that he's blind, and, furthermore, to "leave me alone with her. I want to have some fun." Erwin looks disgruntled and confused as he replies, "Well, that's more than *I'm* having."[33]

So Erwin dutifully goes to Chatterton's table with the message that Bellamy wants to meet her. He also cautions her that she is not to play Rosa this time: "He heard you sing and wants to buy you a drink." Of course, Chatterton is beginning to fall in love with Bellamy, so she no longer adopts such a caustic air when she responds, "Hm. Gee, that's funny." Yet Erwin has more: "You don't know the half of it. He doesn't want you to know he's blind." Chatterton is naturally curious, "Why?" Erwin just shakes his head, bewildered but devoted: "You'll have to go and find out for yourself. Don't ask me."[34] As Chatterton is cozying up to Bellamy, the real Rosa Duchene enters the club, accompanied by her two costars from *Camille*, the wise guys Boyer and Brooke. Rosa knows about the fun they have been having with Bellamy; she appears as morally heedless as they and wants to continue this diversion, only this time she volunteers to go to Bellamy's table and play herself, figuring correctly that he won't be able to distinguish between her voice and Chatterton's imitation of her.

But Chatterton has had enough of this type of fun, so she slips Bellamy a strong drink before Rosa has the chance to get very far in her teasing of the blind veteran. When Bellamy subsequently collapses, his head on the table, Rosa gives up, leaving Erwin and Chatterton to prop him up and out of the club and into a car, at which time Chatterton drives him to her house. When he awakens, she reveals her true identity and the nature of the cruel gag that has been pulled on him. They consequently quarrel, with his accusing her of being a whore (although his word choice is more circumspect), and he demands that she drive him home. This she does, careening down the road at a dizzying speed, angry and hurt at his accusation, for she loves him and she has decidedly proven in her behavior toward both Boyer and her employer Sam Hardy that she is not a whore.

We have no doubt but that they will crash, and of course they do. And, of course, the trauma from the wreck results in Bellamy's regaining his sight. The trauma also makes him realize what an endearing individual Chatterton really is. And, since Chatterton is not an unattractive woman, he is still in love with her after he sees her. Fortunately, neither is particularly hurt in the accident and, by another fortunate circumstance, they are close enough to the Erwin/Bellamy house that they can walk to the front porch. Here they see Erwin coming home in a cab—alone—from the cabaret. As Bellamy and Chatterton agree to meet the next day, and the next, and the next, Erwin is left by himself on the porch, pondering Bellamy's most unexpected reversal of fortune (unexpected to everyone except those of us in the audience who have seen this plot before). But with absolute self-abasement, Erwin shows his delight in the return of Bellamy's vision. In addition, we suspect that

Erwin will loyally continue to work for Bellamy's lumber company, content from this point on to remain forever the second man in line.

Unlike *The Big Broadcast* and *Along Came Youth*, there is little humor in *The Magnificent Lie*, and what little can be found is provided by Ruth Chatterton. Erwin has no witty lines in this, yet his very seriousness and sincerity demand our attention, whether he is patting Bellamy reassuringly on the shoulder or making direct eye contact with Chatterton as he appeals to her for her help.

Privately, Erwin seems to have been in awe of Chatterton; he was very gallant and deferential in his praise of this early feminist whom he saw as forceful, intelligent, and productive. He certainly enjoyed her aggressive sense of humor. In a 1936 interview, he alluded to the fact that Chatteron was a licensed pilot. She had, in fact, flown her own airplane across the country. As Erwin observed to the interviewer: "I once played in 'The Magnificent Lie' with Ruth Chatterton. Most men haven't much subtlety. I know that I haven't. I believe that when someone tells me black is black they don't mean that black is white. But Ruth can handle words like Napoleon handled armies. When it comes to books, music, travel and diplomacy I've yet to listen to her equal. Then, just when you think comfortably, 'Oh, well, all these things are part of a woman's game,' she comes along and turns aviatrix and proves that a woman can be all the things a man can be and do all the things a man can do. And if that doesn't put us at the bottom of the deck, what does?"[35]

NOTES

1. *The Big Broadcast*. Dir. Frank Tuttle. Paramount, 1932.
2. *The Big Broadcast*, 1932.
3. *The Big Broadcast*, 1932.
4. *The Big Broadcast*, 1932.
5. Ted Sennett, *Hollywood Musicals* (New York: Harry N. Abrams, 1981), 151.
6. *The Big Broadcast*, 1932.
7. *The Big Broadcast*, 1932.
8. *The Big Broadcast*, 1932.
9. *The Big Broadcast*, 1932.
10. *The Big Broadcast*, 1932.
11. *The Big Broadcast*, 1932.
12. Stuart Erwin Jr., letter to author, 16 October 2000.
13. *Along Came Youth*. Dir. Lloyd Corrigan and Norman Z. McLeod. Paramount, 1930.
14. *Along Came Youth*, 1930.

15. *Along Came Youth*, 1930.

16. *Along Came Youth*, 1930.

17. *Along Came Youth*, 1930.

18. *Along Came Youth*, 1930.

19. *Along Came Youth*, 1930.

20. *Along Came Youth*, 1930.

21. *Along Came Youth*, 1930.

22. *Along Came Youth*, 1930.

23. *Along Came Youth*, 1930.

24. *Along Came Youth*, 1930.

25. *Along Came Youth*, 1930.

26. *Along Came Youth*, 1930.

27. *Along Came Youth*, 1930.

28. *Along Came Youth*, 1930.

29. *Along Came Youth*, 1930.

30. *The Magnificent Lie*. Dir. Berthold Viertel. Paramount, 1931.

31. *The Magnificent Lie*, 1931.

32. "Just One More Chance" and "Out of Nowhere," both featured in this scene, were Bing Crosby hits of 1931. Both songs were scheduled to be sung by Crosby in the 1931 Paramount feature *Confessions of a Co-Ed*, but "Just One More Chance," the song Chatterton sings here, was deleted from the released print of the latter movie. Its lyrics do fit nicely into the plot of *The Magnificent Lie* at this point: its refrain, which begs the listener to give the singer "Just One More Chance" to prove her love for him, are apropos of Chatterton's developing feelings about her dreamy but duped admirer.

33. *The Magnificent Lie*, 1931.

34. *The Magnificent Lie*, 1931.

35. Martha Kerr, "Women Are Trouble," *Modern Screen* (November 1936): 94.

Two actors with much in common: James Cagney and Stuart Erwin as pioneer airmail pilots in *Ceiling Zero* (1935).

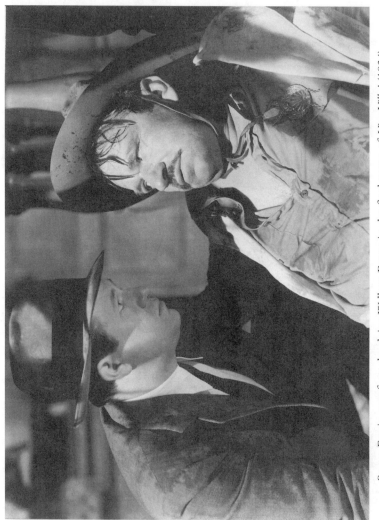

Stuart Erwin comforts the dying Wallace Beery in the final scene of *Viva Villa!* (1934).

Hal Grayson with his orchestra and Stuart Erwin on the set of *The Big Broadcast* (1932).

Stuart Erwin, Dewey Robinson, Edmund Gwenn, Betty Furness, and Robert Armstrong in *All-American Chump* (1936).

The 1955 cast of the television series *Trouble with Father. Bottom:* Stuart Erwin, June Collyer. *Top left:* Merry Anders; *Top right:* Sheila James: "He was very loving and gentle but not maudlin. He didn't like anything phony."

Background from left: Leslie Nielsen and Stuart Erwin. *Foreground from left:* Anne Baxter, June Collyer, and Dana Andrews in an episode of *Playhouse 90,* CBS, c. 1957.

"Film Beauty Marries Comedian." June Collyer and Stuart Erwin shortly before their marriage in 1931.

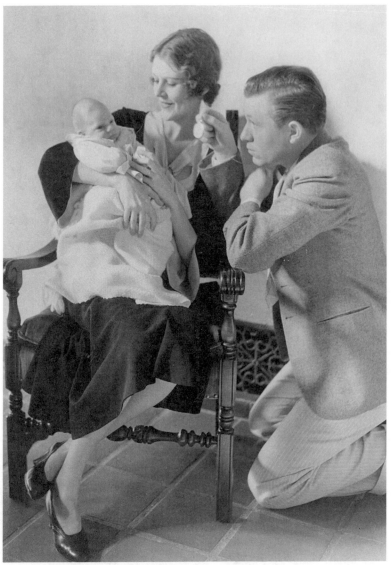

June Collyer, Stuart Erwin, and Stuart Jr., seemingly unamused by his father's pocket watch. November 1932.

Stork Club, 1954. *From left:* The Erwins with their two children, Judy and Stuart Jr.: "He was a wonderful husband and father."

5

WOMEN AND ERWIN

Gatsby turned to me rigidly.
"I can't say anything in this house, old sport."
"She's got an indiscreet voice," I remarked. "It's full of—" I hesitated.
"Her voice is full of money," he said suddenly.

— F. Scott Fitzgerald, *The Great Gatsby* (1925)

He walked amongst the Trial Men
  In a suit of shabby grey;
A cricket cap was on his head,
  And his step seemed light and gay;
But I never saw a man who looked
  So wistfully at the day.

—Oscar Wilde, *The Ballad of Reading Gaol* (1898)

"I'm one who believes that women are smarter than men. Better brains. Quicker instincts. More common sense. Less sentimentality which reduces many a strong man to the sending of lace paper valentines when he ought to be on the field of battle, some kind of a battle. They're better actors too, and I don't mean only on stage or screen. They've got us beat, that's why they're trouble."

—Stuart Erwin, *Modern Screen* (1936)

"He is so kind and gentle of heart, he is always afraid of them. He really admires us more than we deserve, I am afraid."

—June Collyer, *Modern Screen* (1936)

FUN WITH SEX

Throughout his forty-plus year career on stage, on radio, in movies, and on television, Stuart Erwin was not really thought of as a romantic leading man. In many of his films, he was never a serious challenger for the girl against such rugged men as Clark Gable, James Cagney, or even Wallace Beery. However, his reputation as an unworldly, inept, foolish foil to more aggressive types is an inaccurate one. In fact, Stuart Erwin projected a natural gentleness and sensitivity toward women, even when he became irritated at those predatory ladies who he knew were trying to take advantage of him. He also treated many of his female costars with a sly, kidding manner that belied his physical attraction to them. Moreover, there was a decided chemistry between him and the women who acted with him.

For instance, throughout the movie *Palooka* (1934), Erwin and Lupe Velez clearly enjoy themselves while openly ridiculing the censors' blindness to the risqué jokes these clever actors are playing with each other and on their audience. In this particular film, Lupe Velez embodies a quite recognizable type of woman—sensual, flashy, strident—one who achieves an erotic high by delighting in sex with winning athletes. Early in the film, she watches as prizefighter Erwin flattens the current boxing champ William Cagney (Jimmy's younger brother), and she immediately embarks on a campaign to supplant her former lover Cagney with a new lover: Erwin.

She begins her assault on Erwin immediately after his boxing victory by pressing her body against his at ringside. She continues her strategy later in the evening by performing an extremely suggestive song and dance at a nightclub where Erwin has gone to celebrate his victory. Her dress is an appropriate one for a seduction. It is backless, with a V-neckline plunging all the way to her waist. The puffed, frilly sleeves billow as she pulsates to the music. When she raises her arms, she reveals that the dress is well ventilated, not only at front and back, but also at the sides, nearly exposing her breasts in all the directions that it is possible to expose them. It is also clear from this scene that Velez feels no need to confine her stunning body with a bra. Once she decides that Erwin has seen enough of her from a distance, she closes in for her frontal attack by inviting him to her apartment.

What follows is one of the most provocative, blatant, sexually charged scenes in early Hollywood. The scene is especially intriguing when one remembers that *Palooka* was made in 1934, at a time when the Hollywood Production Code of 1930 had become quite strictly enforced. Writing about *The Scarlet Empress*, another movie made in 1934, Andrew Sarris observes that this particular film "shattered the decorum which was spreading over the American cinema like a shroud. Its very outrageousness was an index of the repressive reasonableness of most moviemaking of its time."[1] Such "outrageousness" against "repressive reasonableness" may also be found in at least two scenes in *Palooka*, the first of which begins shortly after Erwin arrives at Velez's apartment, having been unable to resist her enticing ringside proposition. There is nothing either "repressive" or "reasonable" about the mischievous fun that Erwin and Velez are about to have with each other in defiance of the censors.

Indeed, Velez wastes no time, once she has Erwin on her own territory. She settles him on her sofa, hands him a drink, leans over him and, in doing so, renders herself almost topless. Both the camera and Erwin himself are allowed a comfy slide down the neckline of her dress and into her bare skin. While Erwin makes a brave but not always successful attempt to focus his eyes on Velez's face, she executes a serpentine movement from the back to the front of the sofa, reaches to the floor, grabs both his feet, and with one graceful motion places his legs on the sofa. In one of the many symbolic moments that escaped the censors' notice in this particular scene, Erwin protests that he will "ruin" her furniture; however, at this point she is not especially concerned with housekeeping niceties. Indeed, she reassures him of this fact by placing her hand on his thigh. As she nestles against him on the sofa, she tempts him with, "Is there anything else I can do for you?"

ERWIN (clearly discomfited): Gosh—you've been so awfully nice to me—I—

VELEZ (leaning even closer): I could be nicer.

ERWIN: Well—if it's not asking too much—

VELEZ: Yes?

ERWIN (trying desperately to distract himself): I would like a cheese sandwich.

VELEZ (thunderstruck): A cheese sandwich?

ERWIN (talking fast, truly anxious about the effect she is having on him): Yes—American cheese—that's the kind I like best—[Now he irrelevantly trails away] Sometimes I used to eat two or three a day. . . .[2]

But Velez, sensing that her moment of conquest has come, leans forward to kiss him, causing the increasingly nervous Erwin to spill his drink, which pours directly into his lap. Gazing in dismay and embarrassment, he quickly jumps up and examines the front of his trousers; from his waist down to his thighs, they are soaked in liquid.

ERWIN (clearly tickled at the situation, in spite of himself): Oh my goodness.

VELEZ (also tickled, as she reports the obvious): I'm awfully sorry. You're all wet. You must take them off.[3]

When he objects to the removal of his pants, she leads him to the bedroom anyway. As he is about to disentangle himself from her grasp and from his agonizing predicament, she tries once more: "Can I help you?" Here, he throws her a relieved glance: "I'd rather not." Then, afraid that he might have hurt her feelings, he adds, "Oh—it's nothing—I've had wet pants before." Finally, he adds a tag, throwaway line, almost lost as he closes the bedroom door on her, muttering: "I fell in the river once and. . . ."[4] By now, however, it is clear that Erwin is using "the river" figuratively—and that both he and Velez have had a marvelous time with this scene.

The next time they appear together on screen to flout the censors, they are clearly more comfortable with one another. It is obvious that Erwin's Joe Palooka has gained confidence in Velez's presence and that, in fact, he has become her lover. They arrive at a photographer's studio, ready to pose for publicity photos advertising various products; they are dressed for a night on the town, both in fancy evening clothes. As they sit for the photographer, they adopt stiff, formal positions, suitable for the clothing they are wearing. Meanwhile, a sign has been placed in the foreground, revealing just what product the boxing champ Erwin is pitching: Doctor Gray's Gargle. Impatient with what looks like one of those uncomfortable positions assumed by an earlier generation in a nineteenth-century Daguerreotype, the photographer urges, "Give us a little more sex, please."

Without hesitation, Erwin responds, "Sex? How about this?"[5] He then grabs Velez, embraces her, and forcefully, insistently kisses her. He thereby clarifies for the audience members just how they might find Doctor Gray's Gargle useful. He also reinforces his standing as Velez's current lover.

For their next photo, Erwin and Velez wear more casual attire. But this time it is Erwin's appearance that might have given the censors pause for reflection—if they had been paying attention. Velez enters the scene dressed modestly in shorts and sweater; Erwin emerges covered from shoulders to ankles in a revealing, tight-fitting body stocking. It is apparent that he is inappropriately dressed for this occasion because he is carrying golf clubs, although, under the circumstances, no one would be looking at them anyway. At this point, the photographer says, "Now, champ, show us your form." So Erwin obligingly draws back a club as if to swing it, pretending to be oblivious to the absurdity of playing golf clothed only in long underwear.

As Erwin continues to win more and more fights (not realizing that they are set-ups arranged by his manager), he becomes even more self-assured with women and full of fun. Shortly after romping with Velez in front of the photographer, he enjoys the luxury of a manicure given by an attractive blonde. When she finishes, he ostentatiously offers her a $10 bill (this in 1934!). When she protests that she doesn't have change, he condescendingly replies that he doesn't need change. Now it is this woman's turn to feel cozy about the champ: "Thank you, champion. If you want me to come up tonight and give you a polish, why just call Josephine—"

ERWIN (with a straight face): Well—not tonight, Josephine.[6]

Erwin has other plans for the evening; these plans involve a night with Velez, whom he has begun to treat possessively. In fact, Erwin shows how Palooka's growing assurance about his sexual power has transferred itself into other areas of his life. On his way out of the room, he notices that his trainer is resting his head on the fancy evening coat that has become an important part of Palooka's attire since he began his relations with Velez. Erwin whacks the man on the head and grabs his coat, announcing, "If I'd wanted that pressed, I'd 'a sent it to the tailor."[7]

That same night, Erwin, Velez, and Erwin's manager Jimmy Durante spend an unproductive evening at a nightclub, drinking multiple bottles of liquor. Several hours after they have begun these festivities, Erwin and Velez stumble out to the lobby where Erwin, gallantly trying to put Velez's fur coat around her, succeeds in draping it over her head as though he were about to kidnap her. As she is trying to extricate herself and her hairdo from this furry canopy, in charges Cagney, who tries to snatch her coat while taunting Erwin: "I paid for it." But Erwin now feels that he has "paid" for Velez as well, so he becomes belligerent as he challenges Cagney: "Don't you annoy this lady anymore—you understand? This is *my* girl, and I want you to let her alone!"[8]

What Erwin does not realize is that Cagney has accurately predicted Erwin's response; in reality, Velez's former lover is about to get what he has wanted all along: a boxing rematch with Erwin, knowing that if he wins this one, he can also win back Velez's body. And Erwin, for all of his growing worldliness, is still painfully unaware of the extent of Velez's crudeness. He believes that he loves her and that she returns his love; he has ignored Durante's savvy caution, given just hours earlier: "You're just putty in a woman's hands—something to ravish and cast aside."[9]

And Durante is right, for when Erwin does indeed lose his rematch with Cagney, he also loses the sexual allure and attendant danger that Velez has found so intoxicating. So Velez returns to Cagney's bed, while Erwin is reunited with the "nice" girl (Mary Carlisle) that he had left back home in the country before he was lured to the city by the promise of fame as a boxer. The audience knows that Carlisle is a good girl because she represents rural values as opposed to big-city corruption; because she has waited patiently for Erwin to come back, unlike Velez, who would wait for no man; and because she is a blonde and innocent, unlike Velez, the raven-haired temptress. But even in the film's final scene between Erwin and Carlisle, which might have descended into dreadful sentimentality, Erwin cannot resist kidding himself. His face is still bruised from the pounding he has taken from Cagney and his eye is black, so, after declaring his undying devotion to the girl he left behind, he wryly adds: "Gee, but you look nice, Ann. You look twice as good as you ever did—and I can only see you with one eye."[10]

NO CHANCE FOR SEX

Another movie in which Erwin falls for an energetic Latin is *Passport Husband,* a clever, underrated B picture that he made for 20th Century Fox in 1938. This time the exotic recipient of his affection is Joan Woodbury, a Los Angeles native in real life. Woodbury plays Conchita Montez, a dancer/singer in a nightclub where Erwin works as a busboy and where he spends his evenings gazing wistfully at her gyrations, when he is not breaking dishes. By 1938, censorship guidelines were being enforced much more strictly than they had been when *Palooka* was made. So Woodbury in a strapless evening gown is more conservatively dressed as she sings and dances than Velez had been when she had seduced Erwin four years earlier. Yet these two oversexed ladies have similar effects on the hopelessly smitten Erwin.

This time, however, the "good" girl in *Passport Husband* has a much larger role than did Mary Carlisle in *Palooka*. Here, the nice girl is played by the attractive, talented Pauline Moore, an underappreciated actress with a voice as soothing as hot tea laced with peppermint and licorice. In this movie, Moore is a practical nightclub cigarette girl who continually tries to bring the head-in-the-storm-clouds Erwin back down to earthbound reality. Her quiet steadiness provides a nice complement to Erwin's more airborne spirit. To illustrate, Moore waits patiently for him to learn that Woodbury is a schemer with a conscience as twisted as her pitching arm when she hurls dangerously sharp objects at various people who anger her. As he had done in *Palooka*, however, Erwin, in his dealings with women, balances desire with wit, infatuation with facetiousness; and finally, his developing love for Pauline Moore with his conviction that good humor is the best defense against society's corruption.

Early in the movie, Erwin makes it clear that he is fond of Moore, despite his adulation of Woodbury. When nightclub patron Ed Brophy tries to flirt with Moore as she goes by his table selling cigarettes, Erwin demonstrates that he has not forgotten any of his pugilistic skills, for he lands a good punch on Brophy, knocking him down. Erwin quickly regrets his hasty spurt of temper, however, as he tries to bring Brophy around, patting him on the cheek while apologizing: "I didn't want to hurt you, but you needed a lesson in manners. You must learn to respect womanhood." Shortly after, Moore chastises her defender, informing him that his victim is a notorious gangster thug with connections to Woodbury's deported alien boyfriend, Tiger Martin (Douglas Fowley).

MOORE: It was swell of you, Henry, but you might have been killed.

ERWIN (unaware of her meaning): Oh, no. I hit him firmly.

MOORE: But it was very foolish of you.

ERWIN (as though making a speech, declaiming): No man who honors the memory of his mother would permit a mother of the future to be treated disrespectfully. (Now he gives her a knowing, sidelong glance.) And besides, faint heart never won fair lady.

MOORE (sheepishly, obviously attracted to him): Why, Henry.

ERWIN (embarrassed, remembering his crush on the sexy Woodbury): Of course, that doesn't apply in this case, but I believe in proverbs.

MOORE (persistent in trying to bring him to his senses): Yea? Well, do you know this one? Fools rush in where angels fear to tread?

ERWIN (catching the rhythm of these clichés): Yea—I like that one (makes a motion as though he were sewing) and the one a stitch in time saves nine—

MOORE (reminding him of Woodbury's paramour): And you just socked Blackie Bennett's best boy.

ERWIN: Uh huh—and a rolling—(Here he hesitates, does a double take as Moore's words belatedly register. He turns his head away to look in the direction of the nightclub's main floor, turns back, swallows) I did? Oh. (Sits down, numb.)

MOORE: And I still don't understand why they left you conscious.

ERWIN (in a sardonic understatement): Perhaps it was an oversight.[11]

Erwin is about to learn, however, that he will not be paid for the week; this decision is *not* an oversight on the part of the nightclub management, but rather is the penalty exacted from him for breaking so many dishes. When Moore offers to buy the temporarily destitute Erwin a meal, he has no arrogant masculine qualms about allowing the woman to pay. Indeed, he treats her as an equal, with no self-consciousness but instead with a gently kidding, self-effacing tone: "I'll do it if it's agreed I'll pay you back the first week I don't break any dishes." And Moore picks up on his tone, needling him somewhat as she reassures him: "It's a deal. I can wait forever."[12]

But Moore soon discovers that she might have to wait longer than she anticipated, for Erwin is soon fired altogether due to his penchant for destroying nightclub crockery while in the throes of admiration for the lusty Woodbury. However, Erwin is about to receive a lucky blow, for soon after this career setback, he is standing in the nightclub alley pondering his fate when he is hit on the head by a flying diamond bracelet. The jewelry has been thrown from the dressing room window by Woodbury in a fit of pique at her latest admirer, Blackie Bennett (Harold Huber). Naturally Erwin, the lovelorn, returns the bracelet to Woodbury, who invites him back the next day.

A little later, still as airborne as that bracelet had been, Erwin meets Moore at a lunch counter to share with her the meal that she had earlier promised to buy. Their dialogue is reminiscent of Burns and Allen, with the gender roles reversed, as Moore plays straight man to Erwin's seeming non sequiturs. As he enters, Moore is waiting for him at the counter:

ERWIN: Hello.

MOORE: Well, you look happy.

ERWIN: I am. I got fired.

MOORE: So you're happy?

ERWIN: But I'm being hired back again—with a raise. Miss Conchita's fixed it for me. (rapturously) She's *wonderful!* She said she's noticed me at the club.

MOORE (sarcastically): And you've only worked under her nose for three months.[13]

Throughout this scene, Erwin is so befuddled by his obsession with Miss Conchita's generosity that three times he orders walnut waffles and milk, oblivious to each order, filled and placed in front of him by the waiter (Irving Bacon). When he finally awakens to the world, he looks quizzically at the counter, now covered with milk and waffles, and asks Moore, "Did I order all of these? I suppose I can eat 'em if you can pay for them." Now turning his attention from his phantom dream girl to the girl seated next to him, he tells her of his plans to open a lunchroom in his hometown, Hobson Corners. (A Thornton Wilder name, if ever there was one.) Deciding she wants some physical activity, Moore moves away from the counter and announces that she is going to play the pinball machine. Once again, Moore and Erwin do Burns and Allen:

ERWIN (cautioning her against the pinball game): That's gambling.

MOORE: All right, we'll use my nickel.

ERWIN: Oh, but that's why I left my uncle.

MOORE: That's why you left—?

ERWIN: Uh huh.

MOORE: Look, Henry. What has your uncle got to do with my playing this pinball machine?

ERWIN: He invented it.

MOORE: He invented it?

ERWIN: Uh huh. He was quite handy with tools.

MOORE (impressed): Why, the man who invented this machine must be worth a million dollars.

ERWIN: He is. Uncle Charlie invented it as a harmless game and before he realized it, the money just poured in and that's wrong.

MOORE: What's wrong about it?

ERWIN (earnestly): Well, some unscrupulous dealers made a gambling device out of it, so that on 286 nickels it's only possible to get back about 16 1/2 per cent of the original investment. Now you take $14.85 worth of nickels and figure them—

MOORE (confused by the garrulous but morally scrupulous Erwin): Never mind, Henry. Thanks for tipping me off.[14]

Before Erwin realizes that he truly loves the stable, practical Pauline Moore, he is forced to undergo an oxymoronic, pleasurable torture, similar to that which had been meted out to him by Lupe Velez in *Palooka*. But while Velez had wanted only to seduce him, not to marry him, Joan Woodbury as Conchita Montez wants only to marry him, not to make love to him. And both ladies ultimately succeed in their respective goals. When Woodbury discovers that she is about to be deported to South America as an undesirable alien, she is advised by her gangster friends and their lawyer that all she has to do to avoid deportation is to marry a respectable American citizen, thus becoming a U.S. citizen herself and avoiding a long boat ride south.

At first, Woodbury is stumped by the challenge; all of her varied underworld acquaintances have lengthy police records and therefore hardly meet the U.S. government standard for "respectability." Then she fastens on a superb idea; as she watches the newly rehired busboy Erwin gazing wistfully at her, she knows that she has discovered the perfect prey. All she has to do is play upon his sympathy, so she manufactures an inane story to justify why she must immediately become a U.S. citizen. Sobbing, she pleads with the touched Erwin for help. She says that her father in South America has been shot and killed. When Erwin asks when this happened, she replies without hesitation, "Five years ago." Erwin, now totally absorbed in her plight, evidently misses the preposterousness of her answer, so she continues in the same illogical manner. She begs him to save her from those assassins who had murdered her father, explaining that, if she cannot avoid her imminent deportation to South America, she herself will be shot upon her return. Now that she has her prey stunned and tranquilized, Woodbury advances toward her own form of execution; she and her "advisers" beseech Erwin to marry her and subsequently save her life. Dazed, Erwin wanders around in circles for a few seconds. Not wanting to allow her wounded animal to crawl away, Woodbury implores: "I will be such a good wife that you will learn to love me—"

ERWIN: Oh, but I do now—

WOODBURY (genuinely astonished, her scheme working better than she had hoped): Henry! But you never tell me—

ERWIN: I didn't have—[15]

Here Woodbury does not allow Erwin to finish his sentence, for she does not care one bit about how he formerly lacked the opportunity to declare his love. Rather, she grabs him and energetically kisses him. This time around, he does not have a drink to spill on his trousers; instead, he is abruptly and unromantically forced off balance, sits on a convenient nearby chair, and, in the process, ungracefully crushes Ed Brophy's foot under one of its legs.

Jump cut to the next scene of the Erwin-Woodbury wedding, which disintegrates into a brawl when former suitor Blackie Bennett (Harold Huber) kisses Woodbury, who then punches Huber; thereupon, Spike (Edward Brophy) retaliates by hitting Woodbury; Brophy in turn is socked by Erwin, who is trying to defend his bride. At this juncture, the minister demands that all of them leave. Not a propitious beginning for a marriage.

Nor is the remainder of the brief marriage any more pleasant for Erwin. Later that evening as he impatiently paces outside the club, waiting eagerly for Woodbury to finish her work and go home with him, he boasts to her chauffeur that *he* is now her husband. But the chauffeur, who certainly knows her better than Erwin does, remains cynically unimpressed by this revelation. And Erwin is about to know her better himself, but not in the way that he has been anticipating since their ill-starred marriage ceremony. When Woodbury and her entourage finally emerge into the alley, they start to brush by and brush off Erwin, still waiting to take his bride home.

ERWIN: Well, here I am.

HUBER (eternally wanting Woodbury for himself): Yep—here he is.

WOODBURY (now belaboring the obvious): Yes, indeed, here you are. (patronizing him) Conchita like you. You are the nice boy, Henry. Good night.

ERWIN (following her with his eyes in stunned disbelief and despair, and then chasing her): But—you're going home.

WOODBURY (ever the narcissist, not realizing her effect on him): Naturally I'm going home. I live there. Conchita is very tired. I see you tomorrow.

HUBER (in his most ingratiating, but sinister, tone): Don't you worry, Henry. You'll be taken care of.[16]

What Huber means, of course, is that Erwin will "be taken care of" after he has been "taken for a ride" that usually precedes a gangland "rubbing out." Because this is a comedy, however, there is no doubt that Erwin will be rescued before his untimely demise. As indeed he is—by Huber and his lawyer—just before Ed Brophy and Lon Chaney Jr. put the finishing touches to Erwin's good, trusting nature. At this point, the narrative turns even more illogical, because a rival gang is ordered by Woodbury's deported boyfriend Tiger to kill Erwin. Now Brophy and Chaney become Erwin's bodyguards, trying to protect him from his would-be killers so that Woodbury won't become a widow and lose her citizenship status.

Dodging bullets and looking like an escapee from the local jail, Erwin turns up his collar, ducks his face into his lapel, and sidles into the lunchroom, where he sees Pauline Moore and greets her somewhat anticlimactically: "Hello."

MOORE: Aren't you being a fugitive from the dishpan?

ERWIN (still valiantly but improbably trying to hide his face): I had to see you, Mary Jane. You're about the only friend I have in New York. Ever since I got married, somebody's tried to kill me. (Here he looks around furtively.)

MOORE (sarcastically, revealing that she knows about Woodbury's character): I can understand that. Come on, Henry. What's the gag?

ERWIN (confidentially): It isn't any gag. Somebody's trying to kill me. Everything's happened. And now I've even got bodyguards. . . . Spike and Bull. Mr. Bennett says they're to keep me from getting killed, but every time I'm with them, I get shot at. I just gave 'em the slip.

MOORE: Shot at?

ERWIN (casually): Oh, I've been shot at lots of times, but you know, a miss is as good as a mile.[17]

At this point in Erwin's discussion of his near-collisions with disaster, Moore's erstwhile suitor Ted Markson (Robert Lowery) enters. Because Ted is a news reporter, he has had the resources to learn a good deal about Erwin's unfortunate marital situation; Ted even divulges to Erwin his knowledge of the humiliating fact that Erwin hasn't "seen" his bride, except at the club, since their marriage. He also knows that Woodbury had lied to Erwin about her father in South America having been shot. When he apprises Erwin of Woodbury's real reason for marrying him, Erwin registers a mixture of bewilderment and growing awareness that he has been duped. But he is not going to be silenced or shamed any longer.

In the next scene, with the accompaniment of Pauline Moore to give him a new moral center, he propels himself into Woodbury's dressing room to proclaim that he is filing suit for annulment, whereupon Woodbury responds with her usual good humor by hurling a hairbrush at him and Moore. After they have gracefully and in unison successfully ducked this missile, Erwin strolls to a spot next to the door, meticulously picks up a vase filled with flowers, carefully removes the flowers, and calmly tells Woodbury, "This is probably rude and ungentlemanly, but it's the sort of thing that you'll understand." He then executes a Cagneyesque gesture by clutching the flowers in one hand and holding the vase in the other, so that he can toss its water-filled contents onto the face and down the dress of the astonished Woodbury. To ensure that he has done a thorough job, he pitches the contents twice, then carefully places the flowers back into their proper container, returns it to its perch next to the dressing room door, and exits serenely with Moore. Admittedly, the water he so ungraciously dumps is not as messy as

Cagney's grapefruit in *The Public Enemy* (1931), but Erwin's revenge is perfectly adequate for his purpose.

Erwin's triumph is short-lived, however, for when he returns to his apartment, he discovers that Woodbury is moving in with him—lock, stock, and footlockers. In order to thwart his attempt at annulment, she has determined to force herself on him, pretending to be the one wanting to consummate the marriage. Once more he treats her roughly, ejecting her and her footlockers. But unknown to Erwin, his landlady has just opened a telegram addressed to him and learned that he has inherited one million dollars from his uncle. The landlady gives this enlightening bit of news to the frazzled Woodbury as she is about to leave. So again, Woodbury and those footlockers go upstairs, where she declares her undying love to her husband.

Enter the clear-headed Pauline Moore, who knows why Woodbury is sticking around and consequently forms a plan to teach the wanton Miss Conchita a lesson in the school of hard knocks. Allegedly concerned about Woodbury's readiness to be a good, dutiful wife, she tests Woodbury's housekeeping and cooking skills. And, as Woodbury subsequently demonstrates, her abilities in these two areas are evidently somewhere at the nursery school level. Both Erwin and Moore stand around looking vastly amused as Woodbury tackles her scrubbing and cleaning chores with a violence born out of her frustration and anger at the corner into which she has varnished herself.

Meanwhile, Moore has called Western Union, making up her own telegram, which is now delivered to Erwin. The message tells him to ignore the previous telegram's news about his receiving a million dollars, that there was an error, and that he will inherit only one dollar. At this moment, Erwin is thoroughly confused, as he had never even seen the first telegram—the one appropriated by both his landlady and Woodbury. But Woodbury knows the significance of his newly acquired poverty, so, to Moore's delight, she falls for the phony message, once again removing herself and those footlockers from Erwin's premises.

Now that this distraction is out of their way, Erwin can concentrate on the woman whom he has loved all along. Moore confesses her duplicity, informing Erwin that he really *does* have that million dollars. This time it is his turn to confess his feelings, but he has trouble leading up to this declaration. First, he tells her that he will return to Hobson Corners. Then he asks her where she is from. When she replies, "Columbus," he advises her that she should return to Ohio, because New York is no place for a girl like her. As in *Palooka*, the small-town values set the moral standard; Woodbury, like Lupe Velez in the earlier film, belongs in the big city—Moore and Erwin do not. Moore is not ready to return to Columbus, however—at least not without some hint of a future that will include Erwin. So she responds to his counsel with a bitter retort, "Thanks, I'll take your advice." At this point, she walks out on him. Realizing that he has missed his chance, he chases after her. But because of his paralyzing fear of rejection, he has waited too long and she is gone. When he returns to his room, he regrets his inaction: "Now what did I do?" he muses, fully self-aware enough to know the answer.

But Moore is not about to desert the man she loves and who she feels still needs protection from the two sets of gangsters who are trying to bump him off. So she returns and fixes him a glass of milk spiked with liquor, thus priming him for another proposal, although she is the first to mention the word *marry*.

ERWIN: I'm sure glad that you didn't go back to Columbus.

MOORE: So am I. But I have to be leaving tomorrow.

ERWIN: Aw—but you don't have to. Look—I've got a lot of money now and I was going to ask you to—

MOORE: To *what*, Henry?

ERWIN: Well—you've been so awfully good to me—

MOORE (impatiently): You've already said that.

ERWIN: Yea, I know I have, but it's made me realize—

MOORE: What?

ERWIN (trying hard): That I—well—Mary Jane—As soon as this Conchita business is cleaned up, I want to ask you—(hesitates, loses his nerve)—something—

MOORE (tired of waiting for him to finish his sentences): Oh, I couldn't marry you till then anyway.

ERWIN: No, of course not—I—(recognition, does a double take and stands, facing her, still holding the glass of somewhat unhygienic milk): Mary Jane—You mean you will?

MOORE: Uh huh.

ERWIN: Oh, but I haven't even told you that I love you yet, nor how wonderful you are or—(smiles, totally unselfconscious)—well, now I have.

MOORE: It wasn't hard, was it?

ERWIN: No, (now with a determined earnestness and self-confidence) but if you knew how long I've been trying to *say* that. I gotta file suit for that annulment right away. We can't go on a honeymoon with Duke and Blackie popping up to kill me every now and then.[18]

Just as with his revelation to Mary Carlisle at the end of *Palooka*, Erwin refuses to allow the conversation to descend into the sentimental. He undercuts the romanticism of the scene with this sly, self-deprecating remark, while still making his emotional commitment believable.

IT'S ALL IN THOSE LEGS

Another clever but underrated film that represents Erwin's fascination with two women—one decent and practical, the other flirtatious and selfish—is *Mr. Boggs Steps Out* (1937). In this movie he plays Oliver Boggs, erstwhile employee of a company called American Statistics. With a mind like an adding machine, he has just won a bean-counting contest, coming within three of guessing the correct number of beans in a barrel—28,973. With his prize money of $1,500, he moves to Peckham Falls because he has seen an advertisement telling of a barrel factory for sale in this town. (There is something suggestive about the name of the town, but the symbolic suggestion is never really pursued.) Oliver Boggs is a man who has lived an introverted, quiet life, but who is nonetheless fond of people, open to friendships with both men and women, and willing to learn new things.

Arriving by train in Peckham Falls, Erwin walks toward the station, suitcase in hand, eager to buy the barrel factory and embark on a new, more adventurous life. He is thwarted in his stroll, however, when he collides with a beautiful blonde named Irene Lee (Toby Wing, who plays her "bad girl" part with just the right mixture of seductiveness and snobbishness, augmented by her musical, appealing Virginia accent). Although Wing is slender and looks deceptively soft, she takes him by surprise and knocks him flat on his back. Still sprawled on the pavement, clutching his suitcase, he apologizes to *her* for falling down. From his prone position, he removes his hat, while expressing regret, "I'm sorry, so sorry. I didn't see you," he explains. He then pulls himself up, as Toby Wing responds, "Well, I hope you do the next time."

ERWIN (gallantly oblivious to the sound of his next speech): I'd like to very much. You're beautiful. Are you married?

WING: No. I mean, it's none of your business.

ERWIN (still politely carrying his hat, while eagerly, earnestly following her): Oh, but it *is* my business. Do you realize that, according to the recent census, only 60 percent of those who have attained marriageable age are married? And the remaining 40 percent . . .

WING (impatiently turning to face him): *Must* you follow me?[19]

Chastened, Erwin replies, "Oh, I'm sorry. There was no one else to ask." Now Wing is curious. "Ask *what?*" she wants to know. Still bewitched by her presence, Erwin explains, "Where I can find the Peckham Falls Cooperage. You know—where they make barrels." Wing obviously finds that the subject of *barrels* is too proletarian an issue for her to concern herself with, so she answers indignantly, "Do *I* look like I'd know where they make *barrels?*" Here Erwin looks shamefaced and embarrassed, as he shakes his head and replies, almost inaudibly, "No." At this admission, Wing decides that their conversation is over, so she peremptorily dismisses him with an "All right,"[20] and struts off.

Erwin will continue to be obsessed with this sexy blonde, much to his ultimate disillusionment. In the meantime, his love-at-first-sight crush on Toby Wing is about to be complicated by the second woman whom he meets in Peckham Falls. She has the appallingly clumsy name of Oleander Tubbs (Helen Chandler). Although her first name suggests freshness (an evergreen shrub), *oleander* is also poisonous. And the combination of the Erwin/Chandler fictional surnames—Boggs and Tubbs—sounds as if it belongs to a third rate vaudeville act where the performers make music by drumming with spoons on metal buckets. Nor is their first meeting any less awkward than their names. Chandler is running the barrel factory that Erwin wants to buy, and when she first meets him, she sneezes in his face. Ever the professional statistician, Erwin informs her: "The ape can catch a cold from a human and vice versa." To which Chandler indignantly replies, "*Who's* an ape?"

ERWIN: I was merely stating a fact, Miss . . . Uh, what's your name, little girl?
CHANDLER: *Little girl!* I suppose you like fat women![21]

The pairing of Erwin and Chandler is worthy of note. He is soft, low key, methodical, and gentle; she is angular, frenzied, quick, and sharp. In point of fact, Helen Chandler was a skillful, appealing actress, who had worked in the early thirties in pictures such as *Dracula* and *The Last Flight*, both made in 1931. Her forte was the Woman as Victim; she had been especially effective in the latter picture as the only woman in an emotionally lost and wandering group of World War I aviators (Richard Barthelmess, David Manners, Elliott Nugent, and Johnny Mack Brown), trying to find something, anything, in postwar Europe. They adopt her as a sort of pet mascot in their Hemingwayesque journey through Europe in the twenties.

And she was indeed an appropriate choice to accompany these four psychically and physically wounded veterans, as Chandler herself was psychically fragile and brittle, with a nervous, trembling voice that always sounded on the edge of hysteria. She would have made an excellent Temple Drake in William Faulkner's *Sanctuary*, for she had just the right combination of ladylike softness neatly shackled to venality; such a pairing of paradoxical qualities would doubtless have enabled her to play Faulkner's tragically abused heroine. But the part went instead to Miriam Hopkins, a much stronger, more aggressive personality, in the nicely sanitized 1933 film adaptation, *The Story of Temple Drake*.

However, in *Mr. Boggs Steps Out,* Chandler has a lighter role than those to which she had been accustomed, as she falls for Erwin, whose boyish, kind, unworldly manner makes her feel competent, needed, less abrupt; he softens her, takes some of the edge off her. Only a few minutes after being introduced to Erwin, Chandler begins to like him in spite of herself. Holding out to him a bowl of fruit, she offers him an apple. He takes a banana instead, which he methodically peels and inexplicably sucks on throughout the subsequent scene between them. (Whose idea was it to have him eat a banana during their conversation?)

Chandler wants to know more about this strange, diffident man with a twinkle in his eye, so she asks him why he has come to Peckham Falls and why he wants to buy a barrel factory. To this he replies quite forthrightly: "I wanted to see something of life—to be somebody—to find excitement and romance." When Chandler tells him that he won't find much excitement in Peckham Falls, he tells her she's wrong. He mentions having been knocked down by a beautiful blonde who drives an expensive car. Chandler appears both jealous and appalled at this information, as she tells Erwin that the "lady" in question is Irene Lee, a woman of a very unpleasant disposition. Erwin expresses his disagreement with Chandler's evaluation; still pulling at that banana as though it were a lollipop, he says that Irene told him that she wasn't married. To which Chandler hastily replies, "Neither am I."

ERWIN (temporarily removing the banana from his mouth): I'm not surprised.

CHANDLER (defensive): What do you mean?

ERWIN: Statistics reveal that 70 percent of women employed in offices are not married.

CHANDLER (completely won over by his easy, genuine manner): That settles it. I'm going to stay. You need someone to look after you

ERWIN: Oh, that's fine. I feel that with your assistance, I'll be able to cope with anything.[22]

But Erwin is about to discover that he has to cope with more than he ever suspected, when Chandler tells him that the factory he has just bought is nearly broke. She adds that they had only one customer to speak of, a man named Ross (Tully Marshall), and that he is closing his canning and pickle factory. Although Mr. Boggs may be inexperienced with respect to business dealings, he is still a determined, hopeful individual, so he sets off, banana still in hand, to see Ross and persuade him to reconsider. As he is leaving, Chandler throws him the keys to her car, cautioning him to "miss as many things as you can." He smiles confidently as he rushes out. Ever the man who deals with theories rather than with the practical, he reassures her, "Oh, I'm an excellent driver. I took a correspondence course."[23]

When Erwin arrives at the Ross mansion (the banana has thankfully disappeared somewhere), he again encounters Toby Wing as the luscious Miss Lee. She is dressed in white shorts, which barely descend to her thighs and which adhere snugly to her hips, and a light-colored, tight sweater. In this scene with Erwin, Irene's Uncle Ross (Tully Marshall), and Dennis Andrews (Walter Byron), a friend of Ross and hopeful suitor to Irene, there is an effective, humorous use of mise en scène to reinforce our understanding of Oliver Boggs's character. As Erwin approaches the Ross home, he is pictured in the background and on the right; Ross appears in the background to the left of Erwin, but he is just a little closer to the camera; in the right foreground is Andrews. In the left foreground is Toby Wing as Irene. The only character who is completely visible is Erwin. Ross and Andrews are photographed so that only their torsos can be seen. Irene, Ross, and Andrews are standing on the steps of the Ross mansion, so that they appear taller than Erwin. Toby Wing is shot in profile, but only from the hips down to mid calf. Since she is in the foreground, poised on the top step (at least as much as the viewer can see of her), attention is focused on that part of her anatomy which is uncovered. But attention is also focused on Erwin, who has a clear view of her legs. From his position in the background right, he has an unobstructed line of sight to the foreground left, where the camera angle displays two of Toby Wing's most obvious attractions. Even though Erwin is in the background, deep-focus photography is used to reveal his expressions. While he politely holds his hat in front of him, he lets his eyes wander up and down, as though he were trying to decide where to center his concentration. At the same time, however, he gives a slight, impish smile and bites his lip, trying not to laugh.

Although Toby Wing clearly shows us that Irene does not have the same interest in Oliver as Oliver does in her, she nonetheless invites him to a community dance given by her Uncle Ross. Her invitation comes later in the film and is part of a plot hatched by her uncle and Dennis Andrews to steal the barrel business from Erwin, who has just decided that collapsible barrels, invented by Angus Tubbs, Oleander's father, are going to make a profit for the factory.

But, like Lupe Velez and Joan Woodbury in the two previous films, Toby Wing has ulterior motives in pursuing Erwin. Like these two other women, she is hoping to gain an advantage by capitalizing on his gentleness and decency. And, as with Velez and Woodbury, Erwin is at first taken in by her. By the same token, as in *Palooka* and *Passport Husband*, another woman is waiting for Erwin to finally demonstrate his intrinsic goodness and to propose to her by the final scene. In *Mr. Boggs* that woman is Helen Chandler, who is indeed quite bold in her pursuit of Erwin, once she has decided that she really loves him. There is even a quality about her audacious advances that suggests a deep hurt springing from something that Erwin has touched in her.

Such longing can be seen when Erwin comes to the office on his second day on the job. As he sits at his desk, she approaches him and stands to his left, looking at him suggestively. Suddenly, apropos of nothing, she leans over and asks provocatively, "Were you ever in love?" When he smiles shyly and replies that he has never been in such a situation, Chandler offers him an opportunity to do some role-playing. Psychologically, what she does is intriguing. She takes her fantasies about him and reveals these romantic visions to him, an action taking a certain amount of courage, for she exposes herself in this way and makes herself even more vulnerable. She sets up her fantasy as a hypothetical situation: "Well, supposing you saw a pretty girl walking down the street and the wind was blowing—would you look at her face or her ankles?"

ERWIN (hedging): Now, let me understand this. The wind is blow—

CHANDLER (leaning even closer): Perhaps I'd better put it in another way. Supposing you were on a plane and a beautiful girl rushed madly into your arms and said that she was yours—all yours—What would you do?

ERWIN: I'd ring for the porter.

CHANDLER: Mr. Boggs, you belong in the Smithsonian Institute.

ERWIN (with no hint of verbal irony): Oh, I've been there.[24]

At this point, Erwin's Oliver Boggs neither understands why Chandler is acting so aggressively nor comprehends the extent of Chandler's pain. Nor does he catch on when Toby Wing first appears at the barrel factory office to tempt Erwin with her invitation to the community dance. Nor does he pay attention to the fact that Chandler is most certainly jealous and resentful of Wing's presence. In fact, she mimics Wing's snobbish tone when the society lady inquires if Erwin is there. In reply, Chandler flips her head, deigning to look down her nose at Wing: "I'll call him."

When Erwin sees who is awaiting him in the office, he becomes so nervous and flustered that he no longer has any idea what his hands are for; they clearly get in his way as he gazes in awe at Irene Lee, who at least is now wearing a full complement of clothing. Angry, jealous, and halfway in love with Erwin, Chandler leaves with a disgusted flourish, announcing caustically, "I'm going over to the library—read a book on etiquette for the office girl." To which Erwin, hardly listening, replies distractedly, "Yes."[25]

One is reminded of Erwin and Velez in *Palooka* and of Erwin and Woodbury in *Passport Husband*; his awkward shyness with all three of these women is funny. There is something whimsical about his behavior in these three films as he tries to attract the notice of the sensual woman, who is invariably the one to make the first move. And Erwin evidently enjoys trading quips with his leading ladies, whether they are "loose" women on the make or "good" marriageable women. Yet there is also a painful, melancholy quality underlying his behavior with the opposite sex. If he often seems silly and foolish in their presence, he also wants to reach out to them as his equal, to appreciate them, to make them feel worthwhile and important. Further, as he does with the frenetic Helen Chandler, he attracts the decent women in part because he probes deep into their hard, defensive emotional barriers and melts them, without being fully aware of the effect that he is having.

But he is not destined to work such charm on Toby Wing, for she is as self-centered as he is selfless; she has her own reasons for inviting him to be her escort at the community dance. However, for the moment, Wing has Erwin completely fooled; on the surface, she is extremely alluring, with a graceful, elegant carriage, while her cherubic, open face belies the arrogant woman underneath. Still unsuspecting of her true motives, Erwin eagerly accepts and follows her to the door. Her invitation has given him the courage to do some inviting himself, so he asks her to go with him to the movies that evening: "Saturday being the only night that the motion picture palace is open, how would you like to go with me tonight? They are showing the last installment of *Going Wild*, and I'd like to see what happens to Quincy." Miss Lee hadn't expected such reciprocation, so she is caught off guard. But his obvious infatuation validates her high estimation of herself, so she agrees to go. As she is about to leave, Erwin's pragmatism and egalitarianism momentarily surface as he advises her: "You bring your car, and I'll buy the tickets."[26]

But Oliver Boggs will quickly learn some things about Irene Lee and her convoluted idea of what constitutes proper behavior. As with Velez and Woodbury in *Palooka* and *Passport Husband*, respectively, he discovers through an unsettling experience with Toby Wing that not all women are as open and honest with him as he is with them, nor necessarily deserving of his love and consideration. Erwin's education begins on his way to the community dance with Irene. When he sees a car broken down, he orders her to stop so that he can help. While Erwin is peering under the hood, the boy in the car amuses himself by siphoning the gas from Irene's car into his father's car, thus allowing all of those in the disabled vehicle to go on, but leaving Erwin and Wing stranded. She is formally dressed in a long white gown with a neckline that plunges as low as the censors would allow. Around her neck is a white fur piece; on her feet is a pair of high heels meant strictly for sitting and for showing to best advantage the calves of her very lovely legs, but never intended for walking. He doesn't look much more comfortable, dressed in a dark suit; however, it is natural to assume that he doesn't mind the walk quite as much.

In any event, Toby Wing's Irene Lee is really irate. Not only is she physically uncomfortable, but she is angry at Erwin for getting her into this fix in the first place and even angrier at herself for inviting him to come with her. She wants to show herself off and cannot do so on the deserted road that they are now being forced to hike down. As he plods along with her, Erwin doesn't as yet understand the absurdity of his position as the shadowy escort of Miss Narcissistic Personality of 1937, but he is about to learn. Finding a place by the roadside on which to sit, she gratefully eases herself down, rubs her feet, and reveals in her conversation that she hadn't really wanted to spend the evening with him after all:

WING: The next time you turn Good Samaritan, do it alone. It is too hard on my feet.

ERWIN (genuinely puzzled by her attitude): Why, Miss Lee. You act just like you were angry at me.

WING: Oh, skip it. It serves me right. I let myself in for it.

ERWIN: Let yourself in for what?

WING: I came along for the laughs, but now all I want to do is get to the dance, take my bow, and leave.

ERWIN (still willing to give her the benefit of the doubt): Oh, we can't do that. We should stay on with the rest of the folk.

WING: Oh—not *we*—*you*.

ERWIN: I don't understand. You asked me to be your escort.

WING (holding up the palms of both hands): Sure, that was just a gesture on my part.

ERWIN (holding out the palm of one hand, perhaps in an unconscious imitation of her motion): Gesture?

WING: Certainly. That little touch which proves to the natives the Ross family is not ritzy. (At this, she naturally turns up her nose while simultaneously turning away from Erwin)

ERWIN: Then you didn't want to spend the evening with me?

WING: My little angel of mercy—definitely, *no*.

Here, she stands and walks away from him.

ERWIN (left sitting disconsolately): I see.[27]

And so he does. Indeed, he sees so well that, by the time he arrives at the dance with her, he is ready to make a break with both her and the town itself. He announces to the crowd that while he was on the road trying to sell Angus Tubbs's collapsible barrels, he stopped in Washington and registered the patent for Tubbs's invention in daughter Oleander's name. So he willingly gives control of the factory to her. He also takes control in his dealings with Toby Wing, as he confronts her with his observations on her copious character flaws: "Before I leave town, Miss Lee, I am impelled to tell you that you are not as nice as you look." Now it is her turn to be on the defensive, but Erwin won't grant her the opportunity to protest, for he leaves her suspended on the hook from which he has hung her once he has knocked the erstwhile goddess off her pedestal. He delivers the final thrust when he calmly and methodically advises her, "There are over 10,000 institutions of higher learning in this country. I feel it would be well if you were to attend one until you grew up."[28]

Sixty-three years after she appeared in *Mr. Boggs Steps Out*, Toby Wing shared with me some memories of Erwin, whom she really liked, and of her part in the film. She said that she first heard about the part when her agent told her about an interview he had arranged for her for the role. He told her to dress so that she would look the way she thought Irene Lee should look. So Ms. Wing said that she got all dressed up and went to the interview, accompanied by her agent; she impressed Erwin with her alluring appearance and consequently got the job.[29] And she is indeed quite believable, both in dress and in manner, as a beautiful but conceited opportunist.

Erwin is not deceived for long by her external appearance, however. After he has chastised Wing for her immensely immature behavior, he turns to Chandler, who has been in love with him since she first saw him eating that banana in the factory office. Once again, the character created by Erwin is savvy enough to realize where his personal priorities should have been all along. He begins with a compliment, "That's a very pretty dress, Oleander."

CHANDLER: Well, it's a fine time to be noticing it.

ERWIN: You look very pretty, too. Do you know that 90 percent of all men suffer from myopic astigmatism?

CHANDLER: Oliver, what are you trying to tell me?

ERWIN: Well, that—love is blind.

CHANDLER: Well, did *you* know that over 99 percent of married men are controlled by their wives?

ERWIN: No, I didn't know that.

CHANDLER: Well, you will soon.[30]

Recognizing a proposal when he hears one, Erwin smiles bashfully and kisses her with a decidedly passionate embrace. But he next discovers that they are not alone, because people from the dance have come outside to witness their actions. They are grateful to Erwin, for he has just saved their jobs and his factory, so they applaud, calling for him to make a speech. But, as he had in *Palooka* and *Passport Husband*, Erwin undercuts the romantic mood of the scene by his last gesture: He moves toward the crowd, stepping up on a convenient, nearby barrel. As he does so, the barrel collapses, leaving him sprawled on the ground. But he appears unfazed by the crowd's laughter, as he reminds them from his reclining position, "It's collapsible."

And so Oliver Boggs saves Oleander Tubbs from spinsterhood, just as he rescues her from herself—from her psychological wounds, her deep-rooted fears of loneliness, her insecurities. He stabilizes her, gives her courage, helps her define herself.

Notwithstanding the boyish charm and vulnerability shown by Erwin in all three of these movies—*Palooka, Passport Husband,* and *Mr. Boggs Steps Out*—these three share some fine comic elements; we are not to read them as serious or tragic. In this connection, Erwin's self-abasing behavior at the conclusion of each transmits to us his conviction that we should laugh at the characters he has created. After all, these are, for the most part, satiric comedies.

In his book *The 7 Lively Arts*, Gilbert Seldes comments on the criteria for comedy: "The comic film is by nature adventurous and romantic, and I think what endears it to us is that the adventure is picaresque and the romance wholly unsentimental—that is, both are pushed to the edge of burlesque.... The characteristic moment, after all, is when the comedy is ended, and just as the hero is about to kiss the heroine he winks broadly and ironically at the spectators."[31] Indeed, we can see Erwin in all three of these movies as a kind of picaresque hero whose ridiculous adventures finally lead him to a satisfactory, albeit farcical, self-mocking conclusion.

UNREQUITED LOVE: STUCK IN THE MIDDLE

But Erwin was not always so lucky in his pursuit of a woman to appreciate him and to love him. Nor were his relations with women always as zany as they are in the three previous films. Two movies released in 1933 are good illustrations of Erwin's ability to show the sadness of a man who knows that his affection will never be reciprocated. In both *Going Hollywood* and *Hold Your Man* he loses a woman to a more aggressive rival: Marion Davies submits to Bing Crosby in the first instance, and Jean Harlow surrenders to Clark Gable in the second.

Going Hollywood is generally a fun, upbeat movie, unlike *Hold Your Man*, which is almost unrelentingly grim. Marion Davies was a talented comedienne, as was Jean Harlow, but Davies lacked Harlow's hardness and cynicism. Playing a woman named Sylvia Bruce in *Going Hollywood*, Davies has a wistful quality about her that naturally appeals to the softness in Stuart Erwin, who portrays movie producer Ernest P. Baker. This enthusiastic, childlike quality of Davies is evident from the beginning of the movie, when she quits her job as a French instructor at a private girls' school so that she might devote her time to listening to Bill Williams (Bing Crosby) singing on the radio while she fantasizes about how much she loves him. Nor is her wide-eyed eagerness cloying; Davies gives to her character the romantic dreaminess of adolescence without its accompanying predilection for weepy sentimentality.

Even as she later shamelessly breaks in on Crosby's privacy by entering his hotel room, resembling a fan whom we would today call a *stalker* or a *groupie*, she appears neither arrogant, intrusive, nor hysterical. She gently tells Crosby that she has just come by to thank him for what he did for her the night before when she was still at Miss Briarcroft's School, listening to him on the radio. When he tells her that he is packing to go to Hollywood, she decides to follow him by getting on the same train.

But Stuart Erwin is the first to locate Crosby on that train; he enters Crosby's drawing room and timidly tells him how glad he is that Crosby is going to be in his picture. Shortly after Erwin leaves, Davies enters, much to Crosby's surprise and consternation; she persists in thanking him for the favor he did her on the previous night through his radio singing. "I'm terribly in love with you, and I wondered—what are we going to do about it?"[32] she quizzes Crosby. As she is unashamedly declaring her love for him, Erwin reappears, looking for Conroy (Ned Sparks), a movie executive who has been trying to dodge Erwin, tired of hearing Erwin proclaim that movies should be an art, not a business.

But while Davies is throwing herself at Crosby, Erwin is looking carefully but shyly at this woman who is dressed like a schoolgirl in a dark, long sleeved dress with a large, white bow tied at the neck and covering both breasts—which would not be exposed in any event. "You know," he tells her sincerely, "I thought maybe you were an actress, or a beauty prize winner on your way to Hollywood." As he says this, he looks directly into her eyes and she returns his gaze, repaying his compliment without a hint of irony by asking, "Are *you* an actor or a beauty prize winner?"[33] In fact, Davies's earnestness in this movie makes credible the clichéd plot of the unknown hopeful who becomes a movie star when she replaces the leading lady. Although her dancing is lumbering—she looks as though she had taken dancing lessons from Ruby Keeler—her enthusiasm is infectious. And although, like Keeler, she clumps along as if she had fifteen-pound weights attached to her ankles, we can still see how she would be appealing on screen.

The next time that Davies and Erwin appear together, Davies is thoroughly irritated by Crosby's attentions to his leading lady Lili Yvonne (Fifi D'Orsay). So when she meets Erwin outside Crosby's train compartment, she is ready for a frolic with another man. Erwin is only too happy to oblige, as he is armed with two liquor bottles, one in each hand. Brandishing these, he invites her to have a drink with him. We jump to his compartment, where he and Davies are now comfortably settled side by side, on their way to getting pleasantly tanked. Sympathizing with Davies's lovelorn state and crying due to his alcohol-induced melancholy, Erwin tells her of his own lost love, which he vaguely assigns to some time in the past. "I know just how you feel," he says in a sloppy attempt to be comforting. "I was in love once."

DAVIES: What happened?

ERWIN: She married a man from Philadelphia.

DAVIES (awkwardly sympathizing): Oh, that's awful.[34]

In spite of his realization that he is attracted to Davies, Erwin is enough of a gentleman (albeit an inebriated one) to try to commiserate with her. He reassures her that she will eventually be able to land her one true love in the person of Crosby. Indeed, he even helps her to catch him; such cooperation occurs in the scene described in the introduction where both Erwin and Crosby invite Davies to the same party. Only after Erwin has asked her out does Crosby get the idea to do the same. So Crosby suggests that they flip a coin to see who will win her, but he has to borrow the coin from Erwin. It is at this point that Erwin graciously "remembers" a previous engagement for that evening, leaving the way open for Davies to snare Crosby. As the three part—Davies and Crosby happy about the outcome, Erwin resigned to the knowledge that he has undoubtedly lost Davies forever—Erwin does ask Crosby if he might at least have his half dollar back.

So all ends satisfactorily in *Going Hollywood*. Davies is a success in the movie role that Erwin has given her, Davies and Crosby find true love at last, and Erwin is left with—well, with his half dollar and a hit movie—and the comfort of knowing that the latter will probably earn him a lot of money.

It is easy to see how Erwin could fall for Davies in this film, although off screen she was some years his senior and was already showing signs of physical deterioration as a result of her increasingly debilitating alcoholism. One has only to compare her physical appearance in this movie with her bearing and expression in *Show People* (1928), a silent movie made only five years before. In *Show People*, she again plays a movie hopeful; this time she is befriended by a young, handsome William Haines. But in this earlier movie her wistfulness is coupled with a more genuine energy level. In *Going Hollywood*, she seems to be trying too hard, as though she had to pump herself up to the task, especially in her musical numbers. Davies's career was faltering by the time she made *Going Hollywood*; and, although she had hoped that this movie would revive her fading popularity, it did nothing to enhance her reputation.

UNREQUITED LOVE: NO WAY OUT

Whereas *Going Hollywood* is an entertaining, if somewhat dated, musical, *Hold Your Man* is one of the harshest movies that Erwin ever made. It is one of the few roles in which he gives no hint of humor whatsoever. He plays the part of Al Simpson, who is so blindly, madly, completely in love with Ruby Adams (Jean Harlow) that he is eager to overlook her obvious character flaws—moral blemishes which the average man would not even pretend to condone. And he plays the part without a hint of self-consciousness or even a suggestion of embarrassment at Al Simpson's total selflessness. As a result, one feels sympathy for the man's sincerity and its attendant generosity toward a woman who does not seem to deserve such largesse.

The major complication established by the Anita Loos' screenplay involves Jean Harlow's falling for con artist Eddie Hall (Clark Gable) at the beginning of the movie. He and his partner Slim (Garry Owen) have just pulled a con on a stranger, but the stranger quickly catches on that he has been had; he enlists the aid of a cop and the two of them chase Gable into an apartment building. When Gable finds one of the apartments conveniently unlocked, he enters it, where he finds Harlow taking a bath. (Why does she leave her door unlocked when she decides to bathe? Was she expecting some other company?) Although she feigns anger and embarrassment at being discovered, she is still intrigued enough with Gable to protect him from the cop and the con victim when these two enter her apartment looking for him. She is something of a shady character herself, and she knows a kindred spirit when she sees one.

After his pursuers leave and while he is waiting for his wet pants to dry (he had hidden in the tub, pretending to be her husband), he inspects his surroundings and sees a picture of Harlow's boyfriend Erwin, so he knows that he has a rival. But he recognizes Harlow's type, just as she has recognized his, so he has no doubts about his ability to make her surrender to him. But not yet, not now. That will come later, with everlasting consequences. At this moment, when Gable has a chance, he exits her apartment through a back room while Harlow is talking to a female visitor in the front. Once she realizes that she is again alone, Harlow goes to her coin bank and shakes it, pleased when she hears change still rattling inside. The lady knows a thief when she sees one.

She also knows an opportunity for danger and excitement when she sees it, so she arranges to have devoted boyfriend Erwin repeatedly take her to a nightclub that Gable has mentioned by name as one that he frequents. When Erwin first appears in this film, he is supporting Harlow on his arm as they enter the club and innocently asking her why they have to come to this particular place each time they go out. She brushes him off by announcing that she is going to the ladies' room. Here it is apparent that she and Gable are truly meant for each other, for she carries out a maneuver of which Gable would have approved. Once she is in the bathroom and unseen (or so she thinks), she removes some money from her purse, thrusts it down the V-neck of her dress, and throws the purse in with the dirty towels. The purpose behind her apparently odd behavior becomes clear when she returns to the table and tells Erwin that she cannot find her purse. Naturally concerned, he asks, "Was there much money in it?" Pouting, Harlow replies, "Yes, that's what's worrying me. Twenty-five dollars. It was my rent money." As he reaches out to hold her hand, he calms her, saying, "Aw, don't you worry your little head about it anymore. I'll give you the twenty-five dollars for your rent."

HARLOW (feigning reticence): No, Al. I can't let you do that. You're always doing something for me.

ERWIN: I like to do things for you, Ruby. Here—let's have a drink and forget all about it. And tomorrow I'll get you a pocketbook that's got a lock 'n chain on it.[35]

But Harlow's game plan is subverted at this point when a maid at the club (Louise Beavers) appears at their table, Harlow's pocketbook in hand. "I seen you throw this in the dirty towels. Can I have it?" she asks the disconcerted Harlow. Ruby makes a halfhearted attempt at resistance, while we see a close-up of Erwin, whose face registers surprise, disappointment, and anguish as he waves the maid on with a brusque "You can have it." Harlow is now truly on her guard, though all she can manage are a few sputtering, nearly inaudible remarks about the nerve of the maid. Erwin will have none of that, however, for *he* comes to *her* defense, soothing her with, "You don't have to do that to me, Ruby. You can have anything I've got."[36] He reaches into his wallet to give her the twenty-five dollars, pressing it into her hand.

On the surface, his response seems unmanly, wrongheaded, and stupid, but Erwin pulls it off. Never one given to gushing sappiness, his honesty comes through, touching the Harlow character, in spite of her surface hardness. When she asks, somewhat remorsefully, "Ain't you sore at me?" his reply, "No, I'm not sore," reveals that he has both a better command of standard English usage and a better, more forgiving moral sensibility than she. He proceeds to give her an insight into herself as well as an appreciation of his own innate goodness by explaining, "You aren't the kind of a girl you make out to be, Ruby. You've been pushed into these things. I'd like to take you out of all this. You know, Cincinnati is an awful nice place, and I've got a darned good job."[37]

He continues to try to persuade her to look beyond her self-absorption, explaining how "swell" his boss is (we never do learn exactly what Erwin does) and how he hopes that he won't have to travel forever. When he even offers her a home, she blanches, reminding him that she's "been around." Her expression is obviously a substitution for "slept around," which in itself is eu-

phemistic, but 1933 Hollywood, even before strict enforcement of the Production Code, was compelled to use a euphemism to replace another euphemism. But never mind. The thirty-year-old Stuart Erwin, still a reminder
to 1933 audiences of the free spirited Lost Generation, knows what she
means, so he quickly interrupts her, "Let's don't talk about that. Let's talk
about you and me."[38]

It becomes evident at this moment, however, that Harlow no longer
wants to talk to Erwin at all, because she has just seen her risky, adventurous
knight enter the club. So while Erwin continues chattering about the beauties of the countryside surrounding Cincinnati, Harlow has fixated on Gable,
whose attention she hastily grabs. She summons him to their table, explaining to the understandably curious Erwin that Gable is an "old" friend. In
truth, Erwin is generous enough and trusting enough not to suspect anything when Gable asks if he has Erwin's permission to dance with Harlow.
So they leave Erwin sitting alone, as the camera follows their movement onto
the dance floor. It is obvious from their conversation that each has designs
on the other; both are attracted to the danger inherent in beginning a relationship, which clearly is going to involve sex—and soon. Gable's ego is particularly soothed when Harlow hints that she has been searching for him; she
does this by chastising him for not coming to that club—one of his favorite
hangouts—in a month.

"How do you know?" he asks, now alert to her spying activities. Nor is
he at all subtle when he calls her "Sweetmeat" and shows his lack of finesse
as he bluntly invites her to his place for sex: "How about you and I getting
together tonight, huh?" He boldly demands that she dump Erwin by complaining of a "headache" (as in, "Not tonight, dear, I have a headache."—not
that the gentlemanly Erwin would have made demands requiring such a response from her). So Harlow returns to the table with her anxious escort; her
"headache" becomes a "pain in the side," which Erwin is duly concerned
about as he offers to take her home.

But not before he gets taken once again by Gable—this time for the
cost of the check ($2.25) plus ten dollars. Gable proposes that they play "bill
poker," which involves getting the winning "hand" of serial numbers on a
dollar bill—a game allegedly based largely on luck—that is, unless this luck
is bolstered by the bill that Gable has squirreled away for just such opportunities as his most recent sucker presents. After Erwin loses $12.25 to Gable's
"six nine's," Harlow wryly observes to Gable that his bill would certainly be
worth saving.

One has to wonder at this point at Erwin's naiveté; how could a man
live to be his age and not catch on? Yet if one looks closely, it is apparent that

Erwin is playing this scene tongue-in-cheek. He is not that dumb; in fact, he has already demonstrated that he knows the rules of poker, but he has hitherto crafted the character of Al Simpson as a man not given to anger. Rather than display hostility when he is cornered, he either backs off from it (as he has done when Harlow's missing pocketbook turned up) or he pretends that he doesn't get it. He makes the latter choice in this instance.

Gable and Harlow, however, are not especially interested in contemplating the subtleties of Erwin's character at this moment. Their hormones require them to concentrate on other pastimes. In due course, Harlow arrives at Gable's apartment later that evening—and she is still there in the morning. In this connection, Mark Vieira's book *Sin in Soft Focus: Pre-Code Hollywood* presents some historical insights into this film, originally titled *Black Orange Blossoms*. For instance, as the "morning after" scene was originally filmed, Harlow was seen in Gable's dark colored bathrobe.[39] But by the time the movie was released, Harlow had been required to appear the following morning still implausibly wearing the tight-fitting white evening dress she had worn the evening before, when she had begun her date with a different man from the one she ended the night with. She also has kept intact her silk stockings and her high heels. The only obvious part of her apparel that she has removed is her hat and gloves.

As we later piece together the causal links of the plot, we deduce that this is the night Harlow gets pregnant. Since her fancy evening attire looks as fresh and unruffled and form-fitting as it had on the previous evening, the audience is left to assume that the coarse Gable has been very careful in its removal and that she has been equally careful in restoring it early the next morning. Both of these actions seem very implausible. In any case, the decision to change Harlow's "morning after" outfit, wrought by the censorship of the time, makes the events of that night somewhat improbable.

In the meantime, Erwin's character disappears for a while as the focus switches to Gable's illegal activities. He goes to jail for ninety days for getting caught with a stolen car. Harlow doesn't forget him, though, for she loyally visits him, having apparently forgotten about the devoted Erwin, who we assume is traveling somewhere for his unnamed company. But Gable is much more charming and appealing to Harlow than the boring and dependable Erwin, so as soon as Gable serves his time, she participates in another scam with Gable and Slim, his old partner from the early scenes. This time the three try to extort money from a man whom Harlow sets up and leads on. But the con goes horribly awry and turns violent, with Gable slugging the belligerent, overweight, middle-aged man, who lands in the hallway outside the Gable/Harlow apartment. Having disposed of this annoyance,

Gable leads Harlow to a nearby city hall, where they obtain a marriage license, perhaps in the hope that they will settle into respectability and live happily ever after. But not yet.

In the course of the next few incidents, it is possible to see the source of the movie's earlier title, *Black Orange Blossoms*. First, the apartment neighbors discover that the body littering their hall is not merely unattractively lying in disarray but is also dead. Next, a neighbor spots Harlow and Gable in the crowd outside the building and points out Harlow as one who had just recently been seen with the deceased. Harlow tries to run away, but is nabbed; Gable appears to desert her, as he has the good fortune to be faster and therefore disappears into the crowd, leaving her to her fate: pregnant and destined to be sent to a women's reformatory. And Stuart Erwin is still blissfully traveling, somewhere out of camera range.

From this point onward, there is an intriguing motif that informs the film. This motif is part feminist, part anticapitalist, and part naturalistic, with echoes of the fiction of Theodore Dreiser as a part of the third category. The feminist pattern emerges when Harlow arrives at the reformatory and meets other women who are there, like her, because of their submission to the wrong men. From their dialogue, it is clear that all are sexually experienced (one has given birth to her baby in the reformatory, an activity that Harlow herself is painfully anticipating), that all enjoy the comforts provided them by men, and that most have no intention of reforming.

The anticapitalist motif is introduced by one of the inmates, a fiery soapbox socialist, forever raving about the evils of capitalism. As a part of her harangue, she argues that it was their social class that brought these women to this place, that high society dames don't land in reformatories. There is also some bitter social commentary about the options open to women of any class at this time, one of the worst years of the depression. To illustrate, Harlow is pictured being taught skills previously unfamiliar to her. Supposedly, this instruction will prepare her for her reentry into the outside world: she works at a treadle machine learning how to sew, and she is herded with the other women into a room full of stoves where, they are told, they will learn how to bake "angel food" cake. What the well-meaning, aging instructors of these classes fail to teach these ladies is how they are to go about getting money to buy either sewing apparatus or stoves.

Additionally, these prison matrons are reminders to 1933 viewers of the settlement house workers of the teens and twenties, individuals who were often targets of radical social commentators of the day. These leftist advocates were harsh critics of the so-called settlement house social reformers. According to this critical view, these liberal settlement workers allegedly wanted to help the poor immigrant slum dwellers; however, this view also argued that these same reformers were merely do-gooders, interested not in raising the economic status of the poor, but rather in forcing this underclass to assimilate its people into the customs of the more privileged class.

In addition to these echoes of early twentieth-century social criticism, there are also some stereotypical characterizations found among the prisoners; for instance, the women whom Harlow meets represent a partial cross section of lower and working class women, circa 1933. These women contribute to the movie's naturalistic motif. Among these is a young, gentle little black girl named Lily Mae (Theresa Harris), in addition to the aforementioned socialist. There is also a Jewish woman, on whose arm may be seen a dark band prominently decorated with the Star of David. In addition, Harlow is angered to see Gypsy (Dorothy Burgess), a loud, hysterical, preening alcoholic and former girlfriend of Gable's, who has been introduced earlier in the movie when she visits Gable's apartment with Slim and another woman. Gypsy immediately recognizes her rival and she taunts her about Gable, showing Harlow his picture, which she proudly displays. And Harlow, in turn, can do little to retaliate except throw her own insults. The reintroduction of the character of Gypsy serves to remind the viewer of what a jerk Gable can be, for Gypsy boasts that Gable had recently given her money. But the ongoing battle between Gypsy and Harlow—a battle that actually culminates with both women physically assaulting each other—both represents and reemphasizes the desperation of all of these women. Indeed, all of them embody a major tenet of the naturalist philosophy; for such women as these, there is no way out.

Into this gloomy environment comes Erwin, returning to offer Harlow a second chance. And once again, Erwin expertly plays a scene that could have turned maudlin and made him look quite senseless. Instead, he underplays his concern for Harlow. The resultant contrast between her desperation, bordering on hysterics, and his quiet soothing manner, in a voice at times nearly inaudible, leaves the viewer emotionally on edge. Further, although she tells the matron that she doesn't want to see him, and although she reluctantly approaches him after they are left alone, she is clearly torn between her gratitude for him and her certainty that she does not deserve his unconditionally generous offer.

He begins the scene by hesitantly apologizing for not coming to her earlier: "I'd 'a been here sooner if I'd only known about this. I sent you about ten letters from Cincinnati, but they all came back. I only found out this happened when I got back from New York day before yesterday." Here he takes her hand, "Aw, gee, Ruby, I'm sorry."[40] Moreover, Erwin subtlety conveys just what it is that he is sorry for. First and most obvious, he regrets not knowing how to contact her. Next, as we are about to discover, he is sorry for the two circumstances which are clearly causing Ruby so much pain: her incarceration and her pregnancy.

But Harlow will have none of his pity, as she roughly pulls her hand away, replying sardonically, "Thanks, Al." Erwin will not be put off so easily, however, so he continues, "I've got so many things to tell you, I don't know where to begin." Harlow is wary of kindness, for she has received so little in the past. Further, she has found that traditional avenues of hope such as the church offer even less in the way of comfort. So her reply to Erwin echoes the nihilism of the naturalists: "Now don't start to preach. I'm sick 'a preachin'." But Erwin has not a hint of cynicism or hypocrisy in his nature; consequently, he can reassure her, "I didn't come here to preach to you. You mustn't get like that." Once again Harlow becomes arrogant and defensive in her reply: "I'd like to see how you'd get if you were in here for awhile." Her sharp retort gives Erwin the opportunity he needs to offer Harlow a way out: "Ruby, you don't have to stay here any longer. I want you to marry me. They say if you marry me, you can get out on parole."[41]

At this, Harlow turns on him, repaying his kindness with another insult, "So you figured you'd give me a break, eh? That's *nice* of you. Thanks." Ignoring her rudeness, Erwin makes her an offer that seems too good to refuse: "I'm staying in Cincinnati for good now. They made me general manager of the firm. I thought I'd get a little house outside the city, if I could get you to come back with me. Oh Ruby, you'll like it there. You and the boss's dau ..." But Harlow angrily interrupts him, "Why don't you *marry* the boss's daughter." Still remaining calm and soothing in the face of Harlow's mounting, aggressive, irrational hostility, Erwin reminds her, " 'Cause I love you."[42]

By this point, Harlow clearly feels that she deserves not sympathy and love but violence and loathing. Indeed, her self-hatred has become almost too much for her to bear, as she screams, now nearly hysterical: "*Love* me? *Love* me? I could tell you something right now that'd make you turn your back on me and run away from me just as fast as ... "[43]

But Erwin knows what she is about to say. Apparently, one of the matrons has told him about Harlow's pregnancy, because he quickly rejoins, "No, you couldn't." When Harlow insists by saying, "Oh, couldn't I? Well, I'm gonna have a ... " he replies very softly, his last word almost inaudible, "I know what you're gonna say." Then he persists, "Will you marry me, Ruby?" Now truly fearful that she might give in to him and completely baffled by his gentleness, she finally lashes out, "What are you trying to do—be a hero? Or have you just gone crazy? Will you get outta here and forget me?

I never wanna see you again." By the end of their scene together, the last one that they will share in the movie, both Harlow and Erwin have left one with a feeling of utter hopelessness. In fact, one is tempted to jump, a la Woody Allen, into the frame of the film, shake Harlow by the shoulders, and shout, "Take him! Gable is a loser! Come to your senses! Think better of yourself!" But when the matron enters and tells Erwin, "She's simply incorrigible. You'd better go," it is clear that there is nothing anyone can do to save Harlow from herself. After Erwin leaves, Harlow sobs to the matron, "He's too good for me."[44] Yes indeed.

In due course, Harlow is reunited with Gable, who marries her while she is still in the reformatory. They legitimize their relationship just in time for Gable to go to prison; this time, when he is finally released, Harlow is waiting for him, their baby in her arms. And she has good news for the proud, suddenly respectable daddy; Erwin has good-naturedly offered him a job with his firm in Cincinnati, so Gable, Harlow, and baby can live happily ever after. Or can they? Only the most hopeful, romantic idealist would be pleased with this naturalistic ending, satisfactory only on the most superficial level, and probably pleasing to the many fans of Gable and Harlow in 1933.

Twenty-five years earlier, the naturalistic American novelist Theodore Dreiser had written a short story called "The Second Choice." In this story, there is a triangle similar to the one created by Anita Loos in *Hold Your Man*. Although the woman in this story, Shirley, lives a dull, middle-class existence in a small town in Ohio, she is like Harlow's Ruby Adams in that she falls for a good-looking, dangerous, irresponsible man who lies to her, treats her badly, gets her pregnant, writes her a self-serving farewell letter, and deserts her. In the meantime, her boring, phlegmatic, dependable, adoring boyfriend, Barton Williams, waits for her. Like Ruby Adams, Shirley has a very low self-image, so she ultimately settles for Barton when she is forced to admit that her knight-in-shining armor (appropriately named Arthur) will not return. For Shirley, her "second choice" is really no choice at all, and Dreiser makes it clear that Shirley is doomed to spend the rest of her days as a housewife, forever setting the dinner table, waiting for her dutiful husband to return from work and her five children or so to return from their activities.

One incident in the story that clearly defines Shirley's predicament occurs when she visits Barton's place of work. She is determined to return to him, since she has just resigned herself to the knowledge that Arthur will not return, and because she also realizes that she absolutely must have some man to marry. So she approaches him and waits till he looks up from his work, convinced that he still loves her, that he will take her back, and that he still makes her sick. Dreiser's description of the lovelorn Barton could very well be a description of Erwin's Al Simpson: "The infatuation of the discarded Barton was such that it brought him instantly to his feet. In his stodgy, stocky way he rose, his eyes glowing with a friendly hope, his mouth wreathed in smiles, and came over. At the sight of her, pale, but pretty—paler and prettier, really, than he had ever seen her—he thrilled dumbly."[45]

Even though these two women are from different backgrounds and social classes, both are betrayed by con men with whom they have had sexual relations, both are excited by the dangers inherent in their involvement with such men (and the illicit sex just enhances this thrill), and both are offered unconditional love by dull, decent, dependable men. Furthermore, both are attractive, a fact that makes them especially vulnerable to predatory men. But, unlike Dreiser's Shirley, Harlow has navigated so many winding, twisted, deadly roads that she has no illusions and no hope. She is no virgin when she allows Gable to seduce her. Shirley, on the other hand, is an innocent, sheltered, middle-class girl, an only child accustomed to having her own way. So when the charming Arthur takes advantage of her, she tries to convince herself that her beauty will keep him from straying—even as she desperately realizes that the narcissistic Arthur will soon desert her.

Moreover, it appears that both the film and the short story have naturalistic endings. In point of fact, Dreiser's gloomy work seems to have the more naturalistic conclusion, with Shirley trapped both by her biology and by her second-class status as a woman in 1918 America and thus forced to settle for a loveless, unexciting marriage with a steady man who adores her. Since her abandonment by Arthur, Shirley's self-image has dropped so low she is convinced that she deserves nothing better than Barton. He becomes the embodiment of her self-flagellation. Harlow is also convinced of her own worthlessness, but in her situation, it is the good man whom she feels she does not deserve.

Thus, a close examination of *Hold Your Man* reveals an even more insidious tone than the one found in the Dreiser work, for Harlow chooses to marry Gable while simultaneously seeing him led off to prison. Then, when he reemerges as a "new man," ready to accept Erwin's job offer, one is supposed to believe, along with Harlow, that all will be well for the happy couple.

But perhaps not. Harlow's future with Gable will be less secure than Shirley's with Barton. By the movie's finish, Harlow is still speeding recklessly down that narrow, twisted road—with no guardrails and with a one-hundred-foot drop on either side. Her chances of crashing her vehicle through the rail and exiting this pathetic world are quite conceivable. Shirley, on the other hand, will have Barton to stabilize her. Paradoxically, then, Dreiser's conclusion is more optimistic. When Shirley grows out of her adolescent romanticism, she will doubtless come to realize that the world is composed of a series of monotonous events. Harlow will not live long enough to realize anything. Nonetheless, it is still devilishly tempting to give the film a final, satiric, absurd twist by imagining the finish of this snug scenario as something entirely different, with Harlow/Gable/Erwin ultimately establishing a ménage à trois, thus shocking the natives of conservative Cincinnati.

Through all of this, Stuart Erwin gives a remarkable performance in a thankless role, a performance that few actors could have carried off so well. It is especially exceptional when one considers that Erwin is up against that great lover, Clark Gable, and that he easily subjects himself to an insignificant position so that Gable and Harlow can have at one another. But before he concedes defeat, he does gallantly try to win Harlow's devotion, if not her love. Though he knows that the woman he loves is a whore, he still reasons that what she needs is constancy and a chance to think better of herself. He plays their scenes together seriously, without a hint of sarcasm or irony. And because he believes in himself, he believes in her as well. There is not one false note in his pleas to her to accept his love; he is neither foolish nor pitiful, simply honest about his feelings. But Harlow's philosophy is too naturalistic, too rooted in the concept that the outside world is at best indifferent and at worst malevolent. She refuses Erwin's offer of salvation because she knows that there is no such thing.

One has only to contrast Erwin's achievement opposite Harlow in this film with his happy-go-lucky scenes opposite Lupe Velez in the aforementioned *Palooka* to appreciate his flexibility. In *Palooka*, the character played by Velez is also a whore and Erwin knows it, but at the outset of their relationship, he is having too much fun playing around to offer her any semblance of respectability. He kids with her about sex because, at least at first, sex is all he wants. What he wants from Harlow goes way past sex to fix upon something which even Erwin cannot kid her about. He wants to dig deep into her subconscious, to bring into the open her defense mechanisms, to lay bare her soul, to rid her of her psychic pain. In essence, he wants to redeem her from herself, much as he will later save Helen Chandler in *Mr. Boggs*. But Harlow's pain flows too deep; they both know that she would drown him in it. If Stuart Erwin leads us to realize that he will forget the sensual, but self-centered trio of Lupe Velez, Joan Woodbury, and Toby Wing in about a week or so, and that he will even forget the more vulnerable Marion Davies in time, he also silently communicates that he will remember Harlow forever.

A few years after he worked with Harlow, and shortly before Harlow's death in 1937, Erwin had the following curiously ambiguous comment to make about three of his female costars, including Harlow: "Girls like Jean

Harlow, Carole Lombard and Claudette Colbert—you can't expect mere men to talk back to them, to deny them anything they may set their hearts on. Even when they are wrong no man would have the heart to tell them they were anything but right."[46] Perhaps the real-life Erwin would never have pursued quite so eagerly the real-life Harlow. But he was too polite to have put it exactly that way.

NOTES

1. Andrew Sarris, *You Ain't Heard Nothin' Yet: The American Talking Film* (New York: Oxford University Press, 1998), 228.

2. *Palooka*. Dir. Benjamin Stoloff. United Artists, 1934.

3. *Palooka*, 1934.

4. *Palooka*, 1934.

5. *Palooka*, 1934.

6. *Palooka*, 1934.

7. *Palooka*, 1934.

8. *Palooka*, 1934.

9. *Palooka*, 1934.

10. *Palooka*, 1934.

11. *Passport Husband*. Dir. James Tinling. 20th Century Fox, 1938.

12. *Passport Husband*, 1938.

13. *Passport Husband*, 1938.

14. *Passport Husband*, 1938.

15. *Passport Husband*, 1938.

16. *Passport Husband*, 1938.

17. *Passport Husband*, 1938.

18. *Passport Husband*, 1938.

19. *Mr. Boggs Steps Out*. Dir. Gordon Wiles. Grand National, 1938.

20. *Mr. Boggs Steps Out*, 1938.

21. *Mr. Boggs Steps Out*, 1938.

22. *Mr. Boggs Steps Out*, 1938.

23. *Mr. Boggs Steps Out*, 1938.

24. *Mr. Boggs Steps Out*, 1938.

25. *Mr. Boggs Steps Out*, 1938.

26. *Mr. Boggs Steps Out*, 1938.

27. *Mr. Boggs Steps Out*, 1938.

28. *Mr. Boggs Steps Out*, 1938.

29. Toby Wing, letter to author, 10 June 2000.

30. *Mr. Boggs Steps Out*, 1938.

31. Gilbert Seldes, *The 7 Lively Arts* (New York: Sagamore Press, 1957), 23–24.

32. *Going Hollywood*. Dir. Raoul Walsh. M-G-M, 1933.

33. *Going Hollywood*, 1933.

34. *Going Hollywood*, 1933.

35. *Hold Your Man*. Dir. Sam Wood. M-G-M, 1933.

36. *Hold Your Man*, 1933.

37. *Hold Your Man*, 1933.

38. *Hold Your Man*, 1933.

39. Mark Vieira, *Sin in Soft Focus: Pre-Code Hollywood* (New York: Harry Abrams, 1999), 142.

40. *Hold Your Man*, 1933.

41. *Hold Your Man*, 1933.

42. *Hold Your Man*, 1933.

43. *Hold Your Man*, 1933.

44. *Hold Your Man*, 1933.

45. "The Second Choice," in *American Tradition in Literature*, ed. George Perkins and Sculley Bradley, 7th ed., Vol. 2 (New York: McGraw-Hill, 1990), 872.

46. Martha Kerr, "Women Are Trouble," *Modern Screen* (November 1936): 94.

6

THE REPORTER

"I knew you were a reporter—you had that dumb look."

—Kitty McHugh to Stuart Erwin in *Women Are Trouble*
(1936)

The fast-talking, jaded, prying newsman is a familiar character in American film. Actors as varied in style and ability as Pat O'Brien, Adolph Menjou, Lew Ayres, Spencer Tracy, Lee Tracy, Edward G. Robinson, Clark Gable, Cary Grant, Rosalind Russell, James Cagney, Paul Muni, and Glenda Farrell have successfully worked in the genre, each bringing his or her own personality to the role of the probing journalist. When Stuart Erwin depicted such a reporter, as he did in many films, he often combined a cynical need to exploit his sources for his own advantage with an understanding of the frailties of human nature.

VIVA!

One of Stuart Erwin's best-known reporter movies is *Viva Villa!* (1934). In this film, he plays a character almost totally lacking in scruples. It is largely an unsympathetic, complex role that he handles well. Interestingly, he was not the original choice to play the reporter who goes to Mexico and trails after Pancho Villa (Wallace Beery), hoping that Villa will be good, colorful copy. There are various, conflicting stories concerning how Erwin came to play the part of Johnny Sykes in this movie, which was generally successful with both critics and the public.

145

What is not in question is that Lee Tracy, who had been scheduled to appear as the reporter, got into some trouble on location in Mexico, where cast and crew had initially gone for the filming. One movie fan magazine of 1934 simply states that Tracy "spoke out of turn" and that the "clever comedian" Stuart Erwin was given the break that he "could use nicely."[1] On the other hand, the movie critic for *Newsweek*, in a 1934 review, gives the following lengthier, but less accurate, version. For instance, the reviewer states unequivocally but erroneously that *Wallace Beery* replaced Lee Tracy, who had been scheduled to play the *lead*, of all things. (Lee Tracy as Pancho Villa!) No mention is made anywhere in the review of Stuart Erwin, who was the actual replacement for Tracy. Was Erwin so invisible that he disappeared completely from the cast? Yet this review is typical of the way in which Erwin was often completely ignored or simply missed altogether by critics. According to this startlingly mistaken appraisal, published in the issue of April 14, 1934:

> It was probably all for the best that Lee Tracy got into trouble last November—that is so far as the picture "Viva Villa" (M-G-M) is concerned. For it resulted in Wallace Beery's being given the part of the swaggering Pancho, hero of modern Mexico.
>
> On that November morn Mr. Tracy, who was in Mexico to play the lead in the picture, was standing on the balcony of his hotel. A parade came by, the Chapultepec Cadets—Mexico's West Pointers—marching in dress uniforms. "I'd had some drink," Tracy said later. "I began yelling." But the government thought he had insulted their budding heroes. Mr. Tracy was recalled, and Wallace Beery was given the job.[2]

A more reliable version of what actually happened to get Tracy ejected from the country, from the picture, and forever from the M-G-M studio, appears in Todd McCarthy's biography of Howard Hawks. According to McCarthy, Wallace Beery had not only been in Mexico to play the lead from the start of filming, but he had already completed his scenes with Lee Tracy when Tracy was asked to leave the country (narrowly escaping a fine and deportation by the Mexican government). In addition, M-G-M studio boss Louis B. Mayer was incensed when he heard of Tracy's behavior, so Tracy was not only dismissed from the picture but also fired by M-G-M, never again working at that studio.

McCarthy further explains that Howard Hawks, who was in Mexico to direct the picture, claimed that Tracy, always highly strung out, got drunk and "'peed on the Chapultepec Cadets during the Independence Day parade in Mexico City and got put in the can.'"[3] Knowing that reshooting Tracy's scenes would put the film's budget over one million dollars, Mayer decided on some economic reforms. First, he fired Hawks as the director. He then replaced Hawks with veteran director Jack Conway. Mayer also brought the company back from Mexico, and the rest of the movie was filmed in the Los Angeles area. Wallace Beery kept his own counsel about what had occurred, but he flew his private plane from Mexico back to Los Angeles and demanded extra money for having to reshoot Tracy's scenes with Stuart Erwin.[4]

Furthermore, according to Alex Barris in his book *Stop the Presses! The Newspaperman in American Films*, the part of the newsman had to be revised in order to better suit Erwin's personality.[5] If it is true that some script rewriting was indeed necessary, then Beery must have been even more annoyed: one would therefore assume that he had to learn different lines to fit the new exchanges between Villa and Erwin, Tracy's replacement.

In any event, contrary to what the benighted *Newsweek* commentator believed, Stuart Erwin—not Wallace Beery, who had been there all along and who was not happy about having to play his part again—was enlisted to help save the movie. And reliable professional that he was, Erwin gives a memorable performance, especially in the final scene with the dying Beery as Pancho Villa. What is even more remarkable is that Erwin gives a consistent, sound interpretation of Johnny Sykes; he does this in spite of being confronted with the most serious flaw in the film: a script that is weak insofar as the screenplay is constantly shifting the film's tone. To illustrate, Wallace Beery and his sidekick Sierra (Leo Carrillo) continually bump off their enemies, but they play these violent scenes as though they were working in one of Howard Hawks's screwball comedies. The finished film did not turn out as Hawks had hoped it would; however, Hawks, having been fired, was totally disgusted with both Mayer and M-G-M, and doubtless no longer concerned himself with the finished product.

A good illustration of this confusing view of Pancho Villa's character occurs early in the movie when Beery rides into the town where six of his peon friends have just been summarily hanged by some imperious officials of the federal government. Beery orders these six cut down, enlists the help of his comrades to carry them into the courtroom from which they had been sent out only minutes earlier to die, and has each of the bodies propped up in a chair, so that the dead now form a new jury.

This macabre technique of using the dead to replace the living in time and space would be used for good comic effect four years later in *A Slight Case of Murder* (1938) where beer baron Edward G. Robinson tries to go legitimate but winds up with a lot of dead bodies to dispose of. But in this later movie, the dark comedy works; it does so because first, these Damon

Runyon-like murder victims always remain cardboard characters, so that when Robinson's cohorts start moving the deceased around like chess pieces, the results are funny. Next, unlike the people in *Viva Villa!*, none of the characters in *A Slight Case of Murder* are ever caught up in serious class warfare or faced with real evils such as hunger, disease, poverty, and rape. And finally, Edward G. Robinson plays his role earnestly, albeit tongue-in-cheek, without a hint of the smirking, overdone acting often done by Beery in this movie.

Possibly, had Howard Hawks stayed as director, he might have elicited from Beery a performance similar to the one he had gotten from Paul Muni in *Scarface* (filmed in 1931 but not released until 1932. In the interim, Hawks and producer Howard Hughes were actively trying to placate the censors.). When the filming of *Scarface* began, Muni's portrayal was so overwrought and his Italian accent so thick that he was hard to understand. But Hawks persuaded Muni to temper his performance so that he finally gives a more controlled portrayal, adding a lighter touch to the crude character of Tony Camonte, with finally only a hint of that Italian inflection.[6] Like Muni, Beery could have used some directorial advice about underplaying. Beery's Villa would have been more understandable and credible as a violent, ignorant hoodlum, with the humor stemming, as it does in *Scarface*, from the discrepancy between the protagonist's amoral obtuseness and our understanding of his terrifying viciousness.

As the picture now stands, however, Wallace Beery presents a confusing caricature of Pancho Villa. For instance, when he announces that he is going to have a "trial" with the six dead peons sitting (or slumping) in judgment on the federals, the audience can at first feel sympathy with Beery and Company; after all, one of the dead "jurors" is a young boy. But when Beery belligerently announces that his particular justice is going to be a "two for one" ("One peon is killed—I kill two Majordomos or the best that I can find"),[7] his careless attitude is hard to respond to on an emotional level, particularly when the indiscriminate shooting starts. Therefore, Stuart Erwin's performance throughout this movie provides not comic relief as such, but relief from the illogical characters developed by both Wallace Beery and Leo Carrillo.

Stuart Erwin as reporter Johnny Sykes first appears curled up asleep on the train that is held up by Leo Carrillo and other disheveled followers of Villa. Their boisterous arrival jolts him, and, angry at being so rudely awakened, Erwin at first jumps up, assuming a bellicose air as he tries to fight off these intruders. Then, when he realizes that a number of wicked looking firearms are pointed at his head, he becomes uneasy, but willing to try to save himself from the negative effects of a bullet hole through his neck. He gamely admonishes Carrillo: "Now wait a minute, stranger. Wait a minute. If you're looking for money, you're going to be bitterly disappointed. I'm a newspaperman." Searching through his pockets to try to find evidence of his identity before it is stripped from him forever, he tells these obvious cutthroats that he is Johnny Sykes of the *New York World*. Then, apparently irrelevantly, he asks hopefully, "Haven't you heard of me?" When Carrillo responds with the obvious answer, Erwin, still digging in his coat pockets for proof of his increasingly fragile existence, mutters quite seriously, "That's a little disappointing." When he is finally able to ferret out his passport, he nervously presents his picture to Carrillo, verifying that he is indeed a journalist. "All brains—no dough," he reminds the unimpressed Carrillo. Finally, as one of the other bandits grabs Erwin's suitcase and unceremoniously starts to exit the train with it, Erwin concedes, "All right, you can carry it, but no tips."[8]

Throughout this initial encounter with the more dangerous denizens of Mexico, Erwin shows that he is truly fearful of them, all the while maintaining his fatalistic sense of humor. And he is no less fearful when he meets Pancho Villa himself. Johnny Sykes is sitting at his typewriter, writing an accurate account of Villa's bestiality, when he encounters Beery. Unaware that Villa is unable to read, he tries to hide the words; but when Beery admits that he can't figure them out, Erwin thinks fast and makes up some hyperbolic fantasy about Beery's heroic victory over the Federal Army. Nor can he help but use some hyperbole himself when he brags to Beery: "Six million readers hang on my words every morning at breakfast." Meanwhile, the words that Erwin has been busily typing and retyping since his discovery of the gaps in Beery's formal education are shown on the screen: *Now is the time for all good men to come to the aid of Johnny Sykes.*[9]

Since Erwin has fed Beery's overwhelming ego, Beery decides he likes this reporter, so he drags Erwin along with the outlaw band as it flees the Federals. When the reluctant Erwin tries to complain that he needs to stay behind in order to gather news, Beery reassures him that Erwin doesn't need any news—other than Beery himself, that is.

Another way in which Beery feeds his own voracious ego is through exploitation of all the young, attractive women who appeal to his lecherous sensibility. A running "joke" in the movie involves all the women whom Beery would like to marry on a whim—whenever and wherever his libido drives him. And it is Erwin who obligingly performs one of these mock marriages. He presides at this ritual shortly after he has been recruited as one of Beery's merry followers. His rhetoric in this scene is an illustration of flawless timing and well executed intonation, in addition to a hint of nervous tension. In the first part of his performance over the lucky couple (Beery and Katharine De Mille as Rosita), he speaks like the town crier, making a grand proclamation, using exalted diction and trite metaphors: "Hear ye! Hear ye! I am about to unite in matrimony Rosita Morales, the loveliest flower of all Mexico, and that peerless prince of romance—Pancho Villa." Then, without hesitation, he smoothly breaks his rhythm, his diction becomes more common, and he inserts sarcasm that could well have cost him his life, if Beery's mind had not been on other things. Moving naturally from the "peerless prince of romance," he throws this zinger: "and if there's anybody present who objects to these doin's, let him speak up now and he will be buried with full military honors."

CARRILLO (impatiently, not paying attention): Hurry up. It take too long.

BEERY (turning abruptly away from his bride-to-be): Shut up.

ERWIN (mischievous, apparently abandoning the script to deliberately mispronounce one word of these vows): Do you, Pancho, promise to cherish this desert flower for bitter, for worse (quickening his pace) and never stay out after 9 p.m.?

BEERY: I do the best I can.

DE MILLE (adamantly): He come home all right.

ERWIN (abrupt, now brushing her off to finish this phony ceremony): O.K. And Pancho, do you further promise to obey this delicate girl—

Here gunfire interrupts the tender proceedings. As Erwin starts to run away, Beery stops him, admonishing him that he has omitted the most important thing: "Say, 'I pronounce you—I pronounce you—'"

ERWIN (Now really in haste): I pronounce you man and wife. Where's my hat?[10]

Beery is not content to look at only one woman, however. A little later, pausing briefly in the midst of his murderous activities, he meets Teresa (Fay Wray), another young, attractive—but aristocratic—Spanish woman. She is also the sister of Don Felipe (Donald Cook), a vengeful man who will prove to be Beery's final nemesis. But Beery's Villa lacks this foresight, so at this time he awkwardly flirts with her. Just as he thinks he has impressed her with his pleasant self, he rides off to do battle again, waving goodbye to his most recent would-be conquest. Erwin ambles into this scene and, watching Wray wave in return, he warns her: "Unh huh. Don't wave."

WRAY: Why not?

ERWIN (sardonically): One wrong move, and you're married to him.[11]

The next time Erwin appears, it is evident that he is capable of being as much an opportunist in his own way as Beery is in his—except that he lacks Beery's extreme, direct viciousness. While Beery has been occupied with decimating various cities, Erwin has been off getting drunk and falsifying stories about Villa, thus obviating the need to endanger himself through chasing after Villa and his thugs. But he finally catches up with Villa, jumping from horseback onto a train that is carrying Villa and followers to their next fight. He proudly shows the assemblage the headline for a story he has just published, announcing that Villa has taken the city of Santa Rosalia, which is, in reality, a place that Villa has not even occupied yet. When Wallace Beery enlightens Erwin about this fact and inquires about the source of the information, Erwin admits that his informant is a bartender. Never one to be stymied by social amenities such as the truth, Beery helpfully suggests, "Perhaps I can do something."

So the besotted Erwin casts aside any remaining qualms that he might have been holding onto when sober, and asks Beery to save him from embarrassment and protect him from the lie he has just printed. Responding to Beery's offer to do something, he replies, "You can. You can capture Santa Rosalia. Pancho—I'd do as much for you—so help me."[12] And Beery, who has begun to bond with Erwin and who is flattered by Erwin's headline proclaiming a Villa victory, agrees to take Santa Rosalia, even though the town is well fortified.

But the gamble pays off, and Erwin is vindicated when Beery is successful, thus giving Erwin a news scoop several days in advance of the actual event. Yet these two new friends are about to part, at least for the time being, when Francisco Madero (Henry B. Walthall), who has befriended Villa and who is sympathetic to Villa's cause, is elected President of Mexico and tells Beery that he can now disband his army and go home. The scenes that immediately follow this exchange are worth examining in detail since they reveal the differences in acting styles between Wallace Beery and Stuart Erwin.

Although Beery was the far more flamboyant actor—the man with his name above the title who demanded a bonus for having to shoot retakes with Erwin—the scenes where they tell each other goodbye demonstrate that Erwin was in this particular instance a far more subtle, intelligent performer than his costar. Whereas Beery overdoes the weeping sentimentality (in contrast to his remorseless behavior in earlier scenes), Erwin plays his part coherently, revealing anxiety and fear but always showing Johnny Sykes as a man capable of reining in his emotions.

Following Madero's departure for Mexico City, Erwin approaches Beery, who has already done some weepy stuff with Walthall as Madero.

ERWIN (trying to appear matter of fact): Well, I guess it's goodbye then.

BEERY: Johnny, I thought maybe I'd get away from Rosita, and you and me we go have some fun.

ERWIN (still trying to maintain his emotional distance): Nix—it's 9:00. You've gotta go home.[13]

Here Beery appears to be sobbing, while Erwin tries to maintain a more even tone. All the while, however, Erwin also conveys his dread and distrust of Beery. He has seen too much of this outlaw to be deceived by his maudlin display. So when he slaps Beery on the shoulder to encourage him, he shows three conflicting emotions. First and probably foremost, he is still afraid of Beery's degenerate personality, with its wild, unpredictable mood swings. Next, he has also become fond of Beery—albeit grudgingly—and regrets having to leave him. Finally, he does not want to show this fondness and appear weak, for he prides himself on his reputation as a tough, cynical reporter. All three of these emotions are evident as he tells Beery with a certain amount of bravado: "Aw, listen, Pancho. I'd rather be with you than anybody I know. You know how I feel about you—the best company and the swellest pal anybody could ask for." Here Erwin becomes impatient with Beery's histrionics: "Aw, stop crying, will ya?"

BEERY: I ain't no news no more, huh Johnny?

ERWIN (sounding like a coach giving a pep talk, but his voice quivers, partly from fright, partly from genuine pain): You're better than news. You're history. You don't need me anymore.

BEERY: Yes I do, Johnny.

ERWIN (with more feeling than he has allowed himself heretofore): How do you suppose I feel, runnin' out on you? But I've gotta follow the fire alarm—it's my job.[14]

At this moment, Erwin hears the train conductor make his last call for passengers. With this final signal, he comes close to losing control, to revealing his admiration, but he covers himself by hurriedly telling Beery, "Well, so long," and trying to rush away. But Beery refuses to allow him this luxury, so he runs after Erwin, tugging on his arm, like a small child chasing after a parent who has dumped him at school and is now leaving him in the company of strangers. But Erwin is still behaving like the adult that he is—so, pulling away, he insists, "I've gotta go." He then offers Beery his hand, while Beery reciprocates by vigorously embracing him. Although he returns the hug, Stuart Erwin is obviously awkward in the arms of Wallace Beery; he has seen too many men killed by those embracing arms, so he breaks free and mounts the train platform. From this position, he can see Beery tearfully waving goodbye, finger placed tentatively against his lips, once again in a childish gesture.

Meanwhile, Erwin is standing on the platform next to Fay Wray. Regaining his composure, he reverts to his more usual, sarcastic posture when he tells her, "O.K. Princess, you can wave now."[15]

Erwin does not find it necessary to exploit Beery's friendship again until after the assassination of Francisco Madero, the visionary President of Mexico who failed to gauge the extent of his enemies' hatred. In fact, it is Erwin who brings Beery the news, tracking him to a sleazy, fifth-rate hotel in El Paso where he has been living in exile and drinking heavily. When Beery asks Erwin how much money he has, Erwin tells him, "Seven bucks." This amount is apparently enough to get them out of El Paso and on the road. Once more, Erwin finds that Beery's Pancho Villa is good copy, so this time he willingly goes with Villa on his journey of revenge to Mexico City.

Once he arrives in Mexico City, Erwin again witnesses the violence of which Beery is capable, and he files what we may assume are accurate dispatches from the battlefields. He is at his most jaded in a scene where he is typing news of the latest bloodshed and he is approached by Calloway (Francis X. Bushman Jr.) a reporter for the *Saturday Evening Post*. Wearing a light-colored pith helmet (one resembling a modern hard hat worn by construction workers), Bushman introduces himself to Erwin as a writer for the *Post*; at this, Erwin replies sardonically, "I recognize the hat." When Bushman attempts to gather more news from Erwin, asking what is transpiring with Villa, Erwin gives a bitter recitation of Beery's most recent activities: "Well, the transpiring is as follows, sir. Mr. Villa left El Paso three weeks ago with seven bucks—my dough—five men and a hangover. He's gone straight through to here—fighting, scratching, kicking, and scalping. Right now, he's over yonder maneuvering the biggest, daffiest army since Leif the Lucky." In response to Bushman's "Will they hold him back?" Erwin says that Villa is angry with General Pascal for killing Madero.

BUSHMAN: Oh, I see, sort of a personal grudge.

ERWIN (nonchalantly smoking a cigarette): Stick around, Mr. Calloway, and you'll learn something about grudges.[16]

Having filed his latest story about Villa's exploits, Erwin prepares to leave, flippantly telling a fellow newsman not to shoot Calloway in the back. Then he looks once more at the distinctive shape of Calloway's helmet and hurls at the green reporter a final, sharp-edged missile: "Well, Mr. Calloway—Goodbye, good luck. And you'd better hide that hat. They're short of modern conveniences in these parts."[17]

But Erwin is about to lose his colorful subject, because already the aristocrat Don Felipe (Donald Cook) has vowed to kill Villa, not because of Villa's work on behalf of the peons, but because he holds Villa responsible for the killing of his sister Teresa (Fay Wray). Earlier, Villa had attempted to sexually assault Teresa; in her subsequent struggle against him, Sierra had intervened, fatally shooting her. So, although Villa has just been presented a medal of appreciation from the Mexican government, he is about to discover that he should not have ignored one important fact: that not all women, especially aristocratic Spanish women, are infatuated with him.

Moments before Don Felipe's snipers take aim, however, Beery's Villa has been standing in the rain in front of a butcher shop, talking with Erwin about Villa's most recent female conquest. We see Beery and Erwin in a medium shot; then the camera moves in to focus on their conversation. Erwin no longer seems afraid of Beery, as they banter about Beery's reputation as a ladies' man. Erwin also kids Beery about those seven bucks that Beery still owes him. Then, in a reflective moment, Beery invites Erwin to come to the house to see his wife Rosita and their children. When Erwin briefly separates from Beery in order to get his suitcase, the snipers have a clear shot and fire several times. Hearing the gunfire, Erwin quickly turns and runs back to Beery, who has collapsed with chest wounds and who is now propped up in front of the shop.

There follows a radiant, visceral moment, one that burns its way into our emotional core and echoes long afterward. It is a scene that we remember—even though the rest of the film may be forgotten. What we remember is Stuart Erwin crouching next to Beery and hesitantly touching his shoulder. What we remember is Stuart Erwin's gentle, quiet, comforting voice, breaking ever so slightly, speaking Beery's epitaph. Nor does Beery overact in this instance; ever the self-aggrandizer, he knows he is dying but is more concerned with his own obituary than with his physical suffering:

BEERY: Pretty big story, heh, Johnny? Pancho Villa killed. I'm lucky you're here.
ERWIN: Take it easy.

BEERY: What a funny place to die—a butcher shop. (He apparently misses the irony of his location.) Maybe you fix it up more better—huh?

ERWIN (patting Beery's shoulder, more like a father than a comrade): I'll fix it, kid.

BEERY: I hear about big men, what they say when they die. You write something pretty big about me.

ERWIN (with hesitation, gently, his voice cracking): I'll write—Uh—I'll write about how Pancho Villa died with the medal that had once been given him for the rescue of Mexico still around his neck.

BEERY: And the ring Mr. Madero gave me. You write that, too?

ERWIN (still fighting his feelings): I'll . . . I'll throw that in for good measure.

BEERY: What else, Johnny? I like to hear?

ERWIN: Well—I'll . . . I'll (now regaining some of his self-possession, his voice nearly approximating its usual briskness). The peons. From near and far—from north and south—the peons who had loved him came to see him as he lay. They gathered in silence. A tattered multitude kneeling reverently in the streets. And then—once again—the thrilling strains of La Cucaracha rang out on the night air.

BEERY: That's fine, Johnny. You tell me more.

ERWIN: Pancho Villa spoke for the last time. He said—he said—

BEERY: Hurry, Johnny. Johnny, what were my last words?

ERWIN: "Goodbye, my Mexico," said Pancho Villa. "Forgive me for my crimes. Remember, if I sinned against you, it was because I loved you too much."

BEERY: Forgive me, Johnny. What I done wrong?[18]

Despite the discrepancy between what Erwin's Johnny Sykes has just invented and what Beery's Pancho Villa actually says, rather ungrammatically, for his last words, the scene works because both actors make it work; both keep it from being self-pitying and phony. Furthermore, whereas it was Wallace Beery who had earned a reputation as an egocentric scene stealer, it is nevertheless Stuart Erwin who captures this particular scene, making Johnny the passionate heart of the film's ending, not because he is trying to take the moment from Beery, but because, at this particular time and in this particular place, he knows that Johnny Sykes is moved by Villa's imminent death. Yet it is Stuart Erwin's very reticence here that reverberates, and it is his soft, haunting voice—now faltering, now steady—that can still be heard in memory long after the final credits.[19]

Andrew Sarris, writing about James Cagney in his book *You Ain't Heard Nothin' Yet*, makes some observations about Cagney that could very well be applied to Stuart Erwin, notably in this last scene in *Viva Villa!* In fact, Erwin had more in common with Cagney than might at first appear. Sarris offers this very perceptive opinion about Cagney's emotional range:

> Cagney was a very warm actor, one of the few who could make you cry. I am thinking particularly of the moment when he realizes that he has been jilted by Rita Hayworth in *The Strawberry Blonde* (1941), and even more, the moment he "recognizes" Ann Sheridan through the haze of blindness in *City for Conquest* (1940). My heart goes out to him in these scenes, not merely because of his histrionic virtuosity, but because he has fully earned the emotions involved by playing straight and innocent with his characters. Never has he camped up his dopes and stiffs. He was always much too close to them in spirit to condescend to them.[20]

Sarris's analysis with respect to the genuineness of Cagney's emotions is one that fits Erwin's portrayals as well. He too was a very warm, sincere actor, one who could make us cry; the final tribute to Villa is an excellent illustration. Like Cagney, Erwin played "straight and innocent" as he crafted his characters; as a result, he makes us feel as deeply as he does.

Two other films come to mind when we think of Erwin's emotional resonance. Two of these scenes occur in the previously analyzed film, *Make Me a Star* (1932). The first involves Joan Blondell, playing a successful film actress, as she observes would-be but unemployed movie actor Erwin sitting amidst garbage, poking steadily through box lunch containers discarded by movie extras, desperately looking for something to eat. The second shows Blondell afterward buying breakfast for the starving Erwin, sitting across from him in the restaurant and watching helplessly as he tries to hold a coffee cup. Even clutching the cup with two hands, he shakes so badly and strives so hard to hide his misery that we want to sit with Blondell and comfort him.

The second film to touch us is the earlier mentioned *Hold Your Man* (1933), specifically at the point where Erwin visits Jean Harlow, who is serving time in a women's reformatory, and offers to marry her because he truly loves her. And he makes us believe that he loves her, despite her hardness, her callousness toward the world. Moreover, he makes this offer even though he knows that she is pregnant with another man's baby; and he does this even as he faces her violent insults when she rudely, hysterically rejects him. Once again, as he had done in *Make Me a Star*, he refuses to condescend to his character, to play his character as though he were a fool. Like Cagney, Erwin was always too honest with himself to cheat his characters and, as a result, to cheat his audience. So when he finally walks away from Harlow, conceding defeat, we want to reach out and console him because he has not given in to sentimentality. In these three scenes, as well as at the finish of *Viva Villa!*, we want to cry for him because he steadfastly refuses to cry for himself.

In a nice, fitting postscript to this excellent performance in *Viva Villa!*, M-G-M gave Erwin a contract, even as the studio permanently terminated Lee Tracy. In spite of his incisive portrayal, though, Erwin remained modest about his depiction of Johnny Sykes. In an interview he gave late in 1934, he mused rather humbly about the circumstances surrounding his being offered the role, "I'm afraid everybody who saw me was wondering what the part would have been like if Tracy had played it."[21] One has only to study the movie's final scene to realize that by this point most of the audience has simply forgotten Lee Tracy.

HERE COMES THE FLYING BRIDE

Seven years after he replaced the boisterously uncouth Tracy, Stuart Erwin played another newsman, this time a radio broadcaster, Tommy Keenan, in *The Bride Came C.O.D.* (1941). The movie itself, which starred James Cagney and Bette Davis, had mixed reviews; and, as usual, the critics by and large ignored Erwin. In truth, it is not a particularly good movie. Cagney dismisses it quickly in his autobiography, *Cagney by Cagney*. But Cagney, it must be remembered, was critical of most of his movies, pointedly refusing to see nearly all of them, with the possible exception of his musicals. About *The Bride Came C.O.D.* he says, "I have never seen that one, so I have no first-hand information as to how it came out. But I have no reason to doubt Bette's word when her autobiography said, '". . . Jimmy, with whom I'd always wanted to work in something fine, spent most of his time in the picture removing cactus quills from my behind. This was supposedly hilarious. We romped about the desert and I kept falling into cactus. We both reached bottom with this one.'"[22]

Patrick McGilligan, in his insightful critical biography of Cagney, offers a more thorough analysis of what went wrong with the film. After all, unlike Cagney, he apparently saw the completed movie. McGilligan does praise the supporting players, however, including Erwin. These players are the ones who he feels carry the film: "*The Bride Came C.O.D.* is comedy gone amuck—brittle, strained, exaggerated by the truculence of its two stars, the studio's bitch and tough guy, mismatched. The rest of the company is deft and daft: [Eugene] Pallette, [Jack] Carson, Erwin, George Tobias, William Frawley, and Harry Davenport. But Davis is so bristly (wrongly cast here as a light comedienne, not her forte) and Cagney so likewise that what should have been a light concoction collapses from constant overdrive."[23]

As he does with the character of Johnny Sykes, Erwin here creates another newsman, this time a radio commentator (possibly modeled after Walter Winchell) who is flippant and opportunistic. Unlike Johnny, however, the personality of Tommy Keenan as portrayed by Erwin is shallow, more caricature than multidimensional character.

Yet McGilligan's assessment of the secondary characters as "deft and daft" is an appropriate description of Erwin's demeanor throughout. Whenever and wherever he pops into a scene, he brings a welcome, low-key humor to a movie sorely in need of less frantic acting. The film's opening shot reveals Erwin as a true ambulance chaser. He is first seen riding in a police car, his head out the window, as the driver pulls alongside an ambulance. Both vehicles are speeding, but Erwin, now parallel to the ambulance driver, shouts to him: "Hello, Johnny. Got anybody important in there?" When the driver answers "No, Mr. Keenan, just a drunk," Erwin is clearly disappointed: "Why do you bother me with small fry?" Ducking back into the car, he laments to his police buddies, "Just an hour before I go on the air and not one single juicy item. You boys have certainly let me down."[24]

But Erwin's luck is about to change; this luck will take the shape of Allan Brice (Jack Carson) and Joan Winfield (Bette Davis). Erwin exits the police car and enters a nightclub in search of some hot news. He arrives in time to hear an announcement by the unctuous orchestra conductor and songwriter Jack Carson, who bows and bows at the audience while proclaiming to the nightclub patrons his engagement to Bette Davis. But Erwin's Tommy Keenan is initially impressed neither by Carson nor by his pronouncement. Erwin has been around the block too many times to take seriously the soporific airs of Carson, who has the dreadful habit of speaking in puerile rhymes whenever he is given the chance. Joining Davis and Carson at a table, Erwin briefly amuses himself with a cigarette, a glass of champagne, and a pill that he swallows with the help of his drink. He then assumes a tired, world-weary air when he tells Carson: "Sorry, Brice, and no offense, but I can't get excited. You've been engaged to three girls in the last six weeks."[25]

But desperation frequently leads to equally desperate measures, and Erwin is sorely in need of a good, gossipy story to broadcast on his radio show, set to go on the air shortly. Indeed, it is Erwin's inspirational brainstorm that leads to the plot complications around which the remainder of the movie is built. He urges Davis and Carson to elope that evening, even naming the destination—Las Vegas. Ever the pragmatist, he encourages them with this romantic reassurance: "Take it from me—three/fourths of the fun of getting married is getting married. After that, it's just routine." So Erwin gets news for his radio broadcast that evening, as he boasts to his listeners that he has the "greatest scoop ever to come out of the West," and somewhat hyperbolically refers to Carson as the "world's most eligible bachelor."[26] He further arranges for pilot Steve Collins (James Cagney) to fly the happy duo to Vegas. The rest of the movie involves the complications that arise when Cagney is hired by Lucius K. Winfield (Eugene Pallette) to kidnap his daughter in order to prevent her marriage to Carson and fly her instead to Amarillo.

Shortly after Cagney has flown off with his kidnap victim, Carson and Erwin are standing in the airline office, still unsure of what has just taken place, as *both* of them had planned to be on the plane to Vegas, but both have been tricked by Cagney's cohorts into leaving the plane at the last minute. In the mean time, Carson is on the phone talking to Eugene Pallette in Chicago, trying to convince Pallette (playing Davis's father) that he will make an ideal son-in-law. When Pallette—the delightful, portly actor with a voice like a garden rake scraping over gravel—accuses the none-too-bright orchestra conductor of being nothing but a fortune hunter, Carson responds defensively, "Let me tell you something—I paid an income tax of $80,000 last year." To this remark, Erwin has a quick retort: "Even with what you chiseled."

CARSON (not thinking): Even with what I chis . . . (Here he stops in disgust.)[27]

Toward the end of the movie, Erwin reappears in a deserted California mining town where Cagney, Davis, and most of the film's minor characters have assembled to witness the marriage between Carson and Davis. This time, it is Cagney who suggests that these two get married on the spot. But by this time Cagney is metaphorically captivated by Davis, so he arranges for a Nevada judge to marry Davis and Carson in California, knowing that the marriage will not be legal. Since Carson, Davis, Erwin, and the judge believe that they are in Nevada, they are eager for the ceremony to take place, each for his or her own reasons. In particular, Erwin's Tommy Keenan has already told these phantom "forty million" listeners that this charming couple has eloped, so he doesn't want to be perceived as a liar. He also wants the ceremony to be completed before Lucius Winfield gets there to stop it.

The ceremony itself is a wacky one. The Las Vegas judge, who has no idea what state he is in (literally or metaphorically), declares that he is always nervous when he has to marry a couple. Meanwhile, seeing that Erwin is still rudely, disrespectfully wearing his trademark reporter's hat, Carson gives him a disgusted look. Then, in a funny, perhaps impromptu gesture, he plucks it from Erwin's head and hands it to Erwin, who in turn looks at Carson with a disgruntled expression. At the same time, the judge is in a dither over the whole proceeding. Judge Sobler (a play on the word *sober?*) is portrayed with dippy abandon by Harry Holman, a round-faced, cherubic actor who looked like Herbert Hoover and sounded like Bugs Bunny. When Judge Sobler tells the assembled wedding guests that he will have to recite the ceremony from memory because his wife has packed the wrong book, Erwin impatiently urges him, "I don't care if you *whistle* it, as long as it's legal." So Judge Sobler delivers ten seconds of marriage vows, undoubtedly the extent of time allotted him by the Fates to his short-term memory. Still unaware that the marriage is not legal, Erwin hastily exits, but not before advising Carson/Davis: "You made forty million people very happy. Let me know first when you get your divorce."[28]

The remainder of the movies shows the process whereby Cagney/Davis are reunited, thereby proving that they were Truly Meant For Each Other. *The Bride Came C.O.D.* is not an especially memorable picture, but Erwin and the other supporting players provide enough zany, off-the-wall moments to make the movie at least mildly entertaining.

WOMEN ARE EQUAL

Stuart Erwin gives another memorable performance as Matt Casey, a world-weary reporter in *Women Are Trouble* (1936). The plot of this movie, which is a combination of genres—the gangster, the newspaper, the detective, and the romantic comedy—has to do with the repeal of Prohibition and the continuing efforts of racketeers to muscle in on the liquor trade. For instance, some of the opening scenes resemble shots from *Public Enemy* (1931). In both movies, gangsters use violence to coerce liquor dealers into doing business with the underworld. Further, at the beginning of *Women Are Trouble*, one of these liquor store owners is shot and killed on the street, an incident that precipitates most of the action of the rest of the film.

Following the murder of this man, the scene shifts to the police station, where Erwin makes his first entrance as the investigative reporter. He is handcuffed and also incidentally rather miffed at the person responsible for his predicament. When the police chief, Inspector Matson (Cy Kendall), questions Erwin about his unorthodox entry, he replies sarcastically, "One of your smart coppers didn't like a story I wrote." Nonetheless, Erwin is as interested in getting information about the murder of the liquor store owner as he is in the removal of those handcuffs. He also warns Matson about getting too cozy with those racketeers, one of whom has just left the station: "Maybe I'm wrong, but I always figure it isn't good etiquette to discuss spots with a whitewashed leopard—that is, unless you're a tiger."[29]

When Erwin returns to his office at *The Morning Star*, he sees Ruth Nolan (Florence Rice, who resembled Jean Arthur in appearance and in manner), who has been pestering him with her desire to see the city editor Blaine (Paul Kelly). Rice has come to the big city to try to get more challenging work as a reporter. She is young and pretty, with a delicate face and figure; yet all of these attributes belie her tenacity, her determination to do a "man's" job. When she approaches Erwin again with her request to be allowed to see Blaine, he reminds her that Blaine won't hire a girl reporter. As Erwin tells the story, Blaine hired a girl once, and she married him. "Then," continues Erwin, "she left and she hooked him for alimony." Up to this point, Erwin has treated Rice with a sort of offhand casualness, as though she were some household pest that he would like to shoo away but would not want to swat with the latest edition of his paper.

Yet Erwin's Matt Casey keeps his options open. When Rice manages to get inside the newspaper office, thus allowing Blaine to fasten his attention for the first time on the beautiful Ruth Nolan, he is fascinated by her good looks, so he asks Erwin, "Friend of yours?" Erwin appears flustered by this question, but he answers candidly, "I haven't found out yet." Blaine emphatically explains that he doesn't hire females, but Rice's Ruth Nolan is resolute and assertive. She begs to be given a chance to prove herself. Blaine continues to be adamant, and Erwin supports his boss. Although she is in no way ready to give up, Rice decides to leave at this point, giving the two condescending newsmen a parting thrust: "Thanks for the privilege of meeting two such kindly and courteous gentlemen."[30]

Once she is away from their somewhat chauvinist presence, however, Rice proves that she is clever and resourceful. Knowing that she could get some helpful information about the liquor store owner's murder from a member of the Liquor Control Board, she goes to the home of member J. Eldridge, who is just leaving in his car. She follows him to a squalid part of town, arriving in time to see a large truck deliberately push Eldridge's car off a dock and into the water, where he presumably drowns. She rushes back to the newspaper office with the story. She informs Erwin and Kelly that she has witnessed not an accident, as had been reported, but a murder. On the basis of this scoop, Kelly hires her, but he tells Erwin to write the story. She does not appear too disturbed by Erwin's usurpation of her territory, but she does approach Erwin as he sits typing the story that she has given him. "Can't I do anything to help?" she offers. To this, Erwin answers disdainfully, "Yea. Tell me how to spell *assassination*."[31]

While Erwin is busy writing the girl reporter's story, Inspector Matson has arrested Murty (Raymond Hatton), the owner of the truck and the killer of J. Eldridge. Meanwhile, reporters from various papers gather at the police station to await Murty's arrival, including the recently hired Florence Rice. But Erwin is not about to allow a woman to remain in this male-only club, so he takes her aside, assuming an air of confidentiality and secrecy. He advises her to go outside into the alley behind the police station where, he assures her, the big story really is. He does not tell her that he fully intends to remain inside the station where he thinks the actual story will unfold. But Rice falls for his line and drives her car into the back alley. After she leaves, one of the hotshot reporters (Frank Jenks) asks Erwin: "Where'd you send the dame?" Erwin responds with amused pride: "Out in the alley on a snipe hunt."[32]

What none of these clever males have noticed, however, is that in their midst is one man whom no one recognizes—a man with a camera. What they also fail to notice is that hidden in this camera is a gun. As Murty is led into the station, the man with the camera shoots him in the back, fatally wounding him; then the killer runs through the back alley, where Rice has been occupied taking pictures of cats and birds. But this time she inadvertently takes a picture of the man with the camera, thus getting her second coup of the day. But on the way back to the office, she and Erwin are robbed by thugs who take her camera—for reasons that puzzle Erwin, but that she is beginning to understand.

Back in the newspaper office, she gloats over her small triumph: Erwin's plan to get her out of the way has backfired. When she and Erwin report that she got a photograph of Murty's killer, but that the camera was grabbed by muggers who doubtless had a hand in the murder, Kelly is furious at them. He turns on Erwin contemptuously: "You, you stand before me unscratched. Not a bullet in you anywhere. You let them steal our camera and didn't fight to the bitter end for your paper. Why, the old time . . . " Erwin knows what is coming, and he is unimpressed by what Kelly is hinting at. His response is equally mocking: "Yea, I know. The old time reporter would have staggered up here with a stomach full of lead and died just after delivering the camera. But I'm not an old time reporter. Besides, I didn't know Miss Nolan had the picture."[33]

It is Miss Nolan who plays the final, winning card, however, when she reveals with a certain superior air that she has managed to salvage the roll of film with the killer's face imprinted on it. At this bit of information, Kelly, who has just fired her, rehires her; he also orders his staff to print the next issue of the paper with the killer's picture on the front page. He then sends Erwin and Rice (now his fair-haired girl) to go interview the "grieving" widow, Mrs. Murty.

On the way to Mrs. Murty's, Erwin attempts some small talk with Rice. He has discovered that he is attracted to her, but he is unsure of how to approach her. So he begins with a rather unimaginative reference to the romantic nature of the nighttime sky: "Nice night. Lots of stars, aren't there? Big moon. Did they have a moon as big as that back in Northville?" Now it is her turn to be flippant and skeptical. She thinks that he is being nice just so he can set her up to tear her down, so that he can remind her that it was sheer good fortune that enabled her to get the photograph. She is convinced that he still thinks of her as a lucky "small town hick," thus his mention of her hometown of Northville. As with the reporters he portrayed in *Viva Villa!* and *The Bride Came C.O.D.*, Erwin is the big city sophisticate with the hard edge—at least a superficial hardness. Nevertheless, like Johnny Sykes of *Viva Villa!*, Erwin's Matt Casey is a man with a sensitive, gentle side. As he drives Rice to their interview, he shows how this tough, outer layer has begun to unravel.

When Rice tries to put up her feisty defenses against Erwin's efforts to be an attentive companion, he counters with, "C'mon, let's be friends." When she snaps back, "Why should we be friends?" he resolutely tries complimenting her: "Oh, because you got pretty hair, blue eyes, red lips." All the while, he is glancing at her, trying to focus on his driving as well. Next, he confesses that he admires her pluckiness: "And a gosh awful temper that's bubbling all over the place right now. Besides that, I like you."

RICE (truly charmed now, she smiles): Do you?

ERWIN (looking self-satisfied): Sure, and to prove it, I'm inviting you to the Press Club masquerade tomorrow night.

RICE (flattered): Well thanks, but you see, Mr. Blaine has already asked me and . . .

ERWIN (jealous, hurt, wanting to hurt back): Blaine. Hmph. That's one way to get ahead.

RICE (knowing full well the answer before asking the question): What do you mean?

ERWIN: You're pretty good at putting words in my mouth. Figure it out.

RICE: I already have. I think you're the most hateful man I ever met.

ERWIN: Wait'll you get a good load of that Blaine.[34]

By the time they arrive at Mrs. Murty's apartment, the parrying couple have reached a sort of truce and are at least speaking politely, if formally, to each other. They have heard that Mrs. Murty is a tough lady, so Rice warns Erwin to be careful. He reassures her that he'll let her go first. His half-kidding remark turns out to be a quip that they both recall when they are actually face to face with Mrs. Della Murty (Kitty McHugh, sister of the talented comedian Frank McHugh). She gives full meaning to the term "broad" as it is often used to describe a less than genteel lady. She is a short but muscular platinum blonde with features that might be called good-looking were it not for all the makeup that she uses to hide these features—the type of female that high school students of an earlier generation usually referred to as "easy."

In the two reporters' attempts to ingratiate themselves with the formidable Mrs. Murty, Rice clearly takes the lead and keeps it throughout their encounter with her. When Murty accuses Erwin of not being a cop, as he had claimed, but a reporter, Rice chimes in with dismay that Erwin has lied to her as well: that she has just met him on the stairs, where he had claimed he could get her into the apartment because he pretended to be a "copper." She further assures the skeptical, belligerent Murty that she is *not* a reporter.

But Erwin is not to be allowed to hear what Rice claims to be, because Murty slugs him twice, knocking him flat on his back into the hall; then, while he is in this position, she gives him an energetic kick, which lands in some unseen and doubtless unseemly place on his body. Rice clearly enjoys her revenge for Erwin's earlier insults, as she and Kitty McHugh as Murty settle down without the burdensome presence of the male. What they settle down to involves a curious bit of business with McHugh shrieking a blues song to Rice's piano accompaniment. McHugh's wails have the ability to give impalpable pain, similar to the feeling one gets when chalk is scraped across a blackboard. Rice, meanwhile, maintains a plastered smile, though it looks as if she is about to give way to a terrific migraine. What they are doing and why they are doing it will soon be clarified.

By the time Erwin and Rice get back to the office—she with a story and he with a black eye—the dynamics of their relationship has definitely changed. Now she is Paul Kelly's favorite, while Erwin receives nothing but Kelly's derision. As Kelly ridicules Erwin's "sissy" behavior and his letting a woman "scoop" him, Erwin tries to justify himself: "She didn't scoop me.

She doublecrossed me." Perched on top of Kelly's desk, picking at his nails with a file, Erwin makes the following self-mocking resolution: "But I'll get even. I'll find her doll buggy and take all the wheels off. I'll put sand in her powder puff. I'll rip runs in her silk stockings." At that moment, Rice enters, smiling gleefully. Erwin gives her a disgusted look and turns back to Kelly. Making a slashing motion from ear to ear across his neck with his nail file, he tells Kelly: "Here comes my pal."[35]

Rice, in turn, is not about to let her fellow reporter have the final word, so she laughs when she sees his black eye. But she immediately regrets her triumph, apologizing, saying that she wants to explain. At the same time, however, Erwin interrupts her; he will have none of her condescension, as he comes back with: "Now wait a minute. Never explain anything. If you pull a dirty trick or double cross a pal, don't make alibis; just grin and rub it in. You make lots of friends that way."[36]

In spite of his anger at Rice's penchant for humiliating him, Erwin nonetheless admires many of her qualities—qualities that he incidentally shares. He knows a kindred spirit when he sees one. He appreciates her spunk, her intelligence, her wry sense of humor, her imagination; above all, he respects her ability to see a job to the finish, even though she might encounter numerous setbacks on the way. She reveals these outstanding characteristics in the next scene with city editor Kelly as Blaine; she has just returned from her session with Mrs. Murty, the same meeting that has left Erwin looking like a prizefight loser, a victim of Mrs. Murty's fist and foot. In her conversation with Kelly, she reveals how she was able to remain with Mrs. Murty without becoming a victim herself. She had told the widow that she was a booking agent who could get Mrs. M. a three-week vaudeville tour on the basis of her fame as the late Mr. Murty's wife. When Kelly presses her for details, however, asking if she had managed to get a confession out of Mrs. Murty, Rice is forced to admit that her prospective interviewee had been so excited about the prospect of going on the stage that, even with her best reporter instincts, she had been unable to get any substantive information from the horribly untalented Mrs Murty. Kelly is still impressed with Rice's work, however, and her ability to go where her male counterparts have failed to, so he urges Rice to write a human interest story about Mrs. M. and to sign her name to it. In her turn, Rice is so grateful to Kelly for finally acknowledging her worth that she is more eager than ever to go with him to that masquerade ball.

Having had his own invitation to that same ball rebuffed by Rice, Erwin has his own mischievous plan to make the ball lively: he brings Kelly's ex-wife as his date. Furthermore, her face is completely hidden behind a mask, so that Kelly at first doesn't know who this mystery lady is. For his part, Erwin is dressed as a hobo, complete with patches on his pants, floppy scarecrow hat, and false beard. Soon after arriving at the ball, he removes the beard, placing it on the brim of his hat. He leaves it in that position, sporting it during the next few scenes, where it looks like nothing so much as a very large, very silly, very ugly feather. Next, he makes a point of leading his stealth date to the table where Rice and Kelly are sitting. Here he arranges to sit next to Rice, leaving the mysterious masked woman seated next to Kelly. As he eases himself into a chair, he kids his city editor, suggesting that his costume mirrors his salary at *The Morning Star*. One also suspects that, through his tattered dress, Erwin is taking immense pleasure in mocking his own stereotyped movie reputation as an unlettered hillbilly.

Nor can he resist poking fun at Rice, whom he introduces to his date, still artfully disguised: "This is Miss Ruth Nolan. She's always got something up her sleeve—her arm and a knife." Here he makes a slashing motion across his neck, the second time that he has used this gesture to refer to his female nemesis. He also chuckles at his own joke. Then he introduces his date as Madame W, adding, with a giggle, "She used to be Madame X, but she got promoted."[37] Again, he chortles, enjoying himself enormously. He finds it even funnier when Kelly dances with his ex-wife and finally discovers who she is. Meanwhile, he wastes no time in getting reacquainted with Rice, with whom he is becoming more and more fond. While they are dancing, they are interrupted by one of the masked partygoers, who tells Rice that she has a phone call. Neither she nor Erwin suspects anything, so she leaves Erwin, who looks rather confused as he stands alone on the dance floor.

Naturally, Rice has been set up by the thugs responsible for Eldridge's death; as she enters a private room and takes the phone, she is grabbed by one of the disguised villains. Not to worry, however, because she is rescued by Kelly, who has heard he screams and runs into the room just as her attacker vanishes. Cut to the hall outside, where Erwin and Kelly's ex-wife are happily, vigorously skipping hand in hand, like two children who have been let out of school for recess. He is delighted because he has reestablished a rapport with Rice; she is delighted because she has played a neat trick on her ex-husband. His amusement is short-lived, however, when he finds Rice in Kelly's arms. Though they both assure him that he is simply comforting her because she has been frightened, both Erwin and Kelly's ex-wife remain unconvinced. "My, what a charming scene," declares Erwin's companion. Erwin's bitterness resurfaces as he adds, "Yea, it looks like Miss Nolan has a new assignment. I'm sorry we busted in on your little promotion, Ruth."[38]

Even though Erwin takes his date home and Kelly returns Rice to her apartment, these four will eventually play a type of musical chairs and finally get the mates they are most truly compatible with. But not before plot complications resolve everything satisfactorily. Kelly and Rice are kidnapped by the thugs who think the editor and his reporter know more about Murty's murder than they actually do. Erwin traces their whereabouts through the costume company that had supplied one of the kidnappers with his mask. Erwin makes his entrance through an open window, gun in his shaking hand, absolutely terrified but determined to save his city editor and the woman he loves. When one of the gang members once again gets the advantage, it is Inspector Matson who provides the deus ex machina by breaking down the door and saving all three of these well-meaning bunglers from being executed in no time flat.

All then ends happily. Rice and Erwin return to *The Morning Star* office after their marriage at City Hall; Kelly and his ex-wife agree to remarry. And the accomplished boxer, Mrs. Murty? She has become a successful entertainer in burlesque, where she doubtless displays her talents to the deaf.

Stuart Erwin depicts Matt Casey in *Women Are Trouble* as a man accustomed to viewing his own weaknesses with an insight rare among the typical reporter. One has only to look at the difference between his characterization of Matt Casey and his portrayals of Johnny Sykes in *Viva Villa!* and Tommy Keenan in *The Bride Came C.O.D.* to understand this distinction between the hardness of the latter two and the vulnerability of Matt Casey. Sykes and Keenan are by and large self-absorbed manipulators, lacking a conscience and a moral center. With the exception of his stunning speech as Johnny Sykes in the final scene with Beery as the dying Pancho Villa, Erwin paints both Sykes and Keenan as quintessential opportunists. But with Matt Casey, he demonstrates his ability to depict a man who not only has self-knowledge but also has an understanding of the weaknesses of others, specifically in his dealings with Florence Rice and Paul Kelly.

THE ALIENIST AND THE REPORTER

In *The Crime of the Century* (1933), Erwin has another reporter role; in this one, he is a police reporter who solves a murder. *The Crime of the Century*, despite its hyperbolic title, is a neat, tightly crafted movie that provides Erwin with another chance to demonstrate his cynical newsman persona in the role of Dan McKee. Moreover, the film shows his softer, more sentimental side as well, especially in the scenes that he shares with that great beauty of the early thirties, Frances Dee.

The opening credits create an eerie atmosphere, as each of the major performers is seen walking into the frame in silhouette, the name of each actor printed under his/her inky profile. We are then led into a police station where we are introduced to one of the major motifs of the movie: the pittance paid to police officers and their concomitant desire to make a fast buck. We see the police captain Tim Riley (Robert Elliott) and his lieutenant Frank Martin (David Landau) playing cribbage for relatively small stakes, while Erwin looks on and makes sarcastic remarks about their penchant for gambling. We are also given a significant clue about Captain Riley's character when he admits how much he enjoys gambling. As with most murder mysteries, though, we usually miss such clues; then, when we see the movie a second time, we wonder how we could have been so blind.

Interrupting this police pastime is Dr. Emil Brandt (Jean Hersholt). As played by Hersholt, Dr. Brandt is a stereotypical European psychiatrist, complete with an exotic accent of indeterminate ethnic origin. Dr. Brandt reminds one of a typical authoritative "doctor" pictured in early thirties' magazine advertisements touting the amazing health benefits of yeast. Such ads usually featured a photograph of a distinguished physician, portentously advising his well-dressed patient (usually female) of the benefits to her digestive and excretory systems that will accompany her ingestion of Flushes Yeast. But Dr. Brandt wants to discuss murder, not laxatives. While Erwin recognizes the good doctor as the well-known "alienist" about whom he had written a story recently, Dr. Brandt nonetheless does not trust newsmen, as who does in these films? So Erwin is dismissed by the captain, leaving Dr. Brandt to tell his tale.

One is immediately curious about Dr. Brandt when he approaches the two police officers with the interesting news that he wants to be immediately locked up because he is going to commit a murder. The doctor explains how he has come to believe this astonishing fact; he has hypnotized a bank examiner, asked him to steal $100,000, and then ordered the spellbound subject to bring it to his home that evening at 8:15. And the murder itself? That, confesses the doctor, will be accomplished by the insertion of a trocar into the victim's heart, at which time the murderer will keep the $100,000 for himself.

After making his "confession," Dr. Brandt is not especially reassured when both the captain and the lieutenant logically conclude that Brandt will not dare kill, now that the police know of his plans. Just to make sure that the doctor keeps away from that trocar, however, the captain suggests that the lieutenant accompany the doctor home and remain with him. Then, we are given another significant clue—which we undoubtedly miss at this point—

when the lieutenant reminds the captain that he is off duty that evening at 8:30. So, as if he has just remembered that fact himself, Captain Riley offers to relieve Lieutenant Martin that evening at the doctor's home. Thus Riley, not Martin, is present at a significant point in the narrative.

When the scene shifts to Dr. Brandt's house, we learn four intriguing facts about the doctor's situation: first, his second wife (the brassy, healthy, tough, aggressive Wynne Gibson as Freda Brandt) is cheating on him with Gilbert Reid (Gordon Westcott); second, his need for money is exacerbated by Freda's extravagant life style. Next, his secret plan to murder the bank examiner is known by Freda, who has apparently been paying careful attention to the doctor's activities. Finally, we learn that there is a strong conflict between Brandt's college-age daughter Doris (Francis Dee) and her spendthrift stepmother Freda, who looks just slightly older than the typical coed. All of these characters will come under suspicion, in good murder mystery fashion, when the first murder occurs.

And the murder is just about to happen. Its victim arrives, the luckless bank examiner Philip Ames (Samuel S. Hinds). Ames enters with the package of unmarked money, but he does not look at all well. He is obviously in a hypnotic trance, and his face looks as though someone had covered it with a generous portion of papier-mâché.[39] Shortly after Ames's appearance, Captain Riley comes in, as he had previously announced that he would. Moreover, Riley is inordinately interested in looking at the money itself and in subsequently arresting the now prostrate Ames, who looks as though he could not so much as raise his head to say his name, much less offer himself up to be taken away. Nor does the Captain really want to haul off the comatose patient, for Dr. Brandt easily persuades him to forget the entire scenario and allow the money to be returned to the bank.

Now the stage is set for the climax of the first part of *The Crime of the Century*. While Dr. Brandt is emphatically repeating into the ears of the insensible Ames the orders to return the money to the bank, everyone disappears from view, except for Freda, lurking in the shadows and peering anxiously out the windows. We know that Freda would enjoy having the $100,000 for herself, as she has already stolen it once, but was caught by her husband when he searched her purse. So now the money is back in Ames's pocket. Meanwhile, we are puzzled as to just how Ames is going to accomplish the task of returning this cash, for he looks as though he had already passed away some time during the Harding administration.

There follows a scene that we have been expecting: The lights suddenly go out, we hear the sounds of scuffling and struggling, interspersed with muted cries. Freda may be dimly seen fighting off an attacker. The reason that she stands out clearly in the dark is that she has been poured into a white, low-cut, iridescent evening gown, with spaghetti straps barely holding it in place on her well-apportioned shoulders. She glows like a large night-light. Following this encounter with an intruder, she rushes outside, where she sees Erwin from the back. He has been lurking around, good reporter that he is, in hopes that Dr. Brandt will provide a good story. And Dr. Brandt is about to be a better story than Erwin had even hoped for. Mistaking Erwin for her inamorata Gilbert, Freda calls to him. For his part, Erwin is not put off by her error, but immediately follows her into the house.

Since it appears that a fuse has blown, Erwin lights a candelabrum; by this light, they can see one effect of the earlier commotion in the room: Mr. Ames's new condition. "Gee, he's dead," observes Erwin astutely and curiously. Considering Ames's earlier appearance, one might well ask how Erwin could tell. Then they find Dr. Brandt lying on the floor—chloroformed, but alive. Temporarily thwarted in her plan to run off that evening with Gilbert, Freda leaves in order to help her husband upstairs; meanwhile, Erwin naturally calls his paper. By the light of the candles and vigorously smoking his omnipresent cigarette, he tells his listener, "Yea, it's a murder and it's a honey." He adds that he wants to look around "before the dicks muss things up. They don't know it happened yet. Keep a line open for the story. It oughtta be good."[40]

Then, picking up the candelabrum, cigarette hanging from his mouth, Erwin snoops around, searching for clues and generally damaging the evidence before the "dicks" arrive. He also adds an inspired stroke; while he is wandering about with those candles, he hums "Here Lies Love" from *The Big Broadcast*, which he had made the preceding year with Bing Crosby. In that earlier film, Crosby had sung this beautiful love song shortly before he and Erwin decided to commit a joint suicide. Furthermore, they arrived at this decision while gazing at each other over a candelabrum. So Erwin's tuneful humming through his cigarette is a nice, evocative touch, as though he had dug down deep into his previous movie and come back up one year later to reprise the song.

In the meantime, he is finding clues, among them a frayed electric cord and a pin. He also finds Freda, who is still doing her own prying. He sees her pick up a button, which apparently has come from a man's suit jacket, and try to hide it. "Show me where it came from," he orders her. She ignores this command, but while they are standing in the candlelight, he notices that her face is bruised. She feels the bruises, surprised that they are there, but not unaware of how she received them. She admits that someone had tried to choke her; now Erwin knows a lot more than he did previously. He knows that she was in the room when the murder occurred. So too, when she lets slip the word "Gilbert," Erwin recognizes it as the name she had called him earlier. Now he knows even more—that she suspects Gilbert of doing the deed, although she cannot believe that her lover would have actually choked her.

Throughout this exchange between Erwin's police reporter and Wynne Gibson's solidly built tart, the low-key cynicism of Erwin provides an agreeable contrast with the brash defensiveness of Gibson. Furthermore, the foregoing scenes, beginning with Freda's summoning of Erwin into the house, emphasize the focus of the screenplay from this point onward. It is Erwin's Dan McKee, he of the sharp eye and the inquisitive mind, who recognizes clues when he sees (and sometimes trips over) them. It is subsequently Dan McKee who will solve both the first and the as-yet-uncommitted second murder.

But before all of this plot can unravel, we must return to Captain Riley, whom we see strolling into the police station and subsequently learning from the desk clerk of the murder—which coincidentally has only now taken place at the home the captain had just left.

Riley appears surprised at the news.

One who is not surprised, however, is Erwin, as he is the one who has just called the cops. Now that he has completed the confiscation of much of the evidence, he goes to tell Dr. Brandt's daughter Doris of the evening's activities. She is ensconced at a women's college, where most of the students at the residence hall appear to be busy in the academic pursuit of card-playing. In addition, the lobby looks as though it belongs in a southern plantation home rather than in the typical college dormitory. We may therefore assume that it is not only Freda who has been spending the doctor's money.

As Francis Dee's Doris Brandt descends the elegant stairway to greet Erwin and to find out what he is doing there, we see that Erwin is stupefied by her appearance. What he had been expecting to see is not clear, but what is certain is that he is enchanted by her. Holding out his hand, he seems both charmed and flustered. Whereas he had assumed an air of brash superiority over Freda, he cannot find the right tone with Doris. At first, he is eager to convey his excitement, as he greets her with "I've been wonderin' what you'd be like, but I never thought you'd turn out to be so . . ."[41]

Doris is impatient, however, unconcerned about how Erwin had expected her to turn out. Having been summoned from her room, she wants him to get down to business. When she asks him what he wanted to see her about, he is so nervous that he blows the moment, unable to impress her stunningly elegant grace. Erwin always handled such discomfiture with dexterity, especially when it resulted from an encounter with a sexy woman.

At first, he talks too much and too rapidly about irrelevant subjects. He begins with a boast, "Look, Miss Brandt. I'm a newspaperman. Didn't you ever read the front page of the *Record*? Well, that's *me*. I practically *run* that paper." Then, almost as an aside, he adds, "There was a murder pulled off at your house tonight and . . ." Here, Doris falls forward, distraught, and Erwin catches her, aware that he has messed up this conversation. So he tries to make amends by repetitiously reassuring her, "Steady now. Steady. It's all right. It's all right." Naturally, Doris wants to know who the murder victim was.

"One of your father's patients," returns Erwin, "man by the name of Ames. Imagine me springing it like that. Of all the *saps*." He makes a gesture with his closed fist, "Somebody oughtta take me and *sock* me." Doris is not especially interested in Erwin's need for self-punishment, however, for she continues, "What about father?" To this query Erwin replies matter-of-factly but not too tactfully, "Oh, he's all right. Just an overdose of chloroform."

DEE (horrified): *Chloroform?*
ERWIN (taking her hand and pressing it into his): Now, your father's going to be absolutely all right.[42]

Doris insists that they leave right away, so as she and Erwin hurry out of the fashionable lobby, Erwin grabs a handy, nearby coat from off a chair, drapes it over her shoulders, and provides a comforting arm around her shoulder as he leads her out. Whether the coat actually belongs to her is anybody's guess, but since she continues to wear it throughout most of the remainder of the movie, we can safely assume that she at least likes it well enough to keep it on.

Before Erwin can deposit Doris and her coat at her father's home, he utilizes some information that she has just provided concerning her stepmother's "friend" Gilbert, leaving her to go on in the taxi while he visits Gilbert's apartment. Figuring correctly that Freda and Gilbert have long since passed the handshake stage, Erwin decides to use the divide-and-conquer technique to rile both of them and perhaps elicit a confession from at least one. Indeed, his droll, "aw shucks" manner in his meeting with Gilbert catches Gilbert off guard, allowing Erwin to get the results he wants. Erwin has sometimes been compared in manner to Will Rogers, and in this scene, one can indeed hear the similarities, specifically in the slow, deliberate cadence of Erwin's speech patterns.

Erwin begins by telling Gilbert quietly, almost confidentially, that a murder was committed; he also lets Gilbert know that this fact probably is no surprise to Gilbert. Then he surreptitiously cuts a button from Gilbert's suit jacket and shows it to its owner, claiming that the button came from the room in which Ames was murdered. Then, to add to Gilbert's dismay, Erwin further claims that Freda had given him the button with orders to show it to Gilbert. By now, Erwin's victim is ready to convict Freda of the murder, especially when he discovers that the button has been cut off his jacket. He concludes that Freda has set him up to take the fall for her own crime, and that her motive was the $100,000.

Having no more need for the button, Erwin returns it to Gilbert and calls Captain Riley at Brandt's home, saying that he is bringing Gilbert there. When they arrive back at the crime scene, they are surrounded by all of the usual suspects. At this point, Captain Riley pretends that his principal suspect is Dr. Brandt himself, while Gilbert plays out the part of the aggrieved lover, framed by his mistress—a part that Erwin had assigned him. So now Riley is after Dr. Brandt; Doris Brandt is after Riley as she tries to defend her father; Gilbert is after Freda, who he thinks has betrayed him; Freda is after Gilbert in retaliation for his unjust accusations; Dr. Brandt is after Freda because this is the first that he has heard of her affair; and Stuart Erwin is the only one in the scene who is after no one, and who remains calm, surveying with waggish amusement the buffoonery of the doctor and his uninvited guests.

Furthermore, it is Erwin who continues to remain cool-headed enough to find clues. He spots on a chair the suede gloves that the killer was wearing. In addition, he informs Riley that the lights were blown when a pin punctured the lamp cord and a short circuit burned the cord. With a supercilious air, Erwin shows the pin to Riley, appearing indifferent to the fact that this pin is part of the police evidence that Erwin had earlier appropriated. Yet Captain Riley does not appear terribly upset by Erwin's interference with proper investigative procedure, for he now suggests that the assembled suspects reenact the murder—with Erwin as the victim. Riley cleverly assigns Lieutenant Martin the role of the killer and, when the time comes for Martin to grab Freda (who is, unfortunately, playing herself) Erwin points out that the attacker grabbed Freda with his left hand; he has deduced this by the location of the bruises on her face. Here, as Freda begins to remember some crucial facts about the actual event, once more the lights go out, leaving us in darkness. This time it is by flashlight that the body is discovered; it is, naturally, Freda. And the most likely suspect? Dr. Brandt, of course. The motive? His anger at her infidelity.

But wait. At this moment, the movie is interrupted while an announcer appears in order to address the audience. We are about to witness a primitive version of interactive video, as he instructs the viewers to guess the murderer. He tells us that we have sixty seconds to choose. So, while numbers are flashed on the screen to the accompaniment of the sight and sound of a ticking clock, we see the faces of all the major players in the cast; in fact, everyone who has ever entered Brandt's house or even lurked outside is shown, with the exception of Philip Ames himself and the recently deceased Freda. We may assume that the latter character did not darken the house and commit suicide.

Following this original interlude, we find ourselves back at police headquarters, where Doris is still wearing that coat Erwin had picked out for her. Meanwhile, Erwin is busily chewing out the cops, calling them stupid for arresting the doctor. He is rightly convinced that Freda became the second victim because she was about to remember something important about the killer. Indeed, by this time we know that her recollection was related to her feelings when she fought off her attacker in the dark.

But when Erwin is not playing detective, he has time to think about his developing love for Doris. His feelings for her surface in the next scene as he accompanies her in a taxi on the way back to her college. She confesses that she is in no mood to resume her studies, as she complains, "I can't go back there now." Erwin takes advantage of the moment to console her, "Look, honey. You've gotta get a grip on yourself. Stop worrying. I'm not going to let anything happen to your father." To this, Doris replies somewhat ruefully, "What more *could* happen to him?"

"Well," suggests Erwin helpfully, "they could hang him." As Doris gasps, Erwin realizes his faux pas, "Go ahead, sock me." Apparently not wishing for any more violence, Doris continues, "My father didn't kill that man. He didn't kill Freda. I know it. You know it too, don't you?" Here Erwin becomes quite solicitous, "Sure I know it, because you say so."

DEE: That's not a very good reason, is it?
ERWIN: It's good enough for me. (He looks wistfully into her eyes.) But we've gotta do more than know it.[43]

Abandoning romance for a moment, Erwin devises a plan for the two of them to get back into her father's house in order to look for more clues. And with this action they succeed; moreover, they are rewarded when they discover where the $100,000 is hidden. But their elation in finding the murder motive is suspended when they hear someone coming, so they turn out those omnipresent lights and hide in a closet. Their nocturnal visitor is Gilbert, who, Erwin naturally assumes, is the guilty party returning to the scene of the crime to retrieve his stolen cash. Erwin springs the old trick of pretending to have a gun in his jacket pocket as he points it in Gilbert's direction. For his part, Gilbert has not found a whole lot of courage since his last meeting with Erwin, so he dutifully remains under Erwin's command while Doris calls the cops. Captain Riley is particularly interested in the information that Erwin not only has the murderer under his control but also has located the $100,000 as well.

But lo and behold—here comes another guy with a gun; this time it is Doris's brother James Brandt (William Janney), who has been skulking in the shadows outside since early in the movie. Is this another suspect? We have earlier learned that he had quarreled two years earlier with his father over Freda and had thereupon left because of his antipathy toward her. Certainly his past relationship with his stepmother has provided sufficient reason to dispose of her? Ah no—but then why would he want to bump off Philip Ames? Furthermore, why would he be coming back into the house now? Doris and Erwin soon learn the answer to that question, as brother James goes straight to where the cash is hidden. His response to Erwin's curiosity concerning his knowledge of the money's whereabouts is to kiss his sister goodbye as he leaves. "*Hey!*" protests Erwin, unaware of this odd stranger's identity and distressed over such a mystifying, suggestive gesture toward the woman he has begun to hold dear.

But before he can state his intentions toward Doris, he has a murder to solve. In quick order, we eliminate Gilbert when he displays to Erwin and Riley his grotesque left hand; all of the fingers except thumb and forefinger are artificial. Therefore, we can conclude that he would not have had the strength to kill anyone. Riley seems glad to hear Gilbert's excuse; now he can conclude once more, "It is the doctor, after all." Upon hearing her father once again become the prime suspect, Doris, in a fit of pique, pushes away the lieutenant and scratches her hand on his badge. Now she has her own revelation: that's what Freda had been about to say about her attacker, just before her untimely demise—that she had been scratched by something like a police badge. By the same token, Erwin has discovered a playing card dropped by one of the two cops with whom he has frequently kibitzed. Once he determines that the card belongs to Captain Riley, we have the mystery solved at last.

But not quite. Riley has to try to get away, which he does by drawing a gun on the cast assembled for the film's denouement. He runs from the room, closes the door, and fires through it at the various cast members who are now ducking behind the doctor's well-appointed furniture. Finally, we hear a shot that does not come through the door, and we are spared the sight of Riley being arrested, for he has simplified the rest of the plot by killing himself. Now Erwin has another scoop. He calls his paper, "Bill, make that the *late* Captain Riley." He chuckles gleefully as he hangs up the phone. "What a story! Captain of detectives slays two for $100,000. Boy, it's a *wow!*"

Erwin's delight is too much for Lieutenant Martin, however, who lectures Erwin about professional ethics: "That's the trouble with you newspaper guys. You take a story like this and you smear it all over the front page. But how about the hundreds of cops that get killed in the line of duty? What do you do for them? I'll tell you. *Nothing.*" Properly chastened and now subdued, Erwin rejoins, "Sorry, Frank."[44]

So all ends happily for everyone except Philip Ames, Freda, and Captain Riley. Four of the contented survivors—Doris, Dr. Brandt, Erwin, and James Brandt—leave the house arm in arm, Erwin still puzzling over the button that Freda had *really* found at the crime scene. While he is mulling over this question, Doris notes that there is a button missing from his suit jacket. Now that he knows the actual source of the missing button, Erwin manages a sheepish smile, even as he gazes adoringly at Doris. So that when Dr. Brandt asks Erwin how he can ever repay Erwin's kindness, we know the answer before Erwin replies, "Only one way—by becoming the grandfather of my children."[45] Here he looks hopefully at Doris. We assume that she likes the proposal, for at this moment the movie ends.

The Crime of the Century contains no surprises, but it is an effective mystery of the genre, containing good performances by all the leading players. Robert Elliott as Captain Riley does an especially capable job, mixing laconic, world-weary cynicism with feigned surprise as the events, which he has helped to orchestrate, unfold, and then ultimately wrap themselves around him. Also effective is Frances Dee as Erwin's love interest. Dee was not only a lovely ingenue but also a skilled actress, especially adept at portraying women in need of protection. Although Jean Hersholt emerges as a caricature of the typical European doctor, the script doesn't give him too much original material to work with. Finally, Stuart Erwin gives another careful depiction of a reporter always on the alert for a hot, breaking lead, and not especially scrupulous about bending the law in order to be the first with a story. In fact, Frances Dee told reporter Elizabeth Wilson, who was visiting the set while the picture was in production: "I suppose the most important thing about this picture is that it introduces to the screen a new type of reporter, played by Stu Erwin."[46] While Ms. Dee was not entirely accurate in her assessment of the type of character Erwin depicts: there had been others before him who had portrayed this paradoxical combination of cynicism and compassion—notably Lew Ayres in *Okay America* (1932), Erwin nonetheless makes the most of his part.

The Crime of the Century was well received by contemporary reviewers. One contemporary reviewer had these valid observations: "We would have liked to see Lionel Barrymore play the role of the slightly crazed hypnotist-physician played by Jean Hersholt.... As it is, there is something of the earthworm about the Hersholt characterization that tends to rob it of the sympathy invariably gained by Barrymore. However, lest this tends to make you believe there is something wrong with the picture, let us inform you now that it is one of the most intriguing stories of the year, with a mystery motive that is well nigh perfect.... Wynne Gibson, Frances Dee, and Stuart Erwin shine in their respective roles."[47]

NOTES

1. *Modern Screen* (April 1934): 27.

2. "Viva Villa," *Newsweek* 3 (April 14, 1934): 37.

3. Todd McCarthy, *Howard Hawks: The Grey Fox of Hollywood* (New York: Grove Press, 1997), 193.

4. McCarthy, *Howard Hawks,* 195.

5. Alex Barris, *Stop the Presses! The Newspaperman in American Films* (New York: A. S. Barnes and Company, 1976), 99.

6. McCarthy, *Howard Hawks,* 141–42.

7. *Viva Villa!* Dir. Jack Conway. M-G-M, 1934.

8. *Viva Villa!,* 1934.

9. *Viva Villa!,* 1934.

10. *Viva Villa!,* 1934.

11. *Viva Villa!,* 1934.

12. *Viva Villa!,* 1934.

13. *Viva Villa!,* 1934.

14. *Viva Villa!,* 1934.

15. *Viva Villa!,* 1934.

16. *Viva Villa!,* 1934.

17. *Viva Villa!,* 1934.

18. *Viva Villa!,* 1934.

19. Beery could be disarmingly courteous when the occasion called for it, however. Shortly before making *Viva Villa!,* he had been awarded the 1932 Best Actor Academy Award, which he shared with Fredric March. March had received the most votes, but Beery had come within one vote of winning, so, under the Academy rules, Beery was entitled to one of the statuettes. But no one realized this fact until the end of the ceremony, when someone apprised the master of ceremonies, and an award had to be hastily located. Although it looked as though Beery was being given a consolation prize, reporters at the time noted that Beery handled the embarrassing blunder graciously.

20. Andrew Sarris, *"You Ain't Heard Nothin' Yet": The American Talking Film: History and Memory 1927–1949* (New York: Oxford University Press, 1998), 395.

21. William P. Gaines, "Just A Little Bit Timid," *Shadoplay Magazine* (January 1935): 73.

22. James Cagney, *Cagney by Cagney* (New York: Doubleday, 1976), 101.

23. Patrick McGilligan, *Cagney: The Actor as Auteur* (San Diego: A. S. Barnes and Company, 1982), 141.

24. *The Bride Came C.O.D.* Dir. William Keighley. Warner Bros., 1941.

25. *The Bride Came C.O.D.*, 1941.

26. *The Bride Came C.O.D.*, 1941.

27. *The Bride Came C.O.D.*, 1941.

28. *The Bride Came C.O.D.*, 1941.

29. *Women Are Trouble.* Dir. Earl Taggart. M-G-M, 1936.

30. *Women Are Trouble*, 1936.

31. *Women Are Trouble*, 1936.

32. *Women Are Trouble*, 1936.

33. *Women Are Trouble*, 1936.

34. *Women Are Trouble*, 1936.

35. *Women Are Trouble*, 1936.

36. *Women Are Trouble*, 1936.

37. *Women Are Trouble*, 1936.

38. *Women Are Trouble*, 1936.

39. Samuel S. Hinds looked much better by 1938, when he began appearing in the popular *Dr. Kildare* series for M-G-M. He played Dr. Steven Kildare, the wise, kindly father of the often impetuous young doctor, Jimmy Kildare (Lew Ayres). In *Crime of the Century* he looks as though he already needs the ministrations of young Dr. Kildare.

40. *Crime of the Century.* Dir. William Beaudine. Paramount, 1933.

41. *Crime of the Century*, 1933.

42. *Crime of the Century*, 1933.

43. *Crime of the Century*, 1933.

44. *Crime of the Century*, 1933.

45. *Crime of the Century*, 1933.

46. Elizabeth Wilson, "Snooping Over Hollywood: Watching the Stars at Work," *Silver Screen* 3 (March 1933): 73.

47. *The New Movie Magazine* (April 1933): 100.

7

OUTSIDE OF THE MARGINS

Contest director to winner Stuart Erwin, who is playing Oliver Boggs:
"Do you have any way of identifying yourself?"
Erwin: "No—nothing but my birth certificate."

—*Mr. Boggs Steps Out* (1937)

"The single ingredient in American literature that distinguishes it from other literatures of the world is a kind of giddy, illogical hopefulness."

—John Irving, *The Hotel New Hampshire* (1981)

For much of his career, Stuart Erwin played characters who were just slightly off center and unconventional. But it would be a mistake to assume that such men were lacking in intelligence; occasionally what they needed was common sense, but often they were resourceful men of good intentions who ultimately prevailed over the more ordinary individual. In fact, one may see in the characters of Anne Tyler and John Irving, two of our best modern American novelists, the kind of person Erwin frequently portrayed—modern man thrown askew by the vagaries of the twentieth century and by his own unorthodox personality. Although both Tyler and Irving were born in the early 1940s, long after Erwin had already established this offbeat screen persona, the type of character he played fits just as well into the milieu of the late twentieth century as it had blended with the ethos of the early part of the century.

If Stuart Erwin as a young man in the 1930s missed his chance to show his talents as the ideal Jay Gatsby, the quintessential lost soul of the 1920s, host to parties with many liquor- and cocaine-addicted guests, he also failed to live long enough to portray the ideal Dr. Wilbur Larch, the quintessential rebel against the mainstream establishment and, incidentally, ether addict, in Irving's *Cider House Rules* (1985). Likewise, one can just as well picture him as the absentminded, pensive Ezra Tull in Tyler's *Dinner at the Homesick Restaurant* (1982) or as Win Berry in Irving's *The Hotel New Hampshire* (1981). As a matter of fact, Berry is a man perfectly suited to Erwin's style: an unconventional character who in his youth travels around the countryside on his motorcycle with an ancient, odoriferous trained bear named Earl riding in the sidecar.

It is also a point of coincidental interest that F. Scott Fitzgerald and John Irving come together in *The Hotel New Hampshire* at a crucial juncture in the narrative where Win Berry's daughter Lilly concludes that her father *is* Jay Gatsby because he is always pursuing some wild dream—some illusion which he never quite makes a viable reality. His wide-eyed schemes typically end in failure, probably because his character always seems distracted, never totally alive in the here and now. The narrator of the novel, Win Berry's son, comments on his sister's observations:

> "It eluded us then, but that's no matter—" Lilly quoted to us. "Don't you *see?*" she shrieked. "There's always going to be an *It*—and *It* is going to elude us, every time. It's going to *always* get away," Lilly said. "And father's not going to stop," she said. "He's going to keep going after it, and it's always going to get away. Oh, damn it!" she howled, stamping her little foot.[1]

For Erwin's characters, too, something was "always going to get away." But Erwin never stopped trying. And he usually succeeded in pulling the elusive *It* together.

UP FROM THE BOTTOM OF THE BARREL

Mr. Boggs Steps Out (1937) gives Stuart Erwin one of his most idiosyncratic roles as Oliver Boggs, the dutiful employee of American Statistics, a company that proudly proclaims its motto on the office door: KNOWLEDGE IS POWER. FACTS FOR ANYTHING. ANIMAL MINERAL VEGETABLE. Unlike his fast-talking, cynical performances in his news reporter roles, here Erwin gives an understated, earnest, precise interpretation of a man who has devoted all his days to the solitary life of a researcher dealing in facts. He sounds like a metronome in his measured speech patterns— measured, but not at all slow-witted. Indeed, his compartmentalized vision enables him to win a contest at the movie's outset. He has come the closest of any contestant to guessing the number of beans in a barrel. When the contest director announces the winner and gives the correct total—28,973—declaring that Mr. Boggs has guessed within three, Erwin is genuinely upset that he has been off that much, and even goes so far as to take the barrel with him so that he can count the beans for himself. What we have here is an unusually patient, methodical individual. Several years later, James Thurber was to write a story called "The Catbird Seat." Its protagonist, a mild-mannered file clerk named Erwin Martin, has an uncanny similarity to the character of Oliver Boggs as depicted by Erwin. (Thurber's choice of a first name is intriguing, in light of Martin's resemblance to the persona often created by Stuart Erwin.)

Now that he has the $1,500 prize money from the bean-counting contest, more than he has ever had at one time in his life, Erwin decides to quit his stultifying job and go in search of adventure. The spot that he selects for such an enterprise is hardly what the average person would call breathtaking, but Stuart Erwin's Oliver Boggs is hardly the average person. Therefore, when he sees a newspaper ad informing him of a barrel factory for sale in a town called Peckham Falls, he is determined to buy the factory and leave behind his quiet life of solitude. It is an apparently inexplicable choice for a man of Oliver Boggs's reclusive temperament, but Erwin ultimately makes this paradoxical behavior comprehensible.

When Erwin arrives in Peckham Falls, one of the first lessons that he learns as this "new" man, who has only recently redefined himself, is that the $500 he has just spent for the factory will undoubtedly be money lost. It seems that most of the orders for barrels have come from a pickle and canning business that is about to be sold to the Mammoth Packing Company, which is going to use the building as a warehouse. But Mr. Boggs is a resourceful man, accustomed to digging for information, and tenacious in pursuit of what he wants, so he tries to persuade Ross (Tully Marshall), the owner of the canning business, to salvage his factory by taking orders for a new invention: a collapsible barrel. Erwin has just been introduced to this amazing discovery by Angus Tubbs (Spencer Charters), an absent-minded, dithering, eccentric old man and the father of Oleander Tubbs, the young lady who is currently running the barrel factory office. The ingenuity behind the making of this contraption is a feature that Erwin very much admires. Consequently, he hauls one of these barrels to Ross's spacious home, places it on an expensive piece of furniture, carelessly scratching the valuable desk as he does so, and smashes the barrel with a handy golf club, sending a broken part of the club flying across the room, but collapsing the barrel.

Oblivious to the damage that he has caused, he maintains his enthusiasm for this unique container by explaining to Ross how Ross himself can keep his factory open and save money if only he will use these barrels in shipping. Ignoring Ross's growing irritation and sarcastic expression, he further explains how these barrels take up so little space that Ross could ship more merchandise at once, thus underselling his competitors and making a huge profit. Ross remains skeptical, but makes a deal with this idealistic young man. Ross says that if Oliver can show him how he can make one quarter of a million dollars by selling these barrels, then he will be convinced of their desirability and will keep the factory open.

Erwin decides that this is a fair agreement; after all, he is accustomed to dealing with large figures, but only when they appear on paper—not when they confront him in the real world. So Erwin tells Ross's disgruntled factory employees that they can go to work for him. He has deluded himself into thinking that Ross has made a reasonable request—a quarter of a million dollars in barrel orders. Without considering the possible knotty complications that might be tightening around his neck, he tells the workers that he will pay them just as soon as the expected barrel orders come in. The restless laborers, led by Burns (Milburn Stone), look like a group borrowed from a Frank Capra movie: "little," common men as heroes. Not wanting to disappoint these hard workers, Oliver Boggs sets off on a Don Quixote-like quest, not with the faithful Sancho Panza, but with his sample barrel cradled in his arms.

Furthermore, like Don Quixote, he is a man on a mission. Since he has promised Ross's former employees that their jobs with him are secure, he is determined to keep that promise. He travels up and down much of the East Coast, improbably toting that ungainly barrel, but the answer he receives at every office is the same: no one wants to buy barrels. Possibly because his arms are sore from hauling that awkward assemblage of wood and nails, he finally gives the barrel away to a drunk he meets on the street in one of these eastern towns. Erwin at last finds a use for it when he places a stray cat into the increasingly unwieldy crate and unceremoniously hands both barrel and cat to the drunk.

But his inability to promote collapsible barrels is not the worst problem faced by Erwin's Oliver Boggs. He has been lying to the people of Peckham Falls about his success; that is, while he has been on the road, he has been sending them money from his own pocket—money that is supposedly from the sale of these barrels. He is both embarrassed by his failure and horrified at the idea that his money will soon run out, leaving his employees out of work. Yet, on his return to Peckham Falls, he is truthful enough to admit his mistake and courageous enough to address a crowd that could easily and quickly turn into a mob, ready to impale him on his own errors in judgment. Facing the gathering, he promises to pay them just as soon as he has the money.

And initially, his promise seems to be a futile one, that is, until he gets another inspiration from Angus Tubbs. When Angus casually mentions that fruit tastes better in wood, Erwin rushes back to Ross with the idea of manufacturing barrels to store fruit. "Food in wood tastes very good,"[2] he rhapsodizes to Ross, as though he were applying for a job as a writer of doggerel for greeting cards. But for some unaccountable reason, Ross likes Boggs's latest scheme, even echoing Boggs with his own frightful rhymes, and signs an agreement with Oliver for the exclusive rights to purchase all the barrels that Boggs's factory can produce. And, despite attempts by Dennis Andrews (Walter Byron), lawyer for the Mammoth Packing Company, to steal the barrel patent rights from Tubbs and to thus discredit Boggs, Erwin's man of good intentions prevails and saves the jobs of his employees as well as the small town itself. He also gets the girl, Angus's daughter Oleander.

In all of these maneuverings, Stuart Erwin brings into the spotlight the seemingly out-of-focus Oliver Boggs and makes him not only visible but also understandable. Like many of Anne Tyler's protagonists, Boggs trudges hopefully and patiently through the maze of modern existence, sometimes traveling the wrong way down a one-way street, but always arriving at his destination intact and triumphant.

A NUTTY CAMARADERIE

Several years after Oliver Boggs found happiness with Oleander Tubbs and those collapsible barrels, Stuart Erwin would play Lawrence Trent, another contest winner. The movie is *Cracked Nuts* (1941); and, with the inflation that was present in prewar America, his prize has now grown to $5,000. This time he wins—not because he can count accurately the number of beans in a container—but because he has composed a slogan for the Refrigerall Refrigerator, which has sponsored the Refrigerall Opportunity Contest. Just what kind of opportunity this refrigerator affords its owners is never disclosed. (Erwin's alliterative winning slogan: "If it's a Refrigerall Refrigerator, it refrigerates.")[3] This dreadfully dull sentence is acknowledged in a radio studio, where Erwin and other distinguished denizens of Oswego Falls await Lawrence Trent's introduction. The radio announcer (Tom Hanlon) proudly proclaims that the distinguished mayor of Oswego Falls, Wilfred Smun

(Francis Pierlot), will present the $5,000 check to Trent. Like many a politician both before and after, Mayor Smun is a windbag, and the announcer exerts much effort before he succeeds in shutting him up, thus permitting Erwin to go to the microphone and receive his $5,000 award.

All the radio show guests treat the microphone as though it were an electric power line strung across the street in the midst of a thunderstorm. Mayor Smun has to be encouraged to talk directly into it in order to be heard; so too does Erwin as he timidly approaches the speaker's platform. Once these novices get the hang of it, however, they act as if the mike were a deaf person whose ear required a bombardment of loud noise. When the announcer, in his most genial, officious manner, asks Erwin what he is going to do with the money, Erwin stutters shyly into the mike, "I—I—I—I'm going to get married."

ANNOUNCER (in his best patronizing manner): Is the little girl in the audience?

ERWIN: No, she's in New York. I'm going to get her there and fetch her back here and make her the missus.

ANNOUNCER: In New York? What's she doing so far from home?

ERWIN: She's studying typing and things.

ANNOUNCER (wishing he could get on with the conversation): How nice. I'll bet she's a pretty little thing, too.

ERWIN (pleased at the announcer's apparent interest): Oh, you bet she is. Would you like to see her? I've got her picture right here. (He fumbles in his jacket pockets, searching for the visual proof, clearly proud of his girl.) She's very pretty—very, very—*there*.[4]

At this, he happily displays the object of his search; there is a close-up of his pocket watch, with his fiancée's picture comfortably nestled to the left of the timepiece.

The viewer is about to see this paragon of beauty in action, as the scene soon shifts to reveal Erwin's betrothed, Sharon Knight (Una Merkel). Here she is seen in the New York office of patent attorney James Mitchell (William Frawley) busily doing some of those "things" that Erwin had vaguely mentioned to the radio listeners as the subject of her study. It is clear that she has learned some typing skills, for she is composing a letter to an inventor with the exotic name of Boris Kabikoff (a possible send up of Boris Karloff?), who is currently staying at the Cozy Hotel.

We soon learn that the intentions of Mr. Kabikoff (Mischa Auer) are more insidious than cozy, when we see him at his hotel with his fellow conspirator Eddie (Shemp Howard). What these nominal "inventors" are trying to peddle is a smart robot—so intelligent, in fact, that it is almost human—as indeed it is. What makes this robot so clever is that Auer and Howard have an ingenious plan to hide Shemp in this metal contraption, thus making it look as though the mechanical man (whom Auer's Boris Kabikoff names Ivan) can indeed respond to human commands and do human things. Apparently, among these human activities it can perform are excretory functions; a running gag throughout the film involves the flushing noises that from time to time emanate from the robot's metal frame. Nor does the robot look any better than he sounds, for he resembles the Tin Man from *The Wizard of Oz*; that is, assuming that the Tin Man had been sloshed for three days.

The scene shifts back to Una Merkel as Sharon, Erwin's bride-to-be, who has been sent by the business college into an office environment that provides her with ample preparation for her marriage to the peculiar Lawrence Trent. To illustrate, when Auer brings Ivan the robot to visit her boss Frawley, she discovers that mechanical men can perform actions usually associated only with humans, for she is chased—albeit slowly—by the lumbering Shemp Howard hidden within this mass of steel. Auer finds her cowering in a corner, standing on the furniture, with Ivan making his move on her. Auer soothes Ivan's harried forehead by applying a brush as though he were basting a roast, all the while reassuring Merkel that the only thing disturbing her odd admirer is that he is a hyperblondiac—when he sees blondes, he goes mad. But another fascinating feature of the Ivan robot is that he telegraphs these hyper intentions by making a flushing noise just before he begins his assault on unsuspecting, unprepared blonde female strangers.

Having disposed of Ivan the Terrible Tin Man, Merkel encounters another odd inventor. While her boss William Frawley is entertaining Mischa Auer and the robot in his office, she sits outside at her desk, listening to a gangly young man as he balances on what look like ladies' platform heels from a later period. The heels on which he is poised are striped, so that this hopeful client impresses one as a combination of zebra and giraffe. When Merkel inquires as to what use these heels might be put, he informs her that they are just right for looking over heads during a parade. As he awkwardly shuffles out, he collides with Erwin, who has come to fetch his beloved Sharon and take her back to Oswego Falls.

After disentangling himself from the man on short stilts, Erwin hugs Merkel and they sit, whereupon he tells her of his good fortune in winning the contest. He admits that his life in Oswego Falls has been awful without her, but that her absence has given him ambition, thus his prizewinning slogan. "Sit down and I'll tell you about it,"[5] he enthusiastically orders the still-seated Merkel. However, Erwin's Lawrence Trent is about to become an ideal illustration of the cliché "A fool and his money are soon parted." Mischa Auer as Boris Kabikoff and William Frawley as James Mitchell have overheard Erwin tell Merkel that he has won $5,000. Both the phony inventor Kabikoff and the equally crafty Mitchell have their own reasons for wanting to get to Erwin's money. Kabikoff wants it for a nonexistent invention, and Mitchell wants it because his patent business is failing due to his ex-wife Ethel (Astrid Allwyn), who demands back alimony. Mitchell is unaware that Kabikoff's robot acts so human because it is; Kabikoff is unaware of Mitchell's woman problems. Both are aware of a sucker when they see one, though, and they can see Erwin quite well.

When Frawley hurries into the outer office to grab the hoped-for quarry, he finds Erwin energetically kissing Merkel, whom he proceeds to drop ungallantly onto the floor when he is startled by the intruder. As the two connivers have suspected, Erwin is a trusting soul, for he allows them to con him into investing $2,000 of his prize winnings in shares of Ivan, the smart robot. But that's not all. His $2,000 eventually grows into another $3,000 investment when Mitchell later discovers to his great chagrin that his ex-wife's attorney McAneny (Emmett Vogan), of the firm Driscoll, Driscoll, McAneny, and Driscoll, has had Mitchell's bank account attached; thus Erwin's initial $2,000 has disappeared, withdrawn from the private account into which Mitchell had put the check. So now all of Erwin's $5,000 prize money has glided down into the moral abyss created by Auer as Boris and Frawley as Mitchell.

Nor are Erwin's self-created problems over with the loss of all his recent fortune. After signing away his money, Erwin takes Merkel to lunch, where she shows him a telegram from Warren Benson of Imperial Research. It seems that Boris Kabikoff is a former employee of Imperial (hence the exotic Russian name) and that he had disappeared with an incomplete mechanical man. According to Benson's telegram: "He may try to work fake robot racket. Any attempt to patent same will result in injunction suit." Erwin inquires, "What does that mean, *injunction suit*?"

MERKEL: It means a lawsuit, Larry.
ERWIN: I was afraid it meant that.[6]

At this moment, Erwin enlightens her about the loss of not only his $2,000 but also his $3,000. He vows to return to Oswego Falls, cautions her not to tell anyone about the telegram in the meantime, and swears that he will somehow recover his money. As he determinedly rushes out of the restaurant, he demonstrates that he has lost none of his distinctive talent for physical mayhem as he crashes into a waiter, causing dishes to scatter. But he returns a moment later as though nothing extraordinary had happened, and hands the waiter some money, telling him to keep the change.

While Merkel waits for Erwin's return from Oswego Falls, she continues to amuse herself with quirky inventors who have come to see her boss. When we next see her, she is seated at her desk, wearing a pleasantly vacant expression as she listens to a man outfitted with a fireman's hat and beaming at a fire hydrant that he has placed in the middle of the floor. He executes some sort of legerdemain—both verbal as well as physical—as he lectures her on the beauties of this hydrant and the use to which it might be put. "When the atmosphere is condensed, precipitation is caused," he informs the increasingly uneasy Merkel. Opening the front of the hydrant, he starts a fire; from the inside, a flame can be seen ascending as though from a blowtorch. Then, through some sort of mysterious process doubtless understood only by Nobel physicists, the eruption spurts as high as the ceiling, burning a hole in it that allows water to pour down. The overall impression one gets from this visual display is of an indoor rain limited to about three square feet. In fact, throughout this scene, one can imagine the water being surrounded by glass doors, thus allowing Merkel to have her own semi-private shower. Having created a certain amount of soggy havoc, the fireman casually picks up his hydrant and then exits, leaving behind his continuous downward eruption.

Enter two characters from Oswego Falls—Francis Pierlot as Mayor Smun and Will Wright as Sylvanus Boogle. (A name that might have been invented by W. C. Fields.) "We're just having a little rain," Merkel explains to the puzzled visitors. At this interesting bit of news, Major Smun observes that it is not raining outside. But in the next instant he has an epiphany of sorts, does a take, then happily concludes, "*Office* rain. Ain't New York *marvelous!*"[7] The reason that Boogle and Smun are in New York is the result of Erwin's off screen trip to Oswego Falls; they are there to help Erwin and thus to provide a happy conclusion to the movie. They pretend to be wealthy investors who want to corner the market in Ivan shares, provided that Frawley and Auer dump Trent and return his $5,000 to him. All of this happens in due time; Erwin and Merkel return to Oswego Falls to get married; the tricksters are left with their own rope tied around their necks; and Ivan is presumably metamorphosed back into Shemp Howard as Eddie and free to chase blondes sans the cumbersome tin can.

Cracked Nuts is appropriately titled: it is a weird, absurdly funny movie. And although it was released by Universal, a major studio, it was probably relegated to the bottom half of a double bill in 1941 and promptly forgotten.

Today, it has become a cult favorite, its off-the-wall humor doubtless better appreciated now than it was almost sixty years ago. Many silly moments stand out: Erwin's serious demeanor in accepting congratulations for his puerile slogan about the Refrigerall Refrigerator; Ivan's well-timed flushing noises; Merkel's bemusement at the bizarre inventors and their equally bizarre inventions; Erwin's propensity for colliding into people and objects—and not always remaining on his feet. In addition, there are the funny names given to people and places: Boris Kabikoff; Wilfred Smun (the last name sounding like *Smut* in the early scenes), Sylvanus Boogle, the Cozy Hotel. The ex-Mrs. Mitchell has positioned herself into an elegant apartment called the Venus de Milo Arms. Then there is the attorney for the ex-Mrs. Mitchell, McAneny, whose name is uttered throughout with the final syllable sounding like *Ninny*.

So too, there are funny bits of business throughout. Early in the movie, when Erwin proudly shows Merkel's photo to the radio announcer, the picture is not the usual studio photograph, with the woman sensuously shown from the shoulders up in a provocative pose. Rather, we see Merkel seated at her typewriter, looking at the camera somewhat quizzically. Furthermore, whenever Erwin kisses Merkel, something usually occurs to inhibit or interrupt them. He drops her on the floor when his amorous impulses are halted by Frawley's entrance into the office. He leans over the desk to kiss her and, because she is almost out of reach, he knocks over most of the supplies on it. He kisses her on a bench in the park and finds himself being stared at by some interested bystanders, to whom he politely tips his hat. In addition, at the end of the movie, in an effort to show his affection for her in another way, he gently takes the arm of the person who has just come up behind him, looks toward the camera at Frawley, Auer, et al., and says to the individual whose arm he is blithely steering toward the door, "Honey, when we're married—"[8] This person happens to be the black actor Mantan Moreland, who protests that he is *already* married.

But one of the most curious happenings occurs in relation to Shemp Howard and his penchant for blondes. While he is still clad in armor as Ivan, he breaks into a department store and carries out a blonde dummy, but not before a witness has spotted his getaway with what she assumes is a woman he has just killed. The climax of the movie involves a car chase by the police as they speed after Ivan, who they assume will be arrested for murder. One is briefly reminded here of Dennis Hopper in *River's Edge* (1987), albeit a movie with a vastly different, intensely dark, sinister motif, where he plays with a life-sized inflatable female doll, all the while proclaiming that he isn't crazy because he knows that she is not real.

For his part, Stuart Erwin enjoyed working with Una Merkel, with whom he had appeared previously in *Day of Reckoning* (1933), *Have a Heart* (1934), *Checkers* (1937), and *Sandy Gets Her Man* (1940). Shortly after he had starred with her in *Have a Heart*, he told an interviewer that he thought Merkel had "a fine sense of comedy."[9] Certainly, Merkel's whimsical, genteel quirkiness contributed to the overall humorous effect of many of her films. She often seemed to be just on the verge of making all of life's puzzle pieces fit together properly, but sometimes she found to her dismay that the edges were frayed. She would utilize her slightly off-key personality to good effect many years later in the film adaptation of Tennessee Williams's *Summer and Smoke* (1961), in which she played a small but serious role as the pathetically deranged mother of Geraldine Page. One suspects that she would have been an excellent choice to play the aging Southern belle Amanda in another Williams play, *The Glass Menagerie*. But in 1941, the still relatively youthful Merkel was an ideal partner for Erwin in *Cracked Nuts*. Both of them create extraordinary but likeable characters as they muddle along toward a happy conclusion, all the while maintaining their optimism in spite of the double dealing, daffy people they meet on their journey through the heart of New York City's distinctly dark jungle.

ON THE LOOSE WITH MABOOSE

At the beginning of *Killer Dill* (1947) we hear a voice-over narration portentously intoning some facts about the bygone days of gangsters and Prohibition. The unseen narrator takes us back to 1931, when gangland rulers were heroes and people made their own bathtub gin. We see a montage of scenes, purporting to take place in 1931, and we are led into one of those "Joe-sent-me" speakeasies, complete with peephole in place in the door. The narrator also educates us about the light prison sentences given to these gangster heroes, largely due to the efforts of shadowy lawyers. We also note with some amusement that the hairstyles, clothing, shoes, and accessories worn by these Prohibition-era ladies are specifically post-World War II fashions. But no matter. This movie, with Stuart Erwin playing the title role, is not a Warner Bros. underworld flick of the thirties, filled with the gritty realism of a squalid urban setting. Rather, it is an extremely funny send-up of the gangster genre, with pointed allusions to two films starring Stuart Erwin's sometime costar, James Cagney.

The first reference comes with the opening narration itself, reminiscent of the opening montage of Cagney's *The Roaring Twenties* (1939). The second reference also occurs near the beginning, when Erwin goes to a movie with Millie (Dorothy Granger), one of the women who work for him in the ladies' lingerie business. They attend a showing of *Public Enemy Number 21*; the highlight of the action on the movie screen is the squashing of a grapefruit into the face of the onscreen actress by the gangland hero, who tells his victim, "You talk too much." At this not-so-subtle reference to Cagney's *Public Enemy* (released in 1931, the alleged chronological setting for *Killer Dill*), Erwin reacts to the events he is watching by placing his head in his hand and muttering, "Oh *no*." There are at least two possible interpretations of his line. Either he is horrified at the glorification of violence that his character of Johnny Dill is witnessing, or he is surreptitiously groaning at the very obvious, very heavy-handed parody of friend Cagney's early gangster classic. Probably both.

In any event, Dorothy Granger as Millie, Erwin's faithful employee, is fascinated by the movie and intrigued by the rough hero who, she informs the unimpressed Erwin, is a character based on the real-life gangster Big Moroni. (The name sounds less Italian when it is not said aloud; when one sees it in print, one is naturally tempted to add that final *c*. As pronounced by the characters throughout the movie, it rhymes with *baloney*.) "Now *there's* a guy," Granger gushes to Erwin. When he hastily expresses his desire to make a fast exit and not subject himself to any more of this nonsense, Granger demurs, "Are you crazy? This guy's my type."[10] Nor can Erwin believe it when she continues that she could really go for a guy like him. Nor does Erwin's sense of propriety keep him from walking out on the movie, leaving Granger to make her way home alone; he seems especially disturbed by her labeling him a "little boy."

Upon reflection, however, Erwin vows to become less vulnerable to such a demeaning reference and to cultivate a personality that is more like those of these macho guys on the screen. Once outside the theater, he even does a quick, suggestive Cagney imitation when he hitches up his shoulders, a la Cagney in *Angels with Dirty Faces*. (This constitutes another anachronism, as the movie's action allegedly takes place in 1931 and *Angels* was released in 1938. But never mind.) Moreover, the joke here is double-edged. First, Erwin is imitating Cagney's tough guy persona, which was itself an imitation of characters that Cagney had known during his youth in one of New York City's toughest neighborhoods. Cagney, often imitated, was himself a great mimic who ably adapted memories of his childhood friends, neighborhood pimps, and even his own father, an alcoholic who died while he was still in his forties.

Similarly, the other edge of that sword involves Cagney, the very private man, whose personality offscreen was much like Erwin's own character:

modest, diffident, and often self-deprecating. These were aspects of the Cagney personality that Erwin did not have to imitate. The two actors also shared an honesty that translated onscreen into a genuine nobility of spirit, a quality that served as the immutable point around which revolved each scene in which they appeared.

At any rate, Erwin is most concerned now about the fact that he is losing his very beautiful girlfriend Judy (Anne Gwynne) to his crooked but inept lawyer chum Allen (Frank Albertson). So when we next see Erwin, the New Man, he is swaggering into a speakeasy, cigarette hanging from his mouth, and experimenting with his gangster diction and jargon by phoning Anne Gwynne (who he knows is not home because she is out with Albertson). But he figures that talking to himself out loud to an imaginary listener will gather less curiosity from bystanders than speaking indistinct gangland threats to himself. Fortunately, he has a better-than-hoped-for opportunity to practice his newly acquired inarticulate diction when a man appears behind him at the phone, waiting his turn. Sounding like a Damon Runyon character, he spouts some tough-sounding words into the phone, all the better to impress his listener. And, with an appropriately absurd finishing touch, he hangs up the phone, thus allowing his nickel to clink back into place through the opening. Clearly embarrassed at this evidence that there had been no one to listen to him at the other end, he presents a shamefaced expression to the man behind him. But the eavesdropper remains unaware of Erwin's novice status, for after Erwin's guilty exit, this next phone customer shakes his head in awe as he observes, "Those guys always win—even the telephones."[11]

Erwin's next venture into the netherworld does not have quite such a serendipitous conclusion. His foray from Dr. Jekyll to Mr. Hyde begins when he spots two attractive women seated at the speakeasy bar and makes a move on one of them. All is going well with this flirtation, as the woman seems to think that he is the real thing. At this moment, however, Big Moroni (Ben Welden), who has just entered the speakeasy with two of his nefarious colleagues, decides to turn his self-important charm on Erwin's targeted brunette. When she plaintively announces to Erwin "That man's flirting with me," he resolves to try out his new persona by strolling over to Big Moroni—Public Enemy Number 21 himself—and tweaking his nose. Then he pulls out of Moroni's jacket pocket a very large handkerchief, casually wipes his hands on it and, in an ill-considered move, throws it back in Moroni's face. "That's for nuttin', see?" he threatens the astonished Moroni. He then struts back to the bar to rejoin his possible pickup. But his small triumph is short lived when, first, the two ladies leave, and next, when Moroni's two henchmen approach Erwin with the unfortunate news that the gentlemen he has just impolitely assaulted is none other than Big Moroni. Dragging the half-collapsed wannabe tough guy to the big man's table, these thugs present him to the Public Enemy, who pulls a very large, but a very obviously toy pistol on Erwin, announcing in his most menacing tone, "What you did was slow suicide."[12]

But what the luckless Moroni does not realize is that it is not only Erwin for whom the bells of doom are tolling, but also for Moroni himself, inasmuch as his chief rival Maboose (Milburn Stone) has big plans for Moroni's future. Maboose is currently Public Enemy Number 24, but desperately wants to be promoted to a *lower* number—in this case to become Public Enemy Number 23. (Just who is Public Enemy Number 1 is never clarified in the movie, but it never really matters anyway.) So Maboose plots with another of Moroni's distinguished employees, Little Joe (inappropriately named, for this character is played by former wrestler Mike Mazurki), to have Moroni rubbed out for a comfortable cash settlement to be paid to Little Joe. Maboose figures that, with Number 21 wiped away, he will easily be able to drop from Number 24 to Number 23. (Much like the effect of removing one link in a chain, I suppose.)

What is also intriguing about this Public Enemy Number 24 is his name. Milburn Stone's fictional moniker is pronounced just like an English speaker would pronounce the name of the underworld character found in a series of crime films directed by Fritz Lang. Although the German pronunciation requires *Mabuse* to be said with three syllables, with a *schwa* or *uh*-sound as the final, unaccented syllable, the similarities between the two names are striking and perhaps more than coincidental. Lang's notorious Dr. Mabuse is featured in silent films as well as in sound features made in Germany by this great *noir* director. Perhaps Stone's odd designation is an allusion to the Dr. Mabuse of the 1933 release, *Testament des Dr. Mabuse*. In this particular incarnation, the title character is a criminal who controls his vast underworld holdings even while he is confined to a lunatic asylum—and indeed he continues his depraved activities by a type of remote control even after he is dead. If the reference to the weird Dr. Mabuse is deliberate, it is quite appropriate, since the majority of the characters in *Killer Dill* seem sorely in need of asylum, while some of them do, in fact, end up quite dead.

Foremost among those who are mentally challenged and whose fate is terminal is Little Joe. Little Joe in due course rids the plot of Moroni by strangling him and planting his dead body in Erwin's hotel room in a clothes trunk filled with samples of women's clothing. Erwin uses these samples for his models to display as a part of his lingerie business; he is not expecting to find anything there except inanimate objects. And, well, yes, he does find an inanimate object, but only because Moroni has been so rendered.

At first, all Erwin sees is that Moroni appears to be resting in a sitting position with his legs splayed at the bottom of the trunk, so Erwin initially mistakes him for a living stowaway. But when Erwin realizes that Moroni is now indeed a stiff, he is frantic. His first inclination is to try to hide the corpse by folding the unruly legs and arms of the former Public Enemy Number 21 and pushing these limbs back into the trunk. But, even in death, Moroni presents problems for Erwin. The deceased refuses to stay put.

Erwin's dilemma worsens when a customer drops in to pick up a nightgown that his wife has admired; this customer has also spent many years as a house detective and thus might be expected to handle Erwin's thorny situation with professional aplomb. But no. Instead, when he spies the deceased, he promptly faints, collapsing on Erwin, causing both of them to hit the floor. Regaining what little composure he has remaining, Erwin picks himself up and then picks up Moroni, flinging him into a nearby closet. Then, in an inspirational moment, he takes one of his mannequins and places it in the space that Moroni had formerly occupied.

Meanwhile, the house dick is lying prone, resembling a large bear with a protruding stomach. On this ample stomach is a hip flask, a reminder to us that this movie is supposed to be taking place in 1931, when Prohibition was the law of the land. In another creative gesture, Erwin grabs the flask, samples its contents himself, and then gives some to the befuddled bear on the floor. Upon awakening, he starts to accuse Erwin of murder, but Erwin quickly points out the hallucinatory aspects of this sepulchral vision by showing him that the once and former cadaver is really nothing more than a female mannequin. Shaking his head in dismay, the house dick concludes that this last batch of bootleg liquor, which has apparently been comfortably nestled in the flask, is the culprit.

After this intruder exits, Erwin is confronted with a dilemma involving another type of exit: He must now figure out how to dispose of Moroni's potentially embarrassing presence. So he phones the hotel operator and requests her to contact the Herkey-Drive-Yourself Company and to have a truck sent right over. And oh yes, he also needs a porter to come to his room to pick up a trunk. Something in Erwin's voice must have tipped off the operator to an imminent nervous breakdown on the part of her caller, for Erwin's next comment is a sarcastic question in response to her apparent query: "How do I feel? Oh ho ho . . . I feel *fine*, thank you."[13] And he shakily replaces the receiver—edgy, frenzied— looking like nothing so much as a hunted man. If he had thought that being tough was the way to attract women, he is learning differently now.

His next chore is to place the body back in the trunk. Under the circumstances, he accomplishes this physical feat with considerable poise—first dragging Moroni out of the closet and then neatly fitting him into the trunk by folding him up as though he were a collapsible ironing board. All the while, he has to push various items of women's clothing out of the way so as to see more clearly where to deposit Moroni. Finally, he closes and latches the trunk door. With the help of a porter, Erwin wheels the departed into the elevator and out onto the street, where a Herkey-Drive-Yourself pickup is waiting. (Perhaps the company is so called because the name rhymes with *jerky*, an apt adjective to describe Erwin's movements here.) With the trunk and its incriminating contents loaded onto the pickup bed, Erwin takes off through a residential neighborhood, where all the cars parked along the street are 1940s models. So much for even the semblance of verisimilitude and historical accuracy: we have left 1931 for good.

Nor is Erwin's character particularly concerned with chronological setting either. We cut to a close-up of his determined expression as he hunches over the steering wheel, a race car driver bent on winning the Indy 500. As he is speeding along, the trunk/coffin bounces merrily off the back of the truck, landing in the street where curious passersby give it a careful look.

Cut to newspaper headline: *Public Enemy No. 21 Slain. Notorious Gangster's Body Flung at Foot of Policeman.* The paper goes on to describe Erwin as a Jekyll and Hyde salesman. In the best mobster tradition, Erwin is forced to hide out in a hotel room above an establishment called Murphy's Laundry, where he remains for six days without food. Even the mouse that peeks out from his home in the baseboards to grab a bite of cheese is eating better than Erwin, much to Erwin's chagrin. An ability to communicate a controlled anxiety was one of Erwin's fortes, and here he demonstrates this aptitude as he paces the floor, waiting for Judy to bring him something to eat. When she arrives, she brings a welcome hamburger but some unwelcome news: His lawyer friend Allen is going to defend him of the murder charges. That, moans Erwin, will make him the *thirteenth* case that Allen has lost.

Further, once Allen shows up at Erwin's hideout, Erwin is even more convinced that his is a lost cause. Erwin's conviction is the result of Allen's cheerful announcement that he has arranged for Erwin's sensational surrender on the steps of city hall, where reporters have eagerly gathered to await the event. The effusive Allen beams at the increasingly distressed Erwin as he tells him, "This is going to be the biggest surrender since Cornwallis." When Erwin's concerned—but now apparently former—girlfriend Judy wants to know, "Will he have to go to jail?" Allen is smugly reassuring, "Only as a formality. I'll have him out of jail by morning."[14]

As we jump cut to the next scene, we see a close-up of Erwin the following morning, behind bars. Still smug, confident, and supremely happy about the ongoing publicity concerning his client, Allen stands outside these bars, waving in Erwin's puzzled face a newspaper that now proclaims Erwin to be the new Public Enemy No. 21. But Erwin no longer wants to be Public Enemy No. *Anything*; he just wants out. "Tomorrow," Allen assures him.

Jump cut to Erwin still peering out wistfully from behind bars. It is four weeks later. This time the amiable Allen assures him that he no longer has to worry about getting released from jail "tomorrow," for that is when his trial begins anyway. Now all Erwin has to fret about is the distinct possibility that his life will soon be terminated. Hardly the outcome he expected when he began his one-day excursion into the sordid world of racketeering. Nor is Erwin any happier to be out of jail the next day and facing a jury of twelve very hostile-looking people. He dolefully informs Allen that all of the jurors have *bars* in their eyes. However, the women spectators now have eyes only for Erwin; ironically, he has achieved the precise goal that he had sought—to make himself more impressive to the opposite sex. This irony is not lost on him, nor is the knowledge that there is little he can do to court the ladies once he is incarcerated and executed for murder.

As the prosecution displays its witnesses, Erwin's desperation intensifies. The jury hears the damning evidence of the house detective, the hotel porter, Little Joe, even the eavesdropper who had listened in on Erwin's bogus phone conversation: he claims that he heard Erwin threaten Moroni. When it is the defense's turn, things go so badly that Erwin jumps up from time to time, objecting not to the defense witnesses' testimony, but to his own lawyer. The cheerfully complacent Allen calls a series of character witnesses, allegedly to speak of Erwin's reputation for decency; instead, most gush over him, calling him an important, charming gangster—that is, until Judy is called to the stand. At first, Erwin is delighted with her testimony, for she reports that he is a kind, gentle man, incapable of murder. Then the prosecutor proceeds to have at her. He questions her motives by disclosing to a furious Erwin and to the rest of the courtroom that Judy's motives in wanting Erwin cleared are suspect, since she and Allen are engaged. Thus, an exoneration of the accused would be a victory for her fiancé.

All of this is too much for the indignant defendant, who yells at Allen, "Oh—so that's what you were doing while I was in jail." He grabs Allen's throat, vowing, "If I'm gonna die for murder, it's gonna be yours."[15] He doesn't get very far in his assassination attempt, however, because he is subdued by two court policemen. Then, in a sublimely absurd moment, one of the jurors makes an illogical observation, which nonetheless leads to Erwin's acquittal. The juror observes to the court that, since Erwin was unable to choke a 15½" neck (Allen's), he certainly would be unable to break an 18½" neck (Moroni's). What collar size has to do with death by strangulation is a question that no one in the courtroom appears particularly concerned with. Killer Dill is free at last, and Allen is more than delighted to take credit for Erwin's freedom.

But Erwin's gangster days are not yet over. Both rival gangs are again after him, but for different reasons. Maboose and his followers think that Erwin has pulled off a brilliant coup by joining with his lawyer to suborn the juror, so they want Erwin to join their mob. Not quite the conclusion to the trial that Erwin had hoped for. Likewise, the Moroni gang wants Erwin, but for more insidious reasons. Louis Moroni, the brother of the deceased Public Enemy No. 21, wants Erwin's hide in order to avenge his brother. At this point in his exciting new occupation, Erwin thinks that the most prudent action to take would be to return to the ladies' lingerie business. But shots fired in his direction by the Moroni bunch as he leaves his lawyer's office persuade him to rethink his decision. He reluctantly joins the Maboose gang to get protection from Moroni's colleagues in crime.

As Erwin speeds away in a 1930s roadster, followed in another 1930s model car by Moroni's sometime friend Little Joe and another of Moroni's goons, we see that one more time we have entered the twilight zone of no time at all. If time is relative, as physicists tell us, then *Killer Dill* obviously subscribes to this dictum. As Erwin and his pursuers race down the streets of this unnamed, generic city, they pass—and pass again, for the camera tracks multiple times down the same street—roads lined with cars of clearly 1940s vintage. The total effect is marvelously dizzying.

Meanwhile, back at Erwin's hotel room (why he lives in a hotel is never clarified, except perhaps to show that his lifestyle is as unsettled as his nerves), Maboose and one of his gang are poking through Erwin's clothes trunks, admiring the women's clothing that they find therein. (How they got into the room and just why they are there are two other unanswered questions, but these issues don't matter to the plot anyway.) Holding up various garments and unaware of Erwin's occupation in his previous life, Maboose observes, "He must have a harem," to which his fellow mobster replies with grudging envy, "And in all *sizes*!" Maboose also informs his confederate that he is just going to use Erwin for a while. After Maboose has said this, he proceeds to demonstrate that he knows a good underworld cliché by speaking of Erwin's ultimate fate, "Then he goes for a ride."[16] After all, Maboose is still trying to become Public Enemy No. 21, a goal that he will achieve if only he can rub out Erwin.

Having gotten rid of his pursuers (they would not enter Maboose territory), Erwin arrives at his room, where he resumes his tough-talking, mush-mouthed persona in front of his guests. After all, if he wants "protection" from Maboose et al., he must act like one of them. Apparently, his act is enough to convince Maboose that an initiation rite would be appropriate for their novice member, so he proposes to Erwin that they "knock off the Blue Cockatoo tonight. Shove the Moroni gang right out."[17] This is, of course, in the lingo of another gangster cliché, an offer that Erwin cannot refuse.

When the now-famous "killer" enters the Blue Cockatoo, he sees Mr. Jones (Stanley Andrews), a businessman whom he has been trying for a long time to get as one of his lingerie customers. Heretofore, Erwin had been unable to get past Jones's secretary, but now when he approaches their table, he is greeted by Jones and his secretary with a newfound respect born out of fear. Jones orders enough lingerie from Erwin to provide undergarments for the entire student body of a women's college. In the meantime, Maboose and his buddy can see Erwin but cannot hear what he is saying; they assume that he is threatening the gentleman with whom he is speaking. So when Erwin returns and demonstrates that he can also speak in clichés by saying, "I just knocked off an order from one of the toughest guys in underwear," Maboose is naturally curious. "In *what?*" he responds to Erwin's peculiar word choice. At this, Erwin hastily corrects himself, "In the *underworld.*"[18]

We quickly cut to the next scene where one of Moroni's gang is telling Little Joe that they got dispossessed the previous night from the Blue Cockatoo and that Killer Dill is "muscling in" on their territory. So Little Joe proposes to infiltrate the rival gang in order to keep a closer eye on Killer. He says he will pretend to have argued with his own bunch of racketeers so that Maboose will believe he truly wants to change sides. At this juncture, we are probably supposed to remember that Little Joe is used to switching allegiances, for he is the one who began this renewed battle of wills by bumping off Moroni in the first place.

None of this is too terribly important to remember, however, because the scriptwriters have decided by this point to tie down loose ends. They do this by having Erwin learn of Judy's imminent marriage to the loutish Allen and by showing Erwin obtaining a written confession from Little Joe about Moroni's murder. He coerces this confession by holding a water pistol on the unsuspecting Little Joe and confiding to him, "You caused me an awful lot of trouble, you know."[19] But Little Joe never gets a chance to say that he was sorry for causing the Killer so much trouble, because he subsequently gets into a fight with more thugs who enter Erwin's hotel and, as a consequence, takes a dive through the window, landing ten stories away from where he started and effectively finishing his career.

But all is well where Erwin is concerned, for he has saved Little Joe's confession, bad spelling and all, in which Little Joe had admitted that he "kilt" Moroni. He rushes to his lawyer Allen with the evidence he needs to clear his reputation. Allen is not exactly thrilled to see that his client was innocent after all, so in Judy's presence, he tears up the confession. This is all Judy needs to realize that she has accepted the wrong man's proposal, so in the final scene, she returns to Erwin, giving him a long, passionate kiss as her way of apologizing and admitting her foolish mistake. Like so many of his leading ladies before her, she comes to her senses and opts for the right guy.

NOTES

1. John Irving, *The Hotel New Hampshire* (New York: Pocket Books, 1981), 257.

2. *Mr. Boggs Steps Out.* Dir. Gordon Wiles. Grand National, 1938.

3. *Cracked Nuts.* Dir. Edward F. Cline. Universal, 1941.

4. *Cracked Nuts*, 1941.

5. *Cracked Nuts*, 1941.

6. *Cracked Nuts*, 1941.

7. *Cracked Nuts*, 1941.

8. *Cracked Nuts*, 1941.

9. William P. Gaines, "Just A Little Bit Timid," *Shadoplay Magazine* (January 1935): 73.

10. *Killer Dill.* Dir. Lewis D. Collins. Screen Guild, 1947.

11. *Killer Dill*, 1947.

12. *Killer Dill*, 1947.

13. *Killer Dill*, 1947.

14. *Killer Dill*, 1947.

15. *Killer Dill*, 1947.

16. *Killer Dill*, 1947.

17. *Killer Dill*, 1947.

18. *Killer Dill*, 1947.

19. *Killer Dill*, 1947.

8

DEPRESSION-ERA SATIRE

"This great nation will endure as it has endured, will revive
and will prosper. . . . The only thing we have to fear is fear itself—nameless, unreasoning, unjustified terror which paralyzes
needed efforts to convert retreat into advance . . . a host of unemployed citizens face a grim problem of existence, and an
equally great number toil with little return. Only a foolish op-
timist can deny the dark realities of the moment."

—President Franklin D. Roosevelt
First inaugural address, March 1933

HOW TO EARN YOUR BREAD AND BUTTER

On January 20, 1937, President Franklin D. Roosevelt, speaking to the
members of a rain-soaked crowd that had come to hear his second inaugural address, told them: "I see one-third of a nation ill-housed, ill-clad,
ill-nourished." He did not exaggerate. And many of these hungry, homeless,
unemployed citizens blamed the titans of business and industry for their
hardships. Hollywood capitalized on this widespread dissatisfaction with the
seemingly unequal distribution of wealth in America. Throughout the
1930s, moviegoers were treated to a satiric, critical look at the ways of the
wealthy. Some of the best movies of the decade mocked the lifestyles of the
rich. Among the funniest and most incisive were *Easy Living* (1937), *Libeled
Lady* (1936), *My Man Godfrey* (1936), *Dinner at Eight* (1933), and *Holiday*
(1938). Two of these lesser-known satires came from Paramount, the studio

199

specializing in irreverence. Both were made in the early thirties and featured Stuart Erwin: *Strangers in Love* (1932) and *He Learned About Women* (1933). Both movies not only ridicule the rich but also expose the horrible living conditions of the working class: those who are just struggling to get by. Both have a bittersweet tone, their comedy shaded with the suffering of characters who have been cruelly used and exploited by a system which they have watched disintegrating month by month and year after year.

Strangers in Love is the weaker picture, though it does have moments of wit interspersed with caustic social commentary on the suffering of the unfortunate majority living on the margins. It stars Fredric March in a dual role as twins, one evil (Arthur Drake) and the other decent (Buddy Drake). The split personality he displays is similar to the character he played in another 1932 movie, *Dr. Jekyll and Mr. Hyde*, for which he shared the Best Actor Academy Award. (Wallace Beery also won, for his role in *The Champ*.) Fortunately, the evil part (Arthur) dies early in the film, so we are not subjected to the clichéd narrative of good twin/bad twin battling for supremacy all the way to the end. It is the evil one whom we meet first; he is Arthur Drake, whom we see emerging from his luxurious limousine and entering his sumptuous Park Avenue apartment. As in so many depression-era movies scorning the rich, the living space and the accoutrements of Fredric March #1 resemble an art museum interior. And March #1 has a personality to match a museum: he is a cold, unyielding marble statue. He is ruthless with his debtors who get behind in their payments; he is boring (we learn that he is writing a book about his life's passion: Egyptian hieroglyphics); and he is a lecher who cannot keep his moving fingers off his secretary Diana Merrow (Kay Francis). He is not a nice fellow, but that is to be expected; after all, he is rich. However, he also has a bad heart, literally and metaphorically, for which he is constantly taking powders of some sort. Thus, we know that the plot will soon allow him to be dispensed with.

We now leave the mansion of the wicked March #1 and move on to join the common herd on the pavement outside. Stuart Erwin and March #2 (good twin Buddy Drake) are walking past a delicatessen. Erwin as Stan Keeney, military veteran and comrade of March #2, is at his most cynical, ironic best here: a no-nonsense, practical guy with no use for the pretensions of the upper class. His last name, which he takes great pride in pronouncing to strangers, symbolizes his keen wit and sharp mind. As Erwin and March #2 look hungrily into the deli window, Erwin remarks with a forced casualness, "You see that yellow stuff in them squares there? That's *butter*." March #2, unshaven and generally unkempt, unlike March #1, replies equally sarcastically, "What's *butter*?"

They maintain a nice, even, bantering rhythm in the following exchange:

ERWIN: You put it on *bread*.

MARCH: What's *bread*?

ERWIN: It's something you put in your mouth.

MARCH: Who puts it in *whose* mouth?

ERWIN: Don't you remember? You usta use it. (Erwin adopts an eastern, Yankee accent here—an inflection that he loses from time to time during the movie, as he reverts to his native California speech patterns.)

MARCH: Oh, yea. Seems to me I do have a dim recollection. You chew it, don't you?

ERWIN: Something like that. I'd give me right eye for a steak.[1]

At this, March #2 steers Erwin away from the window, but not before Erwin takes one last, longing look at the deli display. Their succeeding conversation is filled with references to their own disillusionment as former soldiers who have fought for their country. The social commentary is obvious; in the early thirties, many young men such as these came back from overseas service to a dying economy and a job market that had no place for them. Although Erwin and March have just served their country in China, back home in America they cannot scrape together enough money to buy one decent meal. So they resort to caustic humor to soften the pangs—both those of frustration as well as those of hunger.

However, Erwin has an inspiration. He suggests that March #2 put the touch on his wealthy twin. Erwin's reasoning is droll, clever, and practical. He urges March: "Why doncha park your pride in the alley and go and see your brother?" At first, March is reluctant: "Ah, I'd almost rather go out and hold somebody up than ask my brother for a cent." But Erwin persists, once again adopting an eastern accent, which he does fairly well. But he keeps losing it, especially in scenes where he gets excited. Here he handles the accent nicely, "Ah, don't be a sap. He's your twin, ain't he?"

MARCH: What's that got to do with it?

ERWIN: Well, it seems to me that a twin oughtta go for twice as much what an ordinary brother'd go for.

MARCH: Haven't even seen the guy in over twelve years.

ERWIN: Then it's a cinch. You got him either way.

MARCH: How do you figure?

ERWIN: Well, if he's glad to see you, a few dollars won't make any difference. If he don't like the color of your hair, well—he oughtta pay you somethin' on account, for having stayed away that long.[2]

Erwin convinces March to go see his wealthy brother. As March leaves
with the parting remark, "Here goes the prodigal," Erwin smiles smugly,
smoking a cigarette (a seemingly affordable commodity during the depression), and quips, "I'll be waitin' here, fella, for half of the fatted calf."[3]

So March #2 goes to see his prosperous twin, March #1; that is, he
heads for Park Avenue to confront his other half. Nor is March #1 at all
pleased to see his down-at-the-heels brother. The two quarrel over money
and over which twin was loved more by their father. In a creaky plot maneuver, March #1 gets so agitated that he collapses, dead from a heart attack.
Likewise, in another equally hoary plot device, March #2 decides that he
will simply assume his rich twin's identity, presumably impervious to the
possible complications in both private and social situations when he tries to
be someone else.

Another improbable event soon occurs when we next see March #2,
who is witnessing a doctor in the process of examining the deceased, whom
the doctor has been informed is Buddy Drake. The poor but decent and
very much alive Buddy has miraculously turned out clean-shaven and
dressed in more formal attire, fooling even his closest servants into believ-
ing that he is Arthur Drake. But if no one else is curious about Buddy
Drake's death, Erwin wants to know more. Having read Buddy's newspaper
obituary, he barges his way in to the sacred Park Avenue building and confronts "Arthur" Drake. He is frantic, bellicose, quarrelsome, and truly upset
about his good friend's death. He is also confrontational; he suspects foul
play since, as he desperately tells "Arthur," he knew very well that Buddy
had a strong heart. Erwin's openness, his genuine distress, pains March, so he
drops his straight arrow deportment and discloses his real identity. Erwin is
elated at this revelation, but he is canny enough to realize that March is
treading in dangerous waters. He cautions March to take what loot he can
and scram.

Some of the hurdles that March #2 encounters are soon erected to
block his way. For example, he has no idea who the woman is who is apparently his secretary, nor who is telephoning him with vague but ominous
threats, nor who the sexy lady is who greets him at his country place (which
appears more Gothic than his Park Avenue apartment), nor what this lady
has on him, although we gather that her blackmail threats concern his ques-

tionable business deals. We also assume that she and the real Arthur Drake had enjoyed a comfortable sexual relationship and that they had much in common, especially their disdain for humanity. We are constantly reminded that March #2—war veteran, poor man, physically fit—is a much nicer guy than his late twin—exempt from war, rich man, physically crippled. But we don't need much reminding; this story is, after all, an indictment of people with a surfeit of money.

March #2 is also thoroughly confused about his past relationship to his secretary's father, Mr. Merrow (George Barbier). He concludes from the cloudy conversations he has with both father and daughter that he had been in business with Merrow, that both partners had lost money, but that he had lost far less than Merrow. He further learns that his secretary Diana Merrow blames him for her father's loss; she suspects that Arthur Drake has stolen money from her father. As his substitute life becomes more and more entangled in the rope that he is slowly wrapping around his neck, March #2 also discovers quickly that his practical, down-to-earth friend Erwin was right: it is a bad, treacherous business to try to embody another person, especially if that person was rich and traitorous.

Some of the skeletons that fall out of Arthur Drake's closet are humorous, however. In one instance, Erwin is walking along the road to Elmview, Arthur's country estate, in order to help out his friend. Since he cannot afford any other means of transportation, he hitches a ride with a man named Clark, who tells Erwin that he is also headed for Elmview. Because Erwin recognizes the name as one belonging to an unseen caller who had earlier threatened his buddy over the phone, Erwin and Clark arrive at Elmview with Clark in a disheveled condition, his glasses appropriated by Erwin— partial evidence that Erwin has roughed him up. In addition, March puts on a belligerent air and berates Clark for the menacing phone message that this person named Clark allegedly conveyed. Yet Mr. Clark (Lucien Littlefield) is a mild-mannered little man who hardly looks like the gangster type and, as it turns out, isn't. Clark is a professor who has come to see March about publishing his Egyptology book. He is evidently not the same Clark who had made the intimidating call.

However, Professor Clark does have a few inner resources which belie his timid soul appearance. After berating March and Erwin for their ungentlemanly deportment, he leaves with Erwin. When Erwin reenters the scene a few moments later, he possesses a black eye, courtesy of the still irate Clark. While March and his secretary giggle over Erwin's unfortunate encounter, Erwin simply concludes, somewhat ruefully, "I never should have given him back his glasses."[4]

But Erwin comes to his buddy's aid after March is forced to write the blackmailing trollop Muriel (Juliette Compton) a check for $24,000; when March orders Erwin to go to her apartment and retrieve the check, Erwin shows his ingenuity together with his histrionic ability. He gets access to her swank place by pretending to be an accident victim and by paying two men to carry him in, casually slung between them, all the while he is moaning about his auto wreck. He even looks authentic, what with that black eye, compliments of Professor Clark. Once he has been laid out on Muriel's chaise lounge, he watches as she helpfully leaves the room to get him some water. While she is gone, he locates the check in her purse, but does not have time to remove it. When she returns with the glass, he uses his best melo-dramatic style, sounding as though he were practicing his elocution lessons, to tell her about the terrible "wreck" in which his wife and daughter were injured, his daughter going through the windshield and his wife screaming out in terror. As he hysterically declaims about how he was pinned to his seat by the wheel while "I struggled and struggled," we see a close up of his foot, definitely struggling and struggling to pull that purse closer and closer to him. Once he has safely eased the check from her purse to his hand, he jumps up, miraculously unhurt, exclaiming, "My wife! My daughter! Your papa's coming!"[5]

Shortly after his passionate run out the door, Muriel recovers enough from her bewilderment at Erwin's wild performance to notice that she has been robbed. But too late: Erwin is gone and so is her $24,000, ill-gotten check. However, March no longer has to worry about such piddling amounts, for by the end of the film all turns out well, with March #2 dis-covering that March #1 had really cheated his good twin out of half his in-heritance. Since the evil but rich March #1 has passed on, March #2 now owns both halves, and will never again have to worry about how to earn his bread and butter. Plus Buddy Drake wins the hand of his devoted secretary. And what about the invaluable Mr. Keeney? Stuart Erwin gets neither the girl nor the inheritance, but we know that his comrade-in-arms will reward his loyalty with a job, and perhaps will even protect him against any future black eyes.

Although the plot of *Strangers in Love* is antique and therefore pre-dictable, it does have the advantage of some good performances by well es-tablished actors: Erwin, Fredric March, Kay Francis, George Barbier as Fran-cis' father, and Lucien Littlefield as the unfortunate case of mistaken identity, Professor Clark. It also gives March a chance to show how well he could play comedy, an opportunity that he was not often given in the course of a long and distinguished career. An interesting sidelight to the movie may be found in the shared stage experience of March and Erwin; in the 1920s, both had worked in the Los Angeles stock company headed by Edward Everett Horton.

Despite its worn out and worn down story, the movie received some good notices. The reviewer for the April 1932 issue of *Photoplay* even takes note that Stuart Erwin is in the cast: "In the capable hands of Fredric March and Kay Francis an old be-whiskered theme becomes an entertaining and amusing movie. You could write the plot blindfolded—twin brothers, one a crook with heart trouble, the other a supposed prodigal but actually a sterling character. But how that boy March shades the characters of the two *Drake* brothers! Stuart Erwin gets over some grand laughs. Good stuff."[6]

As this critic tells us, the movie is not particularly thought provoking; it has no deep hidden meaning. Nonetheless, if there is a moral to this mildly amusing satire, it is possibly found in the belief that you can become rich *and* maintain your morality—but only if you have proven yourself worthy of such rewards while you were still among the poor, hard-working, and honest.

TO THE HIGHEST BIDDER

Whereas Erwin might have continued in poverty had it not been for Buddy Drake's good fortune by the end of *Strangers in Love*, he does not have that problem in *He Learned About Women* (1933). After all, his character in this later film is worth fifty million dollars. A more biting and bittersweet satire than *Strangers in Love*, *He Learned About Women* shows us a variation on the type of character that Erwin had created in *Make Me a Star*: unworldly, isolated, naïve, kind-hearted; in this instance, however, the character he plays, Peter Kendall, becomes the prey of small-minded social climbers rather than the victim of the Hollywood establishment.

Like Fredric March's Arthur/Buddy Drake in the previous movie, Erwin lives in splendor in a sumptuous New York apartment, only his is on Fifth Avenue rather than Park Avenue. But unlike bad twin Arthur Drake, Erwin's Peter Potter Kendall III is a nice guy. The problem with Peter is not that he is rich and dishonest, but that he is rich and disassociated with reality, notably with the plight of the common man. When we first see Erwin, he is in his library, a room large enough to hold thousands of volumes, which it apparently does; furthermore, Erwin appears to have read all of them. Erwin's attorney Drake (Claude King) has gone to see him on a business matter, and we view Erwin from the attorney's perspective: a low-angle shot of him at the top of a tall ladder, large book in hand, frustrated by some factual contradictions he has just come across in his research. We also know that he is a typical egghead because of his physical appearance; his hair is tousled and looks as though he has spent many days unconcerned with the importance of combing it. Of course, he also wears glasses. In modern parlance, he looks like a dweeb.

But he doesn't care how he looks, because he is rich and thus can afford to spend his days reading, comfortably lodged in his library, where no one will see him anyway. He does not have to worry about joining the commoners outside by working for a living. Right now, his major worry involves research he has been doing about the planet Mars. He tells Drake, his attorney, that the authorities differ in their estimation of how cold it gets on Mars. When Drake asks Erwin if he could jump as high as the library ceiling, as he would be able to do on Mars, Erwin replies indignantly that he doesn't live on Mars. To this, Drake quips that Erwin is certainly not living on *earth*. Precisely. But poor Erwin wants to try. He informs Drake that he would like to help others with his fifty million. He even solemnly, knowingly, estimates that there are probably "dozens" of people out there who don't have everything that they need.

Drake thinks that Erwin has the right idea, if the wrong estimate, so he advises Erwin about how to take the first step: he must actually go out of his Fifth Avenue mansion and into the real world in order to experience other people. Although Erwin has lived his whole life in New York, he has visited only three places: the public library, Grant's Tomb, and the aquarium. F. Scott Fitzgerald had it right: the rich *are* very different from you and me. Drake subsequently enlists the aid of his own valet, Wilson (Sidney Toler), to help his young, inexperienced friend in this, his first excursion into reality.

Wilson attacks Erwin from the top down. He changes Erwin's appearance by first, getting him a new hairdo. When we next see Erwin, his hair is slicked down and neatly attached to his head. His glasses are gone, and his suit is formal. Toler questions whether Erwin truly requires these glasses. "Only when I read a lot," is the answer. So Toler keeps them, concluding, "Then you won't need them for some time, sir."[7] What Erwin does need when he ventures all by himself out onto the street is a blueprint for maneuvering through the big city maze. We are to assume that wealthy people never go beyond their doors unless they have a chauffeured car awaiting them just outside. And here is Erwin, on foot, dodging cars and crowds as he walks against traffic signals.

He also needs some guidelines for acknowledging panhandlers. When a down-and-out beggar approaches him, asking for a dime for a cup of coffee because he hasn't eaten in two days, Erwin is so touched that he gives the man a twenty dollar bill, whereupon the man collapses in shock on the pavement. When one considers that *He Learned About Women*, released in 1933, was playing in small towns throughout America, and when one also considers that in 1933 the per capita income of farm households was about $160, Erwin's generosity seems even more remarkable. Perhaps it would have looked simply miraculous to farmers such as Walter Crozier of Haskins, Iowa, who, in the fall of 1932, held an $800 mortgage on his farm, but received $1.90 for it at auction.[8]

Yet it was not just land and possessions that were being auctioned. Erwin's lessons in life's realities are soon continued with a jolt when he comes upon an auction being held on the outskirts of Central Park; being sold at this auction are unemployed people. Totally perplexed, he questions one of the spectators: "I beg your pardon. Is it possible they're selling *human beings?*" The man replies affirmatively, explaining that these are people who are being sold to the highest bidders, to the ones who can pay them the most for the jobs they are receiving from these prospective employers. Had Erwin been told that his favorite planet Mars was made of red and green peppers, he could not have been more stunned at this news. "You mean they need *work?*"[9] he reiterates. The other man's reply emphasizes the desperate state of these unemployed individuals: they are so broke that they will work for any amount that anyone wants to pay.

A woman now steps onto the auction platform. She is modestly dressed in an outfit suitable for an office worker; in fact, the auctioneer makes a few sexist comments about how she would beautify any office. So the bidding begins on the stenographer. The man standing next to Erwin figures that she looks like the ideal type to perform services for him besides stenographic ones, so he bids for her. When it occurs to Erwin what the man has in mind (his Peter Kendall is not *that* inexperienced), he bids for her himself, finally paying the large sum of fifty dollars a week, even though he has absolutely no need of a secretary. Conceding defeat to his bidding rival, the man speaks confidentially to Erwin, slyly observing, "I hope you get your money's worth." When Erwin asks what he means by that, the man chuckles: "*Nothing*. Maybe you *need* a stenographer."[10]

For her part, Erwin's new secretary Joan Allen (Susan Fleming) is naturally suspicious. She obviously has had experience with bosses who demanded that she do more than secretarial work. Therefore, she informs Erwin that she takes dictation sitting in her *own* chair. While they are registering with the auction authorities, we see a portly, former Broadway actress, somewhere between middle age and the nursing home, who is hefting herself onto the auction block. This is Vivian Polidor (Polly), played by Alison Skipworth: in real life, a funny, caustic actress, expert at hurling the appropriate riposte, a kind of British Marie Dressler. She and Joan Allen seem to be friends, the kind that look out for one another. So when Skipworth becomes the object of the bidders' attention, the newly purchased Joan asks Erwin if he will bid on the older lady as well. He protests that he really has no need of her, but Joan insists, confiding in him that the lady is her mother. Naturally, the kindhearted Erwin cannot see mother and daughter separated, so he pays another fifty dollars a week for Skipworth. In answer to this over-the-hill actress' question concerning what she is expected to do in return, he replies that he needs her "as a companion for my children." Thus, the unsuspecting "mother and daughter" are bought for one hundred dollars a week, over half of the annual income for the average farm worker in 1933.

Now that he has them, Erwin is not sure what to do with them. He does not need a secretary, nor does he have any children. When Fleming and Skipworth discover these two facts, they are understandably apprehensive. Skipworth has already had three husbands, so she knows what men are like. So too, Fleming has had some worldly encounters of her own. In addition, when they perceive that Erwin is at loose ends with respect to their future, they don't want to be left hanging from these ends, especially when he invites them to come live with him. But they are poor, desperate, and hungry, and he does look harmless, if not downright helpless, so they resolutely accompany him home. Their resolution becomes less secure, however, when they arrive at his Fifth Avenue address and note that he has to ring to gain admittance, that he doesn't have a key to his own place. He quite matter-of-factly explains in his preoccupied way that he has no need of a key, since he doesn't go out much. By this time, his new employees/boarders no longer seem so astonished by Erwin's idiosyncrasies.

Furthermore, when it dawns on Skipworth that their benefactor is none other than Peter Potter Kendall III, the man who has just inherited a cool fifty million dollars, she develops a decided interest in the future of Susan Fleming's Joan Allen. This future, according to the scheme now being formulated by Skipworth, involves Fleming's marriage to Erwin, thus ensuring that neither one of them will ever have to go up on that auction block again. Skipworth's argument is cunning, practical, and witty. It is also in keeping with the attitude held by the less fortunate class toward the rich as she advises her young friend and fellow conspirator: "Here's a nice young sap, born with a silver spoon in his mouth, a golden rattle in his hand, and a diamond safety pin in his diaper. I say, let's nab him."[11] Fleming is persuaded; it beats going back to be sold again to the highest bidder.

But how to trap him? That shouldn't be too hard, according to Skipworth. She will encourage him to participate in a play whereby he is forced by the script to declare his love for Fleming. Such play-acting will give him the real-life idea, and before the day is out, he will be buying her a diamond ring at Tiffany's. First, however, Skipworth, that old con artist, must set Erwin up. She does this by targeting his shyness, by using her stage experience and her concomitant histrionic ability to persuade him that what he needs to bring him out of his drab existence is some *acting* experience.

As she exhorts him to experience the wonderful world of the theater and the drama, his response to her importunities reveals a social awkwardness that is obvious but also appealing. So Alison Skipworth, standing about five feet five, and weighing around two hundred pounds, entreats Erwin, standing about five feet nine and weighing around one hundred fifty, to come out of his shell. We can see that Skipworth's Vivian (Polly) Polidor has spent many years on stage, broadly gesticulating and gesturing to the highest balcony. Her movements toward Erwin are expansive and broad; his are abashed and diminished. Erwin had a way of pulling back his shoulders, drawing up his elbows toward his chest and pushing both arms backward, all the while apprehensively pressing his fingers together. This he does here, as he carefully recoils from the outspread, ample arms of Skipworth; in addition, as she presses forward into his personal space, he gradually inches backward, fearful of whatever harm she might be thinking of inflicting.

But she only wants to give him *confidence*, maintains Skipworth. What he needs to help him lose his shyness is the experience of the *drama*. Only through *acting* will he be able to unlock his "real" self, that self that needs to come out; that authentic "two-fisted, upstanding, courageous self" that is now buried deep within. And Erwin—the timid, the overwhelmed, the bashful—but the very wealthy, is still unconvinced. He had not really reckoned with this kind of life experience when he had first dared to go out onto the street.

Yet, even as he is protesting to this overpowering figure that he *can't* possibly study drama, Skipworth is preparing a further challenge. She correctly assesses the boyish nature of the man she has chosen as a husband for Fleming, so she reminds Erwin of the nursery tale about the little engine that would not accept the word *can't*, even as it faced pulling a string of cars up a steep hillside. Against such overpowering odds, the little train would not give up, as it chugged up the hill, repeating "I think I can. I think I can. I think I can." Skipworth really gets into the spirit of the little engine's refrain, as she chants its words, all the while rotating her arm in imitation of the motion of the engine's wheel and chugging along across Erwin's well-polished floor, with her bent knees punctuating the enormous efforts of The Little Engine That Could. Furthermore, Skipworth's very proper, very distinctive British accent contributes to the humor of her motions; such humor is achieved through the incongruity between sound and motion that her diction fosters. Although she sounds as if she could easily slip into the part of Hamlet's mother, she looks as if she could be a kindergarten teacher at recess leading her pupils around the playground.

But her technique works. She has indeed appealed to the forever optimistic little boy in Erwin. She makes him join her in her locomotive imitation. Grabbing his arms from behind, locking them onto hers, she becomes the second car on the train, coaxing him into propelling the two of them forward up that steep hill. Now both of them chant in unison, "I think I can. I think I can. I think I can." Then Fleming enters, attaches herself to Skipworth, and the three make an even stranger spectacle as they cavort about the room. They look like the tail end of a chorus line in a third-rate burlesque show. But Skipworth does not much care what they look like, for she sees her plans beginning to bloom with moneyed blossoms. Skipworth now hopes Erwin will get so caught up in the drama, which she has prepared for him to perform, that he will propose to Fleming that day.

Meanwhile, two other characters enter the picture; these two are working on a proposition of their own. One is Eddie Clifford (Gordon Westcott), who operates a legitimate theater and whose business, in best depression-era fashion, is going under; the other is Jonathan Appleby (Grant Mitchell), erstwhile husband of Skipworth's "Polly" Polidor. He tells Clifford that he and Polly divorced over the subject of money: Polly wouldn't give him any. Ah, but there is good news in that respect, Eddie informs him. Eddie has just learned that Polly is living with the disgustingly affluent Peter Kendall, and, accordingly, Eddie has just been inspired to find a way to get some of Kendall's dough.

Wasting no time, they pay a call on Erwin; Polly is not at all pleased to see Appleby, though he pretends to harbor undying devotion for his ex-wife. And Erwin, who is unwaveringly polite to these two intruders, assumes that Fleming's Joan Allen is Appleby's daughter, so he shyly points her out to the doting daddy. Appleby catches on quickly, feigning interest in the "daughter" whom he purportedly has not seen in years, and whom, in reality, he has never before seen in his life.

But Eddie and Jonathan quickly get the attention of Skipworth's Polly; they propose a scheme whereby they will get Erwin to put money into a soup kitchen for the unemployed; then, when that is successful, they will get cash from him to start more soup kitchens—and next, of course, disappear with the cash. Skipworth is still hoping for a marriage between Fleming and Erwin, but she is always amenable to intrigues of this sort, as her former husband knows quite well.

When we next see Erwin and Fleming together, they are working in the soup kitchen, serving meals to the truly downtrodden, many of them elderly—a group which, in fact, was among the hardest hit by the depression. And here we also see how Erwin is beginning to touch Fleming: his decency and generosity toward the unfortunate make her feel like a fraud. Another complication, of course, is that she has fallen in love with him. Nor has Erwin lost his childlike enthusiasm for the game recently introduced to him by Skipworth. He leaves Fleming in the serving line and goes into another room, where a group of disheveled, unemployed, but willing men await him. Erwin promptly assumes his little engine position, leading these men on their own "I think I can" journey up the steep hill. And none of them seem a bit disconcerted by the odd lesson they have just learned, undoubtedly because Erwin is such a heartfelt teacher.

He is also teaching Fleming a few things about human relationships, although he has no concept of the effect he is having on her. Sometime after the opening of the soup kitchen, while Appleby and Clifford are making their final plans to nab $100,000 from Erwin, ostensibly for a chain of soup kitchens, which will naturally never come to pass, Erwin tries to propose to Fleming. However, she won't let him get very far; she is too much in love with him to accept his proposal, for she knows that she does not deserve him. He misunderstands her reticence, assuming that his clumsiness has put her off. He even tells Wilson, "I'm afraid I bungled it."[12] But Fleming is now feeling so guilty that she indiscreetly informs Appleby and Clifford that she is going to warn Erwin of the chicanery that has been taking place right in front of him; of everyone's complicity in taking advantage of Erwin's guileless good nature.

Meanwhile, while Fleming's surrogate "mother," Polly Polidor, has been scheming to help her ex and Clifford confiscate $100,000, Erwin has been planning a surprise of his own for his adopted mother. He has bought her a large bouquet of flowers, complete with a sentimental note in which he wishes her a Happy Mother's Day. At first, he doesn't want her to see the gift, claiming that the present is for the following day. But Skipworth's curiosity is piqued, so when she tells him that at her age she might not have a tomorrow, he shyly, graciously, and gratefully presents it to her. Skipworth is stunned, especially after she reads his note: "Happy Mother's Day from Peter to Mother," her face a study in dismay, sorrow, and grief. Because she doesn't know how to express deep feeling, because she has been so badly battered and used for much of her life, she finds it difficult to let others past her hard outer shell. As a result, all she can think to do is ask rudely, "What is this? Some kind of joke?"[13]

But Erwin's Peter Kendall chooses to ignore her cold response; instead, he replies quite seriously and earnestly: "Oh no. You see, I never knew my real mother, and you've been so kind and helpful that I like to think of you that way." Then, almost apologetically, he adds, "I hoped you wouldn't mind."[14]

This is too much for the hardened old trooper; Erwin has tapped something deep in Skipworth's Madame Polidor, some secret longing that she has been unwilling to let herself feel. His effect on her is similar to the softening effect that his onscreen characters have on his young leading ladies, but with Skipworth there is something more, something that we are, unfortunately, left to guess at. So when Erwin pleads for her understanding, hoping that she will not mind his kind gesture, Skipworth casts an insult, "Well, I *do* mind." At this, Erwin's voice breaks ever so slightly, as he urges, "Oh *please* don't." Then, regaining his self-control and reserve, he adds, "Why, Joan couldn't care any more than I." Skipworth is still ready with a snappy comeback, "Oh, then it's *Joan* you're thinking of—not me."

Still desperately wanting her to appreciate his feelings, Erwin has a quick, honest answer: "That's not true. Whether Joan cares for me or not can't affect my love for *you.*" At his mention of the word *love*, Skipworth begins to choke on her tears. No one has ever treated her this way before. As he did with the character of the gentle, caring, trusting Merton Gill in *Make Me a Star,* Erwin creates a man here whose generosity and love can be neither denied nor ignored. Yet even as Skipworth tries once more to guard against her emotions, her tears belie her words. Moreover, although the camera focuses on her face as she makes this last attempt at insult, we can see enough of Erwin's expression as he watches her to know that he is reading her quite accurately. He realizes her deep hurt, even as she cries out to him: "Let me tell *you* something. Thanks for all this, but I don't *want* it. And I'm not at all flattered that you should think that I'm old enough to be your mother. . . . And then there's *another* thing. There's *another* thing."[15] On this line, she crosses the room, sits down, covers her face with her hands, and sobs. Erwin slowly follows her, kneeling by her chair, looking up to her as though he wants to say something to comfort her.

But at this moment, something frustrating occurs within the film's narrative structure. The scene ends with an abrupt shift to a scene between Skipworth and Erwin, who are interrupted by Gordon Westcott as Eddie Clifford; Eddie is most eager to tell them that there is a bank messenger outside. What is particularly annoying about this precipitous cut is that we never learn *what* this other thing is that Skipworth has referred to in the previous scene where she sits before Erwin, weeping. We are led to believe that there might be somewhere in her past a horrible loss, something which she has never been able to put behind her. Did she have a child of her own? If so, did the child die? Was she indeed someone's mother? Or are her tears ones of regret that she never had a child? Whatever the cause of her grief, we want to know more, but we are not given the chance.

What has become clear to us, however, is that Skipworth has become a different woman; she has reclaimed some inner decency that has doubtless been there all along, a morality brought to the surface by Erwin's great kindness. Thus, when Erwin rushes out to meet the bank messenger, who has come with the $100,000 for the chain of soup kitchens, Skipworth turns on Clifford with every bit of regal dignity that she can gather. She announces that it's all off, that they are not going to take his money. She explains to a skeptical, unimpressed Clifford, "The boy is too fine, too decent to be swindled."[16]

Furthermore, Skipworth has the courage to follow through with her resolution. As Erwin returns with a travel bag filled with money, Skipworth tells him all—how Clifford and Appleby planned to skip the country with the cash, never intending to use it for soup kitchens. She also bravely admits that she too is a thief. At this, Erwin anxiously asks about Joan. "Not Joan," replies Skipworth adamantly, also volunteering that Joan fell in love with Erwin. "She *did*!" exclaims Erwin ecstatically, seemingly ignoring all that Skipworth has just confessed. But as the next scene reveals, he has caught everything she has said. At this moment, however, he is also concerned for his beloved's safety, for she is now in the custody of the nefarious Appleby. The ever resourceful Clifford has the solution; he will see that Joan comes back unharmed for a price: Erwin's $100,000. Naturally, Erwin agrees to the ransom, precipitating Clifford's speedy exit from the scene.

The following exchange between Erwin and Skipworth is beautifully underplayed. It demonstrates Erwin's sensitivity toward his fellow actors and his ability to read their emotions and to react to their feelings. It also shows his capacity for expressing much with no words. Not only does he listen to others' language—both spoken and unspoken—but he also exhibits tension with his whole body. As he listens to Skipworth's attempts to make a chastened escape from his life, he makes us understand his own pain through his understanding of Skipworth's pain.

After Clifford has disappeared to ransom Susan Fleming's Joan, Skipworth gently picks up her Mother's Day bouquet. She has just admitted to

Erwin that Joan is neither her daughter nor Appleby's daughter. She nonetheless clearly cherishes the flowers, though they are tormenting her because she perceives them as symbolic of her treachery—and of the possible, but unrevealed, loss of her own child. As though begging for Erwin's forgiveness, she asks, "May I take these?" Erwin does not hesitate in his response, "Of course. They're yours." As Skipworth turns to leave, Erwin wants to know, "Where are you going?"

"Away," is her soft-spoken answer.

"Why?" asks Erwin; as he does so, we feel that he really wants to know. "Haven't I caused you trouble enough?"

But Erwin quietly puts a stop to Skipworth's pathetic need for self-punishment. "Oh, you can't go now, Mother. I need you."[17] And he does, as she in turn needs him.

Throughout this exchange, there is a kind of emotional rhythm that can frequently be felt in many of Erwin's more serious encounters with other performers. The rhythm is slow, the pace is steady; the beat does not feel forced, as though it had been imposed arbitrarily upon a tune for which it is inappropriate. In short, the feelings generated are honest. We can see the genuineness of these feelings in Erwin as he listens to Skipworth, occasionally turning from her to face the camera, his expression revealing an inner conflict, one that has issued from his adopted mother's recent revelations. He is hurt by the betrayal of those whom he has trusted, but he recognizes Skipworth's hurt as well; furthermore, he desperately wants her love.

The remainder of the movie descends into slapstick, resulting in a tonal shift that is jarring. For instance, Appleby suddenly turns into a good guy when he discovers that Clifford is going to doublecross Erwin and not return Joan; rather, as Clifford smugly informs Appleby, he is going to take Joan and the $100,000 and head north, keeping Erwin's girl for himself. Because Appleby cannot dissuade Clifford from these evil intentions, the reformed ex-husband of Madame Polidor phones Erwin, tipping him off as to Joan's location in Clifford's theater. There follows a chase with, on one side, Erwin and those unemployed men whom he has been encouraging toward self-improvement; and, on the other, Clifford and his cronies. They batter one another across the stage of the theater, up into the flies, through the orchestra pit, and into the theater's empty seats. Erwin unquestionably defeats Clifford in hand-to-hand combat, he wins Joan back, and he tells Skipworth that she will naturally come to live with them. As for Appleby, Skipworth takes him back, now that she has seen his redeeming qualities. Perhaps all four will live together.

And Erwin as Peter Kendall, like Fredric March as Buddy Drake in *Strangers in Love*, proves that the rich can be just like real people, after all. But, as with the earlier movie, *He Learned About Women* constantly reminds us of the dark side of the American Dream: of the indisputable fact that hard work and good intentions do not pay off for everyone; and that, as President Roosevelt had informed Americans in his first two inaugural addresses, inequality of opportunity continued to exist in depression America.

NOTES

1. *Strangers in Love*. Dir. Lothar Mendes. Paramount, 1932.
2. *Strangers in Love*, 1932.
3. *Strangers in Love*, 1932.
4. *Strangers in Love*, 1932.
5. *Strangers in Love*, 1932.
6. "Strangers in Love," *Photoplay* 41 (April 1932), 52.
7. *He Learned About Women*. Dir. Lloyd Corrigan. Paramount, 1933.
8. T. H. Watkins, *The Great Depression: America in the 1930s* (Boston: Little, Brown and Company, 1993), 119.
9. *He Learned About Women*, 1933.
10. *He Learned About Women*, 1933.
11. *He Learned About Women*, 1933.
12. *He Learned About Women*, 1933.
13. *He Learned About Women*, 1933.
14. *He Learned About Women*, 1933.
15. *He Learned About Women*, 1933.
16. *He Learned About Women*, 1933.
17. *He Learned About Women*, 1933.

9

SOME CONCLUSIONS

Here was a new generation, shouting the old cries, learning the old creeds, through a revery of long days and nights; destined finally to go out into that dirty gray turmoil to follow love and pride; a new generation dedicated more than the last to the fear of poverty and the worship of success; grown up to find all Gods dead, all wars fought, all faiths in man shaken. . . .

—F. Scott Fitzgerald, *This Side of Paradise* (1920)

You are all a lost generation.

—Gertrude Stein

Be a good listener. It's astounding how many people want to talk and how few are willing to listen. A good audience is a joy forever.

—Stuart Erwin, *Hollywood* (1937)

REDEFINITION AND VERSATILITY

One of my favorite cartoons features a man seated at his computer, his hand resting on a key. He is reading on the screen some lines from the eleventh-century *Rubáiyát of Omar Khayyám*; this particular excerpt provides him with the following sage advice: "The Moving finger writes; and, having writ, Moves on: nor all thy Piety nor Wit shall lure it back to cancel half a Line." Then we shift to the second frame of the cartoon, which shows the same man now looking at a blank screen, having apparently hit the delete key.

217

I suspect that there is a lesson here somewhere, one that conveys a truth about our times. If we don't like what we are reading or seeing or hearing, we can eliminate the offending annoyance with one keystroke, or reduce the size of our window, or close out our window completely. Or we can fast forward through the boring parts of the latest hit movie we have rented on video. We can scroll through a book or article that we are reading online. We can also skip the boring lead-ins to the long, omnipresent jokes or riddles or tall tales forwarded to us via email by friends, relatives, slight acquaintances, and people we have never met but who know someone whom we knew forty years ago in high school. We can, if we choose, also skip the joke altogether, because doubtless we received it two weeks before from someone else.

Moreover, when we send our own email letters, we rarely bother with spelling, punctuation, and inclusion of minor sentence parts such as subjects. We figure that these letters will not last until the water gets hot, so why worry about something that is so impermanent? If we teach English, as I do, we hesitate to assign to our literature students a novel that is very long, because we have learned that 250 pages is about the maximum length they can read, provided they are given at least three weeks in which to finish it.

We are not able to settle down for very long to accomplish a single chore, for we become impatient when the task takes too much of our time and concentration. If it does, we just delete it from our memory files and try something simpler. And when our students complain that they cannot focus on their assignments because they have two full-time jobs, are the sole providers for their numerous children, are enrolled in five academic classes, and can study only between the hours of midnight and four a.m., we understand how they feel.

We live in fragmented times, measuring out our lives by the number of minutes we allot ourselves for each of the many responsibilities we tackle each day. And because we parcel a certain portion of ourselves out to each person according to the degree of intimacy we have with that individual, we tend to distance ourselves from most people, to treat others with cynicism, apathy, or both.

One is tempted to say that the world in which Stuart Erwin worked so hard in order to create lasting, credible characters who gave of themselves freely, honestly, and yes—patiently—to others, was an entirely different world from ours. Yet Stuart Erwin grew up in fragmented times as well. Born at the beginning of the last century in an isolated, rural part of California, he found himself as a young college freshman in the early twenties absolutely terrified and totally confounded by the vast size and the fast pace of the University of California at Berkeley. Moreover, he came of age in the post-World War

I decade of disillusionment; in addition, he was, by his own admission, a member of that wild Lost Generation. It was a generation, as Ezra Pound observed in his 1920 poem "Hugh Selwyn Mauberley," that had learned of the world's impermanence and fragility, that saw its monuments cast in the brittle medium of plaster. It was an impatient generation, much like our own, unwilling to undertake any task that required it to lose time.

So too, the social and technological changes that were occurring just after the Great War made many youth feel that they were indeed suffering from momentum shock—from what Pound had referred to as an "accelerated grimace." These two words actually hint at the painful, obsessive hedonism of the youth of the twenties, the leer of the skull, the memento mori, the constant reminder to the Lost Generation that what they had lost in their plunge over the smirking abyss was their lives. Stuart Erwin possibly first sensed this awesome change when he left home to attend the university. Then, when he decided that acting was vital to his happiness, he began his journey into the professional theater at a time when both the form and content of modern plays were changing. The forms were experimental, often seemingly incoherent and absurd; the content reflected the frustration and desperation of Erwin's generation. Frederick J. Hoffman, writing about the decade in his book *The 20's*, comments on the feelings prevalent at this time: "The mood of futility, the shrugging of shoulders over questions of moral imperative, were in large part a consequence of the war. The postwar generation felt honestly that it had been victimized by a gross and stupid deception. . . . In much of the literature of the twenties there was a continuous statement of rejection; this was in part a naïve awakening to the existence of new forms of evil in the world, but it also served as an indignant protest against a civilization that had played a bad joke on itself."[1]

If the anything-goes youth of the 1920s rejected the earlier, prewar standards, it also celebrated a new, innovative age. By the time Stuart Erwin left the stage in 1928 to make his first movie, motion pictures, like the theater, were entering a transitional period, moving from silents to sound. Actors who could speak as well as pantomime were much in demand. And because Erwin already had a good deal of stage experience, he had no trouble with the speaking parts in his early films. Even so, he was still confronted with change, with a world that was continually breaking apart and realigning itself. Many of his films of the late twenties and early thirties demonstrate this fragmentation of his own day.

For instance, movies in which he appeared between 1928 and 1933 often deal seriously with the hard economic times of the early depression, yet at the same time they treat humorously and casually the easy accessibility of illegal booze in these waning days of Prohibition. Many of the characters he created during this period spend a good deal of time getting drunk. So too, these early films also have a daring quality, free of pre-Code Hollywood censorship. Much of the dialogue and many of the situations found in this early talkie period were risqué. The language was filled with double entendres; the situations were often morally questionable. Erwin and his early costars played around with material which they simply could not have attempted some thirty years later.

For instance, Erwin's 1929 movie *Sweetie* has him sunbathing naked (albeit in a long shot), with Helen Kane taking aim at his rear with her shotgun. He staggers drunkenly through such Prohibition-era movies as *Up Pops the Devil* (1930), *The Magnificent Lie* (1931), and *The Big Broadcast* (1932). In *Dangerous Nan McGrew* (1931) he tries extremely hard to propose to Helen Kane, but initially, all he can manage is a series of questions to her in which he inquires as to how much she cares for, first, cucumbers, and then, bananas. Both of these anxious lovers decide that they prefer bananas to cucumbers, which they decidedly do not like at all, presumably because cucumbers are not as soft as bananas. Their conversation, only outwardly about food, exemplifies the dizzy, iconoclastic quality to these early movies, in which madness is the norm and no one ever seems surprised by moral inconsistency. In *Palooka* (1934), Erwin has another sexy lady to play with, as he romps with Lupe Velez, peers down the neckline of her braless dress, disappears into her bedroom in order to remove his wet trousers, and soon afterward becomes her lover.

Likewise, by the early thirties, the role of the American male in motion pictures was being altered and subsequently redefined. The rugged, tough-talking type was replacing the handsome, cultured refined sort, which had been so popular in the twenties. By the mid-thirties, Clark Gable, James Cagney, Spencer Tracy, and Edward G. Robinson had replaced William Haines, David Manners, and Ramon Novarro as audience favorites. Even Ronald Colman and William Powell, more polished actors than Gable, Cagney, Tracy, and Robinson, remained popular but had, for the most part, turned to light comedy and away from serious romance. Into this environment came Stuart Erwin, whose versatility bridged the gap between the less aggressive, more boyish males of the twenties and the tough, hardened, cynical men of the thirties. In the late twenties and through the thirties, he played bashful, timid men, often painfully afraid of declaring themselves to the women they loved; yet he also played caustic, antisocial, amoral men of the world. Sometimes he illustrated both of these characteristics simultaneously, as he created complex—but rarely confusing—individuals. Moreover, unlike the affected, fussy, effeminate male comics of this decade such as Edward Everett Horton, Grady Sutton, and Franklin Pangborn, Erwin never camped his characters; even in his wildest, most farcical roles, he created multidimensional, masculine individuals.

From the mid-thirties and throughout the forties, Hollywood would become tamer, less daring, more aware of criticism from educational and religious groups with respect to movie content. Irreverent comics such as W. C. Fields, Mae West, and the Marx Brothers were straitjacketed and, while not exactly hauled off by the censors to the asylum for the wicked, were so cleansed that they looked tired, helpless, and worn down. And although Stuart Erwin continued throughout the thirties and forties to make a variety of films from many different genres, the characters he played from the late thirties onward seemed more subdued, less frantic; more mellow and comfortable with themselves, less urgent in their need to be accepted. So too, like Fields, West, and the Marxes, he faced increasingly inflexible studio bosses: men who refused to give up the tight control which they enjoyed over their actors. Indeed, in 1944, Erwin lost the opportunity to play Elwood P. Dowd in *Harvey*, a role which author Mary Chase had crafted with him in mind, because the studio refused to release him from his contract. Furthermore, just a few years later, Warner Bros. caved in to the dictates of Will Rogers's widow, with disappointing results for Erwin when he missed the chance to portray Will Rogers, another role for which he would have been ideally suited. In fact, the last movie in which Erwin appears to be having a really good time while he mocks the pretentiousness of people who take themselves too seriously is *Women Are Trouble*, which he made for M-G-M in 1936. Only two of his movies in the forties—*Cracked Nuts* (1941) and *Killer Dill* (1947)—contain glimmers of that preposterous foolishness that his early Paramount comedies could boast of. Having lived through the postwar despair of the twenties and the social criticism and satire of the thirties, Erwin had to redesign and reidentify himself by the late forties and early fifties. But it was not easy; as a later generation would also discover, the world was moving faster than it ever had at any time in human history, with the invention of the atom bomb breaking apart older, optimistic beliefs in mankind's progress.

Furthermore, with the publication in 1949 of George Orwell's *1984* and its fears of a totalitarian state attendant upon technological advances capable of deleting the past, Americans would become even more afraid of the future. In addition, with the increasing paranoia that prevailed in America throughout the forties came a concomitant darkness in American movies; such darkness was not limited to film noir but could be seen even in domestic comedies of the post-World War II period. One good illustration is

The Jackpot (1950), which features James Stewart as the harried breadwinner who wins a radio contest by getting the answer ahead of time from an informed source and thereby, through cheating, gathering in a bundle. The questionable ethics purveyed in this overwrought comedy offer an intriguing preview of the quiz show scandal in the fifties involving the vastly popular *Twenty-One*.

Another good instance of silly domestic goings-on is Erwin's *Heading for Heaven* (1947). In this one, he is the nominal head of a household that includes his wife (Glenda Farrell), who firmly believes in the efficacy of seances as a means to talk to the dead, his freeloading brother-in-law, and his daughter. The ridiculous plot lacks the gracefully inspired derangement and impudence of Erwin's early thirties movies. The film's one good moment comes when Erwin delivers a deadly accurate, impromptu kick onto his brother-in-law's rear. Here we can see the old devilment at work one more time, but sadly, the moment is not repeated, and the movie descends into predictability.

But by the fifties, Erwin had reassembled the pieces of his own fragmented time and of his own suspended acting career; in his television series *Trouble with Father*, in which he played a husband, father, and school administrator, he would return to the unassuming, susceptible boyishness of his earliest movies. However, the twenty-plus intervening years marked a decided difference in his approach. The stuttering shyness of the past had become the wry amusement of a man well adapted to the present. The giggling lunacy of the well-intentioned young man of the twenties and thirties had become a twinkle in the eye and a chuckle from the middle-aged high school principal. The naïve child-man beset by troubles from worldly con artists had become a caring parent whose best intentions often went comically awry. The woman whom he loved, sometimes in vain, had become his real-life wife June Collyer, an attractive, down-to-earth lady, who evidently returned his love. Although Stuart Erwin had always been a most genial actor, basically at ease with himself, he had also mellowed with age, grown into someone whom you could feel comfortable with, whom you could bring your troubles to with no embarrassment whatsoever.

A GENTLE, UNDERSTANDING
MENTOR AND COUNSELOR

One of those who felt such comfort in his presence is Sheila James, a talented, savvy child actress who appeared with Erwin on television in the fifties. Today, Ms. James is a Harvard-educated lawyer and a California state senator. But fifty years ago, she played Erwin's younger daughter in *Trouble with Father*, which ran on television from 1950 till 1955. When I asked her to analyze the type of person he was, she replied that he "had a gentleness" with not even "a hint of cynicism."[2] She further agreed that he was indeed "extremely comfortable with himself" and certain of his own identity. She also alluded to the fact that he "had married a woman allegedly above him in class and seemed easy with it." Thus, despite his modest, self-effacing response to an interviewer who, years before, had asked him how he had happened to win the hand of popular debutante June Collyer, Erwin doubtless never questioned why she had so eagerly decided some twenty-one years earlier to be his wife.

Further, we can see that his tendency throughout the years to kid his costars as well as himself must have come naturally, for Ms. James maintained that he "had a twinkle in his eye" and that he "was ready for mischief at times." She also sensed that he had an intrinsic sense of humor when she observed that he was both "loving and funny." Although she repeatedly used the word *gentle* to describe him, she also noted that he was "not maudlin. He didn't like anything phony."

Perhaps such inherent integrity is the one attribute that helps to explain why Erwin seemed so uncomfortable as the unlettered hick in *Pigskin Parade*. The only truly sincere part of his performance may be found in his scenes with Judy Garland, where these "loving and gentle" qualities as described by Ms. James, his surrogate daughter, emerge quite openly. It is entirely possible that Erwin was seeing the fragile teenaged Garland as a surrogate daughter.

From Sheila James's account, Erwin also appears to have been what modern psychologists calls an *enabler*—that is, one who makes others feel important. In fact, his own real-life son told me that his father had been his mentor and his inspiration. By the same token, Stuart Jr.'s television counterpart said that she herself "loved him," and that, just like her real parents, he "made me feel worthwhile, productive, appreciated." She added that he got along "extremely well" with the other cast members and was very professional. In addition, she said that both he and his wife conveyed the importance of such professionalism to her. Moreover, since she kept in touch with both of the Erwins after the series ended in 1955, she presumably continued to view them as supportive surrogate parents.

Ms. James's opinions are shared by Stuart Erwin Jr., who lovingly recalled his father as "modest and self-effacing and down to earth. He was a terrific guy. He loved people and he wanted to get to know them instantly.

He loved to talk to strangers as much as to friends. It was difficult to get him in and out of the supermarket in under an hour. Dad was great to those he worked with, from his directors and co-stars to the assistant grips. And, for his family, he was a wonderful husband and father!"[3]

Indeed, from my correspondence with Stuart Jr., it is clear that the son truly admired and loved his father. He reaffirmed what Sheila James remembered as the supportive qualities of both of the Erwins. For instance, in the early fifties, when Stuart Jr. was a student at Brown University, Stuart and June maintained an apartment in New York City where their children hosted friends from school. Stuart Jr., recalls that his "parents loved entertaining them all, and were the most popular Mom and Dad, by far. They were very proud of us." He adds that "we were a very close and loving family." Furthermore, Sheila James's pleasant recollection that Erwin made her feel "worthwhile, productive, appreciated" is supported by Stuart Jr.'s own reminiscence of his parents' guidance and encouragement: "They were very proud of us. In my case, Dad was thrilled with my career at Brown and very proud of my being an officer on a destroyer. He was very pleased when I followed him into show business, although relieved that it was as a producer rather than actor. They loved us and their grandchildren, as we loved them."[4]

So in short, here we have Stuart Erwin, the private man—loving, funny, gentle, professional—much like the characters he portrayed on screen. And we also have Stuart Erwin, the private man—plainly at ease with himself but remarkably modest. In fact, when I asked Ms. James to comment on Erwin's observation, made in 1952, that he often felt invisible, she replied that he was indeed that self-effacing—an adjective also used by Stuart Jr. to describe his father.

William Schallert, a veteran of dozens of movies and television shows, provided me with a further perspective on the private Stuart Erwin. Schallert responded to my inquiry about his experience in working with Erwin by writing some entertaining reminiscences; his memories precede the *Trouble with Father* days. In 1947, Schallert appeared with Erwin in an industrial film called *Doctor Jim*. According to Schallert, the movie was made by the John Deere Tractor Company; in it, as Schallert recalls, "I played a farmer whose wife was ailing after drinking milk from our cows. Stu Erwin, who played Dr. Jim, dropped by to check on her. He asked me some leading questions about my cows and I suddenly got what he was driving at and in that moment of revelation uttered the memorable line: "'Bang's Disease!!'—which is another name for undulant fever. Dr. Jim had the cure, of course, and all ended well. . . . Stu Erwin was a charming actor of the 'aw shucks' school—low key and very real and honest in his performance. . . . He was also a nice guy, as I recall."[5]

As I have tried to emphasize throughout this book, "real" and "honest" are indeed two appropriate adjectives for Erwin; there is rarely a false note in any of his performances. No matter what the decade—whether the 1920s or the 1960s—no matter what the role, no matter what the size of the part, he played fair with his characters, even the most peculiar of them. Whether the role was comic or serious, he never mocked or ridiculed them; therefore, we believed in them because he believed in them himself. While it is somewhat difficult to accept the idea, as Sheila James does, that a man as shrewd and intelligent as Erwin was did not have "a hint of cynicism" anywhere in his nature, it is nonetheless possible that he was able to maintain such a forthright, idealistic hopefulness, even into his middle age. Perhaps this underlying, ever-youthful optimism and integrity in his nature are the qualities that account for others' perception of him as a warm, genuine, honest individual—both on screen and off.

By the 1960s, Erwin's movie appearances were limited to only three theatrical features: *For the Love of* Mike (1960), *Son of Flubber* (1963), and *The Misadventures of Merlin Jones* (1964). None are particularly memorable, although in his role as a police captain in the last picture he shows some of the michievous spark of thirty years before, particularly when he chuckles as he contemplates something that he finds funny. But he is about sixty pounds heavier than he had been in the 1930s, and he looks tired, perhaps because he is frazzled by worry over what he is doing in such a basically muddled, messy movie. Maybe because the subject matter of theatrical movies had begun to change so drastically by the 1960s, Erwin turned more and more to television during his last decade.

But he did not live long enough to see the decade's end, to witness the shattering of old taboos with the advent of such 1969 groundbreaking movies as *Midnight Cowboy* and *Easy Rider*. Moreover, though Erwin was only sixty-four when he died in 1967, he lived through some of the most cataclysmic events of the twentieth century: World War I, the moral vacuum of the 1920s, the Depression, World War II, the atomic bomb, and Korea. He also lived to see a society broken apart by Vietnam. Was he disillusioned by the world of the rebellious sixties? Or did he see it as simply an extension of the disgruntled youth of his own generation of the twenties? On the other hand, was he so upset by the children of the sixties that he, like Jay Gatsby, would have wanted to repeat the past?

It is doubtful that Stuart Erwin looked back on his life with any serious regrets, for one feels that he was not a man given to the sentimentality that often accompanies nostalgia. Yet if one looks closely at some representative episodes of *Trouble with Father*, one is struck by the number of veteran character actors appearing with regularity on the series. Many of these were performers who had made movies with Erwin, sometimes as far back as the early thirties. In the case of Willie Best, the well-known black actor who had a continuing role in the series, one sees a thread stretching all the way to Best's appearance as a laundryman in *Up Pops the Devil* (1931). Although Best shares no scenes with Erwin in that movie (Best actually has more screen time than Erwin does), both appear in the cast. Likewise, other veteran actors who were featured in the series include Alan Mowbray, Raymond Hatton, Margaret Hamilton, Chester Clute, Margaret Dumont, Florence Lake, diminutive Harry Hayden and his real-life wife, the statuesque, imposing, not-to-be-trifled-with Lela Bliss (playing Harry and Adele Johnson, the Erwins' neighbors), Don Beddoe, and Ben Welden. All of these actors except Alan Mowbray and Lela Bliss had made at least one movie with Erwin.

However, not everything on the show involved a backward look at movie history; there were some daring, forward-looking moments as well. One good illustration of this is found in the role played by Willie Best. While he does act as a kind of servant and handyman for the Erwins, and while he is somewhat deferential to Erwin (he calls Erwin "Mr. Erwin"; Erwin calls him "Willie"), there is a camaraderie between Erwin and Best that jumps over those hurdles of race that had been erected years earlier and that continued to prevail with a vicious fervor throughout the fifties. For instance, Erwin never hesitates to show his fondness for Best by affectionately touching him, even occasionally putting his arm around Best's shoulders. Furthermore, whenever the two engage in slapstick and Erwin sees that Best might be in physical danger, he shows genuine concern for his black buddy, trying to keep him safe from harm.

One must recall the mood of the times in order to fully appreciate the rapport between these two actors of different races. During this same period, another well-known entertainer, Eddie Cantor, would receive a good deal of hate mail for a small, simple, thoughtful gesture which he made toward Sammy Davis Jr. on the *Colgate Comedy Hour*, broadcast on February 17, 1952. When Davis had finished his number to enthusiastic applause, Cantor came on stage, equally impressed by the achievement of the young black performer, still relatively unknown to the general public. Noting that perspiration was running down Davis's face, Cantor took his own handkerchief from his breast pocket and wiped the forehead of young Davis. Following the broadcast, malicious mail flooded NBC. The writer of one representative example violently protested: "Eddie Cantor: How dare you mop that coon's face with your handkerchief on national TV?"[6] In light of this national mood, then, Erwin's ongoing, comfortable relationship with Willie Best is even more stunning.

Trouble with Father takes an even bolder step in the attitude shown toward Best by the two girls who play Erwin's daughters (Sheila James and Ann Todd). At least Eddie Cantor and Sammy Davis Jr. were both male, so that there was nothing sexually threatening about Cantor touching Davis. But *Trouble with Father* introduces another, more dangerous element. Both girls on the show treat Willie Best as an equal, with Sheila James and Best often in league together against her parents. And with the older daughter, Ann Todd, Best would come ominously close to a serious violation of acceptable 1950s standards for relations between a black man and a white woman. Since Todd is supposed to be a teenager still in high school, the continuing compatibility between the two might have been interpreted by a disapproving audience as unmistakably polluted with a taboo sexual element.

For example, in one such defiant episode, Best climbs through a second story window and sneaks into Todd's bedroom at night in order to help her escape from her room, where she has been sent by her parents as a form of punishment. They spend some time alone together in her bedroom, plotting their strategy. Neither seems at all self-conscious about their potentially compromising situation, nor do the Erwins exhibit any indignation when they finally learn about the mischief enacted by Best and their older daughter, an attractive, delicate, and vulnerable young woman.

That Stuart Erwin starred in a series with such unorthodox, farsighted liberal ideas for the conservative fifties says much about his character and his courage. In addition, though he apparently was not one to dwell on the past, at the same time he remained loyal to those he had known and worked with during his first years in Hollywood. Besides his commitment to his profession, to his fellow actors, and to his art, he also continued to manifest this attribute of adaptability, notably in the remarkable, egalitarian quality he displayed toward everyone throughout his long career, a quality especially befitting the civil rights movements of the sixties.

In short, during the five decades in which he performed, he handled the diversities of his particular world and of its changing times most expertly, from the hip flasks and bathtub gin generation of the late twenties to the pot smoking, make-love-not-war children of the mid-sixties. Whereas our world is the impermanence of cyberspace and the impatience nurtured by computer speed, Erwin's was the impermanence of the 1920s postwar despair and the impatience nurtured by dreams crushed when America's economic foundations collapsed, burying the hopes of the age. True, his was in many ways a different world from ours, but he would have understood us. And he would have done his best to make us see both the humor and the sadness in our era, as he did so well during his own lifetime—again and again and again.

NOTES

1. *The 20's: American Writing in the Postwar Decade* (New York: The Free Press, 1962), 23.

2. All quotations from Sheila James are from a letter to author, 24 March 2000.

3. Stuart Erwin Jr., letter to author, 12 October 2000.

4. Stuart Erwin Jr., letter to author, 16 October 2000.

5. William Schallert, letter to author, 6 July 2000.

6. Herbert G. Goldman, *Banjo Eyes: Eddie Cantor and the Birth of Modern Stardom* (New York: Oxford University Press, 1997), 277–78.

APPENDIX

STUART ERWIN ROLES THAT NEVER WERE
BUT THAT SHOULD HAVE BEEN

Although Stuart Erwin had at least two bitter career disappointments when he was denied the opportunities to play roles that had been tailored for his talents—specifically the parts of Elwood P. Dowd in *Harvey*[1] and Will Rogers in *The Story of Will Rogers*—there were other parts that he could have interpreted equally adroitly. The following is a list of characters—all of whom appear in plays, novels, or short stories—that he was capable of handling extremely well, either in movie or in stage adaptations. Some of these works have actually been made into motion pictures; some have never been filmed. In any event, Erwin would have been the ideal casting choice for each of these characters. But it appears that no one ever offered him the opportunity.

- Jay Gatsby in F. Scott Fitzgerald's *The Great Gatsby* (1925). Erwin had just the right mixture of dreamy naïveté and moral amnesia to play Fitzgerald's protagonist. Had the movie been filmed in the thirties, which it wasn't, Erwin would have been the ideal age for Gatsby.
- Willy Loman in Arthur Miller's *Death of a Salesman* (1949). By 1960, Erwin would have been just right to play Miller's lost, hopeless Willy. Erwin could have handily demonstrated his understanding of Willy's cringing bluff and bravado; further, since Erwin had such a shrewd awareness of human limitations, he would have allowed us to see quite clearly the reasons that Willy Loman's pathetic life had

added up to nothing. Yet he would have treated Willy with empathy, never condescending to him.

- Erwin Martin in James Thurber's short story "The Catbird Seat" (1945). As far as I know, this amusing work has never been adapted for stage or screen. Thurber's patient, dependable, unobtrusive, methodical, mild-mannered file clerk, who challenges and defeats an aggressive, overbearing woman, was a role perfectly suited to Stuart Erwin's personality.

- Bartleby, in Herman Melville's story "Bartleby the Scrivener" (1853). Melville's alienated character, who withdraws more and more from life, engaging in increasingly absurd behavior, displayed that combination of dark humor combined with pathos which Erwin handled so well in so many roles.

- Charlie Wales in F. Scott Fitzgerald's story "Babylon Revisited" (1931). Here is the quintessential lost soul of the Lost Generation, a man who spent the decade of the twenties living in a drug- and alcohol-induced haze and who is now desperately trying to reclaim his life. As Stuart Erwin showed in many of his Prohibition-era movies, he could play such lonely, dissipated men quite skillfully. Given a chance, Erwin undoubtedly would have made Charlie Wales into a sympathetic yet tragically doomed character. Although the work was filmed in 1954 under the title of *The Last Time I Saw Paris*, it was Van Johnson who was cast as Charlie Wales; and he looks as though he were in pain throughout the entire movie. It is a boring adaptation, one which took many liberties with the original story. Stuart Erwin would have brought life to the tale.

- Barton in Theodore Dreiser's story "The Second Choice" (1918). The Second Choice of the title is the dull, phlegmatic Barton: the devoted, romantic, forgiving, but predictable guy whom the heroine chooses because she cannot have her first choice, the dangerous Arthur.

- John Singer in Carson McCullers's *The Heart Is a Lonely Hunter* (1940). The deaf-mute protagonist of this novel is another character whom Erwin would have brought vividly to life, revealing the pain of a man adrift, cut off from the world.

- Joe in William Saroyan's *The Time of Your Life* (1939). The philosophical centerpiece of this play is Joe, sitting in a San Franciso waterfront bar, untiringly listening to the illusory hopes of the various outcasts who enter the bar. James Cagney played the role in the 1948 movie version, the last independent production that he made with his brother William as producer. Erwin might have given a more laid back, less energetic interpretation of Joe the philosopher than Cagney does, but Joe's ruminations about life and his optimistic, if somewhat occasionally ironic, humor were nonetheless suited to Erwin's gentle, understanding temperament.

NOTE

1. He did, however, get the chance to play Elwood P. Dowd in summer stock throughout New England in 1950.

FILMOGRAPHY

1. *Mother Knows Best*. Dir. John G. Blystone. With Madge Bellamy, Louise Dresser, Barry Norton, and Lucien Littlefield. SE as Ben. Fox, 1928.
2. *New Year's Eve*. Dir. Henry Lehrman. With Mary Astor, Charles Morton, Earle Foxe, and Florence Lake. SE as Landlady's Son. Fox, 1929.
3. *Speakeasy*. Dir. Benjamin Stoloff. With Paul Page, Lola Lane, Henry B. Walthall, and Warren Hymer. SE as Cy Williams. M-G-M, 1929.
4. *Thru Different Eyes*. Dir. John G. Blystone. With Mary Duncan, Edmund Lowe, Warner Baxter, and Natalie Moorhead. SE as a reporter. Fox, 1929.
5. *Dangerous Curves*. Dir. Lothar Mendes. With Clara Bow, Richard Arlen, Kay Francis, and David Newell. SE as a Rotarian. Paramount, 1929.
6. *The Exalted Flapper*. Dir. James Tinling. With Sue Carol, Barry Norton, Irene Rich, and Albert Conti. SE as Bimbo Mehaffey. Fox, 1929.
7. *The Sophomore*. Dir. Leo McCarey. With Eddie Quillan, Sally O'Neill, Stanley Smith, and Russell Gleason. SE is uncredited. Pathé, 1929.
8. *Sweetie*. Dir. Frank Tuttle. With Nancy Carroll, Helen Kane, Stanley Smith, and Jack Oakie. SE as Axel Bronstrup. Paramount, 1929.
9. *The Trespasser*. Dir. Edmund Goulding. With Gloria Swanson, Robert Ames, Purnell Pratt, and Henry B. Walthall. SE as a reporter. United Artists, 1929.
10. *This Thing Called Love*. Dir. Paul L. Stein. With Edmund Lowe, Constance Bennett, Roscoe Karns, and ZaSu Pitts. SE as Fred. Pathé, 1929.
11. *A Pair of Tights*. Dir. Hal Yates. With Harry Bernard, Marion Byron, Anita Garvin, and Edgar Kennedy. SE is one of the cast in this two-reel silent comedy. Hal Roach, 1929.

12. *The Cock-Eyed World.* Dir. Raoul Walsh. With Victor McLaglen, Edmund Lowe, Lili Damita, and El Brendel. SE as Buckley. Fox, 1929.

13. *Men Without Women.* Dir. John Ford. With Kenneth MacKenna, Frank Albertson, J. Farrell MacDonald, and Warren Hymer. SE as Radioman Jenkins. Fox, 1930.

14. *Young Eagles.* Dir. William A. Wellman. With Charles "Buddy" Rogers, Jean Arthur, Paul Lukas, and Virginia Bruce. SE as Pudge Higgins. Paramount, 1930.

15. *Paramount on Parade.* Dir. Dorothy Arzner and Otto Brower. With Iris Adrian, Richard Arlen, Jean Arthur, and Mischa Auer. SE in a cameo appearance as himself. Paramount, 1930.

16. *Dangerous Nan McGrew.* Dir. Malcolm St. Clair. With Helen Kane, Victor Moore, James Hall, and Frank Morgan. SE as Eustace Macy. Paramount, 1930.

17. *Maybe It's Love.* Dir. William A. Wellman. With Joan Bennett, Joe E. Brown, James Hall, and Laura Lee. SE is Brown of Harvard (uncredited). Warner Bros., 1930.

18. *Only Saps Work.* Dir. Cyril Gardner and Edwin H. Knopf. With Leon Errol, Richard Arlen, Mary Brian, and Charley Grapewin. SE as Oscar. Paramount, 1930.

19. *Along Came Youth.* Dir. Lloyd Corrigan and Norman Z. McLeod. With Charles "Buddy" Rogers, Frances Dee, William Austin, and Evelyn Hall. SE as Ambrose. Paramount, 1930.

20. *Playboy of Paris.* Dir. Ludwig Berger. With Maurice Chevalier, Frances Dee, O. P. Heggie, and Eugene Pallette. SE as Paul Michel. Paramount, 1930.

21. *Love Among the Millionaires.* Dir. Frank Tuttle. With Clara Bow, Stanley Smith, Richard "Skeets" Gallagher, and Mitzi Green. SE as Clicker Watson. Paramount, 1930.

22. *Happy Days.* Dir. Benjamin Stoloff. With Charles E. Evans, Marjorie White, Richard Keene, and Martha Lee Sparks. SE as Jig. Fox, 1930.

23. *No Limit.* Dir. Frank Tuttle. With Clara Bow, Norman Foster, Dixie Lee, and Thelma Todd. SE as Ole Olson. Paramount, 1931.

24. *Dude Ranch.* Dir. Frank Tuttle. With Eugene Pallette, June Collyer, Mitzi Green, and Jack Oakie. SE as Chester Carr. Paramount, 1931.

25. *The Magnificent Lie.* Dir. Berthold Viertel. With Ruth Chatterton, Ralph Bellamy, Sam Hardy, and Charles Boyer. SE as Elmer. Paramount, 1931.

26. *Working Girls.* Dir. Dorothy Arzner. With Judith Wood, Paul Lukas, Frances Dee, and Claire Dodd. Paramount, 1931.

27. *Up Pops the Devil.* Dir. A. Edward Sutherland. With Willie Best, Joyce Compton, Richard "Skeets" Gallagher, and Carole Lombard. SE as the inebriated stranger. Paramount, 1931.

28. *Misleading Lady.* Dir. Stuart Walker. With Claudette Colbert, Edmund Lowe, Robert Strange, and George Meeker. SE as Boney. Paramount, 1932.

29. *The Big Broadcast.* Dir. Frank Tuttle. With Bing Crosby, Leila Hyams, George Burns, and Gracie Allen. SE as Leslie McWhinney. Paramount, 1932.

30. *Make Me a Star.* Dir. William Beaudine. With Joan Blondell, Ruth Donnelly, Charles Sellon, and Sam Hardy. SE as Merton Gill. Paramount, 1932.

31. *Two Kinds of Women.* Dir. William C. de Mille. With Adrienne Ames, James Crane, Claire Dodd, and Josephine Dunn. SE as Hauser. Paramount, 1932.

32. *Strangers in Love.* Dir. Lothar Mendes. With George Barbier, Kay Francis, Fredric March, and Lucien Littlefield. SE as Stan Keeney. Paramount, 1932.

33. *Hollywood on Parade.* Dir. Louis Lewyn. With Bing Crosby, George Burns, Gracie Allen, and Gary Cooper. SE in a guest appearance. Paramount, 1932.

34. *The Face in the Sky.* Dir. Harry Lachman. With Spencer Tracy, Marian Nixon, Sam Hardy, and Russell Simpson. SE as Lucky. Fox, 1933.

35. *Under the Tonto Rim.* Dir. Henry Hathaway. With Raymond Hatton, Fuzzy Knight, Ken Taylor, and Fred Kohler. Paramount, 1933.

36. *Crime of the Century.* Dir. William Beaudine. With Frances Dee, Robert Elliott, Wynne Gibson, and Jean Hersholt. SE as Dan McKee. Paramount, 1933.

37. *International House.* Dir. Edward Sutherland. With Peggy Hopkins Joyce, W. C. Fields, George Burns, and Gracie Allen. SE as Tommy Nash. Paramount, 1933.

38. *Hold Your Man.* Dir. Sam Wood. With Jean Harlow, Clark Gable, Dorothy Burgess, and Muriel Kirkland. SE as Al Simpson. M-G-M, 1933.

39. *Day of Reckoning.* Dir. Charles Brabin. With Richard Dix, Madge Evans, Una Merkel, and Isabel Jewell. SE as Jerry. M-G-M, 1933.

40. *Going Hollywood.* Dir. Raoul Walsh. With Marion Davies, Bing Crosby, Fifi D'Orsay, and Patsy Kelly. SE as Ernest P. Baker. M-G-M, 1933.

41. *The Stranger's Return.* Dir. King Vidor. With Tad Alexander, Lionel Barrymore, Beulah Bondi, and Irene Hervey. SE as Simon. M-G-M, 1933.

42. *He Learned About Women.* Dir. Lloyd Corrigan. With Susan Fleming, Alison Skipworth, Sidney Toler, and Grant Mitchell. SE as Peter Potter Kendall III. Paramount, 1933.

43. *Before Dawn.* Dir. Irving Pichel. With Dorothy Wilson, Warner Oland, Dudley Digges, and Gertrude Hoffman. SE as Dwight Wilson. RKO, 1933.

44. *Viva Villa!* Dir. Jack Conway. With Wallace Beery, Leo Carrillo, Fay Wray, and Donald Cook. SE as Johnny Sykes. M-G-M, 1934.

45. *Bachelor Bait.* Dir. George Stevens. With Rochelle Hudson, Pert Kelton, Richard "Skeets" Gallagher, and Burton Churchill. SE as Wilbur Fess. RKO, 1934.

46. *Chained.* Dir. Clarence Brown. With Joan Crawford, Clark Gable, Otto Kruger, and Una O'Connor. SE as John Smith. M-G-M, 1934.

47. *Have a Heart.* Dir. David Butler. With Jean Parker, James Dunn, Una Merkel, and Willard Robertson. SE as Gus Anderson. M-G-M, 1934.

48. *The Band Plays On.* Dir. Russell Mack. With Robert Young, Leo Carrillo, Betty Furness, and Ted Healy. SE as Stuffy. M-G-M, 1934.

49. *The Party's Over.* Dir. Walter Lang. With Ann Sothern, Arline Judge, Patsy Kelly, and Catherine Doucet. SE as Bruce. Columbia, 1934.

50. *Palooka.* Dir. Benjamin Stoloff. With Jimmy Durante, Lupe Velez, Marjorie Rambeau, and Robert Armstrong. SE as Joe Palooka. United Artists, 1934.

51. *The Hollywood Gad-About.* Dir. Louis Lewyn. With Baby Peggy, Frankie Darro, Buster Crabbe, Ginger Rogers. SE in a guest appearance. Paramount, 1934.

52. *After Office Hours.* Dir. Robert Z. Leonard. With Constance Bennett, Clark Gable, Billie Burke, and Harvey Stephens. SE as Hank Parr. M-G-M, 1935.

53. *Ceiling Zero.* Dir. Howard Hawks. With James Cagney, Pat O'Brien, June Travis, and Isabel Jewell. SE as Texas Clarke. Warner Bros., 1935.

54. *Absolute Quiet.* Dir. George B. Seitz. With Lionel Atwill, Irene Hervey, Raymond Walburn, and Ann Loring. SE as Oscar "Chubby" Rudd. M-G-M, 1936.

55. *All American Chump.* Dir. Edwin L. Marin. With Robert Armstrong, Betty Furness, Edmund Gwenn, and Harvey Stephens. SE as Elmer. M-G-M, 1936.

56. *Pigskin Parade.* Dir. David Butler. With Patsy Kelly, Jack Haley, John Downs, and Judy Garland. SE as Amos Dodd. 20th Century Fox, 1936.

57. *Women Are Trouble.* Dir. Earl Taggart. With Paul Kelly, Florence Rice, Cy Kendall, and Kitty McHugh. SE as Matt Casey. M-G-M, 1936.

58. *Exclusive Story*. Dir. George B. Seitz. With Robert Barrat, Wade Boteler, Madge Evans, and Raymond Hatton. SE as Tim Higgins. M-G-M, 1936.

59. *Small Town Boy*. Dir. Glenn Tryon. With Dorothy Appleby, Clara Blandick, George Chandler, and Joyce Compton. SE as Henry. Grand National, 1937.

60. *Sunday Night at the Trocadero*. Dir. George Sidney. With Reginald Denny, Gaylord Carter, George Hamilton, and Marge Champion. SE is uncredited and plays himself. M-G-M, 1937.

61. *Slim*. Dir. Ray Enright. With Pat O'Brien, Henry Fonda, Margaret Lindsey, and J. Farrell MacDonald. SE as Stumpy. Warner Bros., 1937.

62. *Second Honeymoon*. Dir. Walter Lang. With Tyrone Power, Loretta Young, Claire Trevor, and Marjorie Weaver. SE as Leo McTavish. 20th Century Fox, 1937.

63. *I'll Take Romance*. Dir. Edward Griffith. With Melvyn Douglas, Margaret Hamilton, Grace Moore, and Helen Westley. SE as "Pancho" Brown. Columbia, 1937.

64. *Dance Charlie Dance*. Dir. Frank McDonald. With Jean Muir, Glenda Farrell, Allen Jenkins, and Addison Richards. SE as Andy Taylor. Warner Bros., 1937.

65. *Checkers*. Dir. H. Bruce Humberstone. With Jane Withers, Una Merkel, Marvin Stephens, and Andrew Tombes. SE as Edgar Connell. 20th Century Fox, 1937.

66. *Mr. Boggs Steps Out*. Dir. Gordon Wiles. With Helen Chandler, Walter Byron, Toby Wing, and Tully Marshall. SE as Oliver Boggs. Grand National, 1938.

67. *Hollywood Handicap*. Dir. Buster Keaton. With Warner Baxter, Edgar Bergen, Charles Butterworth, and June Collyer. SE as himself in an uncredited guest appearance. M-G-M, 1938.

68. *Three Blind Mice*. Dir. William A. Seiter. With Loretta Young, Joel McCrea, David Niven, and Marjorie Weaver. SE as Mike Brophy. 20th Century Fox, 1938.

69. *Passport Husband*. Dir. James Tinling. With Pauline Moore, Douglas Fowley, Joan Woodbury, and Harold Huber. SE as Henry Cabot. 20th Century Fox, 1938.

70. *Hollywood Cavalcade*. Dir. Irving Cummings. With Alice Faye, Don Ameche, J. Edward Bromberg, and Alan Curtis. SE as Pete Tinney. 20th Century Fox, 1939.

71. *It Could Happen to You*. Dir. Alfred L. Werker. With Gloria Stuart, Raymond Walburn, Douglas Fowley, and June Gale. SE as Mackinley Winslow. 20th Century Fox, 1939.

72. *The Honeymoon's Over.* Dir. Eugene Forde. With Marjorie Weaver, Patric Knowles, Russell Hicks, and Jack Carson. SE as Donald. 20th Century Fox, 1939.

73. *Back Door to Heaven.* Dir. William K. Howard. With Aline MacMahon, Wallace Ford, Patricia Ellis, and Van Heflin. SE as Jud Mason. Paramount, 1939.

74. *Our Town.* Dir. Sam Wood. With Frank Craven, William Holden, Martha Scott, and Thomas Mitchell. SE as Howie Newsome. United Artists, 1940.

75. *When the Daltons Rode.* Dir. George Marshall. With Randolph Scott, Kay Francis, Brian Donlevy, and George Bancroft. SE as Ben Dalton. Universal, 1940.

76. *Sandy Gets Her Man.* Dir. Otis Garrett and Paul Girard Smith. With Baby Sandy, Edward Brophy, Jack Carson, and William Frawley. SE as Bill. Universal, 1940.

77. *A Little Bit of Heaven.* Dir. Andrew Marton. With Sig Arno, Gloria Jean, Noah Beery, Jr., and Monte Blue. SE as Cotton. Universal, 1940.

78. *The Bride Came C.O.D.* Dir. William Keighley. With James Cagney, Bette Davis, Jack Carson, and George Tobias. SE as Tommy Keenan. Warner Bros., 1941.

79. *Cracked Nuts.* Dir. Edward F. Cline. With Una Merkel, Mischa Auer, William Frawley, and Astrid Allwyn. SE as Lawrence Trent. Universal, 1941.

80. *Drums of the Congo.* Dir. Christy Cabanne. With Peggy Moran, Turhan Bey, Don Terry, and Ona Munson. SE as Congo Jack. Universal, 1942.

81. *The Adventures of Martin Eden.* Dir. Sidney Salkow. With Glenn Ford, Claire Trevor, Evelyn Keyes, and Dickie Moore. SE as Joe Dawson. Columbia, 1942.

82. *Blondie for Victory.* Dir. Frank Strayer. With Penny Singleton, Arthur Lake, Larry Simms, and Jonathan Hale. SE as Pvt. Herschel Smith. Columbia, 1942.

83. *He Hired the Boss.* Dir. Thomas Z. Loring. With Evelyn Venable, Thurston Hall, Vivian Blaine, and William T. Orr. SE as Herbert Wilkins. 20th Century Fox, 1943.

84. *The Great Mike.* Dir. Wallace Fox. With Robert "Buzz" Henry, Carl "Alfalfa" Switzer, Pierre Watkin, and Gwen Kenyon. SE as Spencer. PRC, 1944.

85. *Pillow to Post.* Dir. Vincent Sherman. With Ida Lupino, Sydney Greenstreet, William Prince, and Johnny Mitchell. SE as Captain Jack Ross. Warner Bros., 1945.

86. *Doctor Jim.* Dir. Lew Landers. With Barbara Wooddell, William Wright, Hobart Cavanaugh, and William Schallert. SE as Dr. James Gateson. John Deere and Co., 1947.

87. *Killer Dill.* Dir. Lewis D. Collins. With Anne Gwynne, Frank Albertson, Mike Mazurki, and Dorothy Granger. SE as Johnny Dill. Screen Guild, 1947.

88. *Heaven Only Knows.* Dir. Albert S. Rogell. With Robert Cummings, Ray Bennett, Brian Donlevy, and Bill Goodwin. SE as the sheriff. United Artists, 1947.

89. *Heading for Heaven.* Dir. Lewis D. Collins. With Glenda Farrell, Russ Vincent, Irene Ryan, and Milburn Stone. SE as Henry. Eagle Lion Films, Inc. 1947.

90. *Strike It Rich.* Dir. Lesley Selander. With Rod Cameron, Don Castle, Ellen Corby, and Lloyd Corrigan. SE as Delbart Lane. Allied Artists, 1948.

91. *Father is a Bachelor.* Dir. Abby Berlin and Norman Foster. With William Holden, Coleen Gray, Mary Jane Saunders, and Charles Winninger. SE as Pudge Barnham. Columbia, 1950.

92. *Moochie of the Little League.* Dir. William Beaudine. With Kevin Corcoran, Reginald Owen, Alan Hale Jr., and Frances Rafferty. TV movie, 1959.

93. *When Comedy Was King.* Dir. Robert Youngson. With Roscoe "Fatty" Arbuckle, Wallace Beery, Billy Bevan, and Charles Chaplin. SE in archive documentary footage. 20th Century Fox, 1960.

94. *For the Love of Mike.* Dir. George Sherman. With Richard Basehart, Arthur Shields, Danny Zaidivan, and Armando Silvestre. SE as Dr. Mills. 20th Century Fox, 1960.

95. *Son of Flubber.* Dir. Robert Stevenson. With Fred MacMurray, Nancy Olson, Keenan Wynn, and Tommy Kirk. SE as Coach Wilson. Buena Vista, 1963.

96. *The Misadventures of Merlin Jones.* Dir. Robert Stevenson. With Leon Ames, Annette Funicello, Connie Gilchrist, and Tommy Kirk. SE as Police Captain Loomis. Buena Vista, 1964.

97. *Shadow Over Elveron.* Dir. James Goldstone. With Don Ameche, Jill Banner, Vic Dana, and James Dunn. SE as Merle. TV movie, 1968.

BIBLIOGRAPHY

Albert, Katherine. "How to Become A Hollywood Hostess in One Easy Lesson." *Photoplay* 37 (December 1929): 32–33, 127–128.

"Back Door to Heaven." *Photoplay* 53 (October 1939): 6.

Barris, Alex. *Stop the Presses! The Newspaperman in American Films.* New York: A.S. Barnes and Company, 1976.

Bederman, Gail. *Manliness and Civilization.* Chicago: University of Chicago Press, 1995.

Behlmer, Rudy, and Tony Thomas. *Hollywood's Hollywood: The Movies About the Movies.* Secaucus, N. J.: Citadel Press, 1975.

Benayoun, Robert. *The Look of Buster Keaton,* ed. and trans. Randall Conrad. New York: St. Martin's Press, 1983.

Blum, Daniel. *A Pictorial History of the American Theatre 1860–1970,* 3rd ed. New York: Crown, 1969.

Brooks, Tim, and Earle Marsh, eds. *The Complete Directory to Prime Time Network and Cable TV Shows: 1946–Present.* New York: Ballentine Books, 1999.

Burnham, David. "Mr. Sycamore." *The Commonweal* 37 (November 17, 1942): 144.

Cagney, James. *Cagney by Cagney.* New York: Doubleday, 1976.

Cather, Willa. "Paul's Case." Pp. 406–21 in *Literature: An Introduction to Fiction, Poetry, and Drama,* 7th ed., edited by X. J. Kennedy and Dana Gioia. New York: Longman, 1999.

Chapman, John, ed. *The Burns Mantle Best Plays of 1949–1950.* New York: Dodd, Mead and Company, 1950.

Cook, Ted. "Cook-Coo Gossip." *The New Movie Magazine* 6 (July 1932): 33.

"Crime of the Century." *The New Movie Magazine* 7 (April 1933): 100.

Dooley, Roger. *From Scarface to Scarlett: American Films in the 1930s.* New York: Harcourt Brace Jovanovich, 1981.

Dreiser, Theodore. "The Second Choice." Pp. 864–877 in *American Tradition in Literature*, 7th ed. Vol. 2, edited by George Perkins and Sculley Bradley. New York: McGraw-Hill, 1990.

Eames, John Douglas. *The Paramount Story.* New York: Crown, 1985.

Erwin, Stu. "My kids won't let me!" *American Magazine* 153 (June 1952): 17–19, 90–93.

Eyman, Scott. *Print the Legend: The Life and Times of John Ford.* New York: Simon & Schuster, 1999.

Fitzgerald, F. Scott. *The Great Gatsby.* With foreword and study guide. New York: Charles Scribner's Sons, 1961.

Gaines, William P. "Just A Little Bit Timid." *Shadoplay Magazine* (January 1935): 50–51, 73.

Gilder, Rosamond. "Mr. Sycamore." *Theatre Arts* 27 (January 1943): 20.

Goldman, Herbert G. *Banjo Eyes: Eddie Cantor and the Birth of Modern Stardom.* New York: Oxford University Press, 1997.

"Have a Heart." *Photoplay* 47 (April 1935): 13.

Hewitt, Barnard. *Theatre U. S. A.: 1668 to 1957.* New York: McGraw-Hill, 1959.

Hoffman, Frederick J. *The 20's: American Writing in the Postwar Decade.* New York: The Free Press, 1962.

"How Hollywood Entertains." *The New Movie Magazine* (November 1931): 53, 109–110.

Hughes, Glenn. *A History of the American Theatre 1700–1950.* New York: Samuel French, 1951.

Irving, John. *The Hotel New Hampshire.* New York: Pocket Books, 1981.

"It Could Happen to You." *Photoplay* 53 (October 1939): 8.

Katz, Ephraim. *The Film Encyclopedia.* 2nd ed. New York: HarperCollins, 1994.

Kennedy, David M. *Freedom from Fear: The American People in Depression and War, 1929–1945.* New York: Oxford University Press, 1999.

Kerr, Martha. "Women Are Trouble." *Modern Screen* (November 1936): 54, 93–94.

Leider, Emily Wortis. *Becoming Mae West.* New York: Farrar, Straus and Giroux, 1997.

Maltin, Leonard. *The Great Movie Shorts.* New York: Crown, 1972.

Mann, William J. *Wisecracker: The Life and Times of William Haines, Hollywood's First Openly Gay Star.* New York: Penguin Books, 1998.

Mantle, Burns, ed. *The Best Plays of 1942–1943.* New York: Dodd, Mead and Company, 1943.

————, ed. *The Best Plays of 1943–1944.* New York: Dodd, Mead and Company, 1944.

————, ed. *The Best Plays of 1944–1945.* New York: Dodd, Mead and Company, 1945.

McCabe, John. *Cagney.* New York: Alfred A. Knopf, 1997.

McCarthy, Todd. *Howard Hawks: The Grey Fox of Hollywood.* New York: Grove Press, 1997.

McGilligan, Patrick. *Cagney: The Actor as Auteur.* San Diego: A. S. Barnes and Company, 1982.

McIlwaine, Robert H. "Small Town Boy." *Modern Screen* (July 1937): 12–14.

————. "Homespun Hero." *Modern Screen* (March 1939): 46, 80.

Modern Screen (April 1938): 65.

Mordden, Ethan. *The Hollywood Musical.* New York: St. Martin's Press, 1981.

Parish, James Robert. *Hollywood Character Actors.* Carlstadt, N. J.: Rainbow Books, 1979.

Perry, Hamilton Darby. *Libby Holman: Body and Soul.* Boston: Little, Brown and Company, 1983.

Photoplay 40 (July 1931): 56.

Photoplay 41 (December 1931): 96.

Proctor, Kay. "How to be a Howling Social Success." *Hollywood* (December 1937): 22–23, 59–60.

Ragan, David. *Movie Stars of the '30s.* Englewood Cliffs, N.J.: Prentice-Hall, 1985.

————. *Who's Who in Hollywood.* 2 vols. New York: Facts on File, 1992.

Sarris, Andrew. *You Ain't Heard Nothin' Yet: The American Talking Film: History and Memory 1927–1949.* New York: Oxford University Press, 1998.

Schallert, Edwin, and Elza Schallert. "Hollywood High Lights." *Picture Play* 37 (February 1933): 63.

Screen Book 14 (June 1935): 66.

Seldes, Gilbert. *The 7 Lively Arts.* New York: Sagamore Press, 1957.

Sennett, Ted. *Hollywood Musicals.* New York: Harry N. Abrams, 1981.

Shipman, David. *The Story of Cinema.* New York: St. Martin's Press, 1982.

"Stars' Hopes for 1932." *Screen Book Magazine* 8 (February 1932): 25.

"Strangers in Love." *Photoplay* 41 (April 1932): 52.

"Stuart Erwin." *Modern Screen* (April 1934): 27.

"Stuart Erwin." *Screen Album.* (winter 1939): 39.

"Stuart Erwin, the Lovable Yokel of 115 Films and TV, Dies at 64." *New York Times* 22 (December 1967): 31.

Stuart, Gloria. *I Just Kept Hoping.* Boston: Little, Brown and Company, 1999.

"Studio News." *Silver Screen* 5 (February 1935): 68.

Tibbetts, John C., and James M. Welsh, eds. *The Encyclopedia of Novels into Film*. New York: Facts on File, 1998.

Vieira, Mark A. *Sin in Soft Focus: Pre-Code Hollywood*. New York: Harry N. Abrams, 1999.

"Viva Villa." *Newsweek* 3 (April 14, 1934): 37.

Watkins, T. H. *The Great Depression: America in the 1930s*. Boston: Little, Brown, and Company, 1993.

Williams, Henry B. ed. *The American Theatre: A Sum of Its Parts*. New York: Samuel French, 1971.

Wilson, Elizabeth. "Snooping Over Hollywood: Watching the Stars at Work." *Silver Screen* 3 (March 1933): 73.

Winters, Yvor. "Robert Frost: or, the Spiritual Drifter as Poet." *Sewanee Review* 56 (1948): 564–96.

"Women Are Trouble." *Photoplay* 50 (October 1936): 123.

INDEX

245

ABOUT THE AUTHOR

Judy Cornes, a native of Kansas City, Missouri, holds B.A. and M.A. degrees in English from the University of Missouri in Kansas City and a Ph.D. in English from Southern Illinois University. Since 1973, she has been a professor of English at Odessa College in Odessa, Texas, where she teaches classes in composition as well as in literature. Her teaching interests include eighteenth- and nineteenth-century novels written by women and minorities, film history and interpretation, and the study of early twentieth-century magazine advertising as it reflects social and cultural history. In 1977, she was the recipient of a National Endowment for the Humanities grant to study Russian novels at the University of Virginia. Her article on the films in the *Blondie* series appeared in *American Classic Screen* (1982).

She currently lives in Odessa with her husband, Frank, and their cat, Peta.